SPEAKING RIGHTS TO
POWER

SPEAKING RIGHTS TO
POWER

Constructing Political Will

Alison Brysk

OXFORD
UNIVERSITY PRESS

OXFORD
UNIVERSITY PRESS

Oxford University Press is a department of the University of Oxford.
It furthers the University's objective of excellence in research, scholarship,
and education by publishing worldwide.

Oxford   New York
Auckland   Cape Town   Dar es Salaam   Hong Kong   Karachi
Kuala Lumpur   Madrid   Melbourne   Mexico City   Nairobi
New Delhi   Shanghai   Taipei   Toronto

With offices in
Argentina   Austria   Brazil   Chile   Czech Republic   France   Greece
Guatemala   Hungary   Italy   Japan   Poland   Portugal   Singapore
South Korea   Switzerland   Thailand   Turkey   Ukraine   Vietnam

Oxford is a registered trademark of Oxford University Press
in the UK and certain other countries.

Published in the United States of America by
Oxford University Press
198 Madison Avenue, New York, NY 10016

© Oxford University Press 2013

Library of Congress Cataloging-in-Publication Data
Brysk, Alison, 1960–
Speaking rights to power : constructing political will / Alison Brysk.
pages cm
Includes bibliographical references.
ISBN 978–0–19–998266–0 (hardback : alk. paper)—ISBN 978–0–19–998267–7
(pbk. : alk. paper)   1. Human rights.   2. Communication in politics.   I. Title.
JC571.B758 2013
323—dc23
2013001329

1 3 5 7 9 8 6 4 2
Printed in the United States of America
on acid-free paper

To wit: history admits no rules; only outcomes.

What precipitates outcomes? Vicious acts & virtuous acts.

What precipitates acts? Belief.

Belief is both prize & battlefield, within the mind & in the mind's mirror, the world. If we *believe* humanity is a ladder of tribes, a colosseum of confrontation, exploitation & bestiality, such a humanity is surely brought into being....

If we *believe* that humanity may transcend tooth & claw, if we *believe* divers races & creeds can share this world as peaceably as the orphans share the candlenut tree, if we *believe* leaders must be just, violence muzzled, power accountable & the riches of the Earth & its Oceans shared equitably, such a world will come to pass. I am not deceived. It is the hardest of worlds to make real....

Yet what is any ocean but a multitude of drops?

     —David Mitchell, *Cloud Atlas*, Sceptre/Random House (2004), 528–529

CONTENTS

LIST OF TABLES

PREFACE

Like all of my research, this book was catalyzed by a moment of connection that forced me to think more deeply about issues of chronic concern: a conversation with representatives of the Sudanese People's Liberation Movement (SPLM), exiled in South Africa. I was in South Africa in October 2006 to research an earlier project on the changes in South Africa's foreign policy since its liberation from apartheid. In this process, I met several South African academics and displaced African activists who were trying to find a constructive role for the new South Africa in neighboring wars, dictatorships, and refugee crises.

The Southern Sudanese SPLM exiles I met, through a South African academic who had been helping with practical governance training, were internationally educated survivors of the civil war that had killed millions of their fellow Southerners. They had been appealing to the international community for over a decade and had just begun to gain some recognition. Through this experience, they were already as familiar as I with international human rights standards, institutions, and donors. What they wanted to know from me was how to connect with American and international publics and policy makers, and the lessons of my previous decade of work with relatively successful Latin American human rights movements.

For the first time, I saw that my retrospective analyses of symbolic politics could shift a struggle still unfolding, and that the victims and advocates wanted conceptual strategic guidance as much as practical solidarity. We talked about how to frame rights claims within the canon, about imagery of Africa, discussed bridging narratives of genocide with other communities, and analyzed the different transnational identities of human rights defenders. But I felt that my answers and my own understanding were scattered. As is fitting for a book about the power of communication, this book constitutes an extended reply to their questions. Their own struggle has abated with the achievement of independence, though conflict and violence continue. But I hope that the next time someone wants to know how to reach hearts and minds to stop and heal massive suffering, we will have a better answer in these pages.

ACKNOWLEDGMENTS

This book stands upon the shoulders of a veritable human tower of power, to whom I am immensely grateful. Their collective academic, material, and moral support made it possible to survey this inspiring territory from a great height, although of course none are responsible for the content of my reports.

First and foremost, a series of extraordinary research collaborators contributed to the content. My graduate research assistant at UC Irvine, Madeline Baer (now faculty at San Diego State), was a critical partner for the work on trafficking, Colombia, norm entrepreneurs, and a co-author on FGM. My current doctoral student Natasha Bennett at UC Santa Barbara has done stellar research on the performance cases, political theory, the Arab Spring, campaigns against the death penalty—and she brilliantly organized the manuscript both conceptually and logistically. While an undergrad at UCSB, Antonio Gonzalez ably prepared an enormous range of case studies on the Dreyfus Affair, Spanish Civil War, Darfur, Congo, and male feminists. My studies of interethnic solidarity began with a coauthored project with UC Irvine doctoral student Daniel Wehrenfennig (now director of the Olive Tree Project). Research on the use of new media in Iran drew upon the research and activism of UCI doctoral student Eric Mosinger. My interest in the US use of political parody was sparked by the insightful senior thesis of UCI undergraduate James Kuo (now staff at the Colbert Report). UCI undergrad Sherry Park did tremendous primary research on Japanese American politics, while Aran Aghapour prepared an incisive analysis of dueling Diasporas on the UCI campus. Eileen Filmus of UCSB thoughtfully researched essential background on altruism, humanitarian movements, and social psychology. Another talented UCSB undergrad, Emily Michaels, prepared thorough case studies on Kony 2012 and US civil liberties campaigns. UCSB student Sarkis Yacoubian offered important information and perspectives on the Armenian community. My work on human trafficking developed in collaboration with co-editor Austin Choi-Fitzpatrick (University of Notre Dame and Central European University). My thinking on norm entrepreneurs, Aung San Suu Kyi, and Médecins Sans Frontières were shaped by co-author Claude Denis (University of Ottawa).

I am grateful for the insight provided by interviews with Floyd Mori of the Japanese-American Citizens' League, Peter Bouckaert of Human Rights Watch,

Tenzin Tethong of the International Campaign for Tibet, and for their permission to publish them. Several colleagues provided insightful readings that immeasurably improved the manuscript, including Wayne Sandholtz (USC) and Gershon Shafir (UCSD).

Portions of the project were developed and sometimes published in previous forms with the much-appreciated sponsorship of several universities, journals, and presses. A previous version of "Why We Care" was published in Mark Goodale's edited collection, *Human Rights at the Crossroads* (Oxford University Press, 2012). A comparative case study of FGM and gender-based asylum appears in "Changing Hearts and Minds: Sexual Politics and Human Rights," in Thomas Risse, Steve Ropp, and Kathryn Sikkink (eds.), *The Persistent Power of Human Rights: From Commitment to Compliance* (Cambridge University Press, 2013). It was based on workshops sponsored by the University of Wyoming in 2009 and the Free University of Berlin in 2010. The analysis of frame shift in FGM draws upon "New Rights for Private Wrongs: Female Genital Mutilation and Global Framing Dialogues," with Madeline Baer, in Clifford Bob (ed.), *The International Struggle for New Human Rights* (University of Pennsylvania Press, 2008). Prior versions of the analysis of trafficking were presented in "Beyond Framing and Shaming: Human Trafficking, Human Security, and the International Human Rights Regime," *Journal of Human Security*, Fall 2009, as well as my co-edited volume with Austin Choi-Fitzpatrick, *From Human Trafficking to Human Rights: Reframing Contemporary Slavery* (University of Pennsylvania Press, 2012). Analysis of interethnic solidarity, and the studies of African American and Jewish Americans derive from "My Brother's Keeper? Inter-Ethnic Solidarity and Human Rights," with Daniel Wehrenfennig, *Studies in Ethnicity and Nationalism*, Spring 2010. Related work on interethnic solidarity was prepared for a 2009 workshop organized by Michael Goodhart and Anja Mihr and funded by the University of Pittsburgh. The case study of Colombia originally appeared as "When Words Fail: Communicative Action and Human Rights in Colombia," *Colombia Internacional*, No. 69, Spring 2009, based on a generous invitation from the Universidad de los Andes, Bogota in 2008. The initial analysis of the use of new media in Iran and China was presented at the 2010 conference, "Global Citizenship," at the invitation of Michele Micheletti and the University of Stockholm. The paper "Human Rights as Global Social Imagination" was prepared under the auspices of the 2010 MacKay Lecture at Dalhousie University, Novia Scotia.

Since 2010, my scholarship has been generously funded by the Duncan and Suzanne Mellichamp Chair in Global Governance at UCSB, and this project would not have been possible without their vision and support. My 2011 fieldwork in India was supported by the Fulbright Senior Specialist program at Ravenshaw University, Orissa. I am also grateful for the collegial support of

Professors Mano and Bidyut Mohanty (India Institute for Social Studies) and Matt Schutzer (New York University) throughout my time in India.

Many thanks to my editor Angela Chnapko and Oxford University Press for once again providing a helping and a guiding hand for my research. I would like to thank Peter Mavrikis from Newgen, the anonymous peer reviewers for notably thorough and constructive suggestions, and the editorial staff for swift, professional, and sympathetic editing. Many thanks to Random House for permission for the opening epigram from Cloud Atlas, and to Shobha Das of the Minority Rights Group for the cover photograph. Ruben Dominguez, doctoral student at the University of Salamanca and visiting fellow at UCSB, has provided much-appreciated social media management.

I have been blessed and sustained for half a century by a rich network of family and friends, who have all contributed in diverse ways to this book. Among my friends, I must highlight a few who have taught me the meaning of care so profoundly they have become fictive kin: my godfather Robert Bettinger, soul sister Carol Wise, and big brother Gershon Shafir. My parents, neighbors and friends in a dozen cities where I have lived, dozens of colleagues throughout the republic of letters, and fellow travelers in the global village have nourished, supported, and inspired me. But it would take another book to recount their wonders and my love for them.

So I will simply follow the golden thread through this tapestry of four generations of mothers and daughters. My daughter, Ana Brysk Freeman, has inspired me to think deeply about the power of social media, human rights campaigns for sexual and gender equality, and the ethics of recognition. My older daughter, Miriam Brysk Freeman, has walked her own path of scholarship as she led her graduating class at George Washington University, and invited me to share her work at the Villa Grimaldi Human Rights Memorial in Santiago, Chile. During the course of writing this book, my family lost two mothers and gained two daughters. On December 28th, 2011, my daughters' grandmother Therese Donath passed away—and on the same day, my sister's daughter, Isadora Brysk Cohen, was born. Six months later, in May 2012, we lost my own grandmother Rhea Tauber, at the age of 104. She migrated from Odessa to Ellis Island in 1912, to found a veritable dynasty, and became a teacher, writer, and world citizen whose footsteps I hope to follow. In September 2012, we gained a new life, my brother's daughter Lara Ani Rebecca Brysk. She is the descendant of refugees from both the Armenian and the Jewish Holocausts—and also, on both sides, physicians and musicians who try to heal the world's pain.

With this book, I try to honor the contributions and aspirations of all of these members of my personal, academic, and global communities. Here it is; everything I know so far.

A.B.

SPEAKING RIGHTS TO
POWER

INTRODUCTION

Rhetoric for Rights

If I am not for myself, who will be?
But if I am only for myself, what am I?
And if not now, when?
—Rabbi Hillel,
first-century Jewish sage

How do we come to care about the suffering of strangers, and how can that care construct a world that protects human dignity? The struggle for human rights depends on recognizing suffering, connecting to its victims, and mobilizing political will to transform the power structures that are the source of abuse or neglect. We are defined as humans when we stand for something beyond ourselves, stand together with others, and—as Hannah Arendt put it in the face of the radical dehumanization of the Holocaust—"act in concert in the public sphere" (Arendt 1972: 143). In a previous era, this project seemed to depend mostly on mobilizing direct grassroots challenges to state power—in Alinsky's phrase, "reveille for radicals" (1969). But in our times, the struggle for human rights depends increasingly on mobilizing persuasive rhetoric to garner global solidarity—speaking rights to power.

Yet we do not fully understand how to speak rights to power. Sometimes "naming and shaming" brings down dictatorships; at other times, an enlightened world community ignores well-documented genocides. We need to know when speaking up for rights matters; we need to analyze the successful strategies and appeals that have defied the odds and brought attention and action to far-flung human rights struggles. Although this power of speech has its limits, it is a universal human capacity, a long-standing concern of political theorists from Aristotle to Habermas—and speaking rights is often the only power available to the dispossessed. This book will try to show how far speaking rights can go in securing them, and how certain forms of communicative appeals can foster greater recognition of wrongs—and build political will to address them.

Human rights are both a motive and a means for constructing cosmopolitan compassion. Human rights propose universal and equal freedom, protection, and empowerment—making the world safe for an ethic of care. Care is the opposite of domination; it is speaking love to power. We manifest care in individual actions, social attitudes, transformations of communities, and political campaigns for human rights: at home, abroad, and across borders. A growing body of treaties, laws, institutions, and movements seeks to safeguard our universal human dignity—a secure base of protection and freedom that culminates in the capacity to care. The meaning of human rights is limned in the destruction of care by every form of oppression. At the climax of Orwell's *1984*, the protagonist's loss of humanity is signaled when he loses the capacity for solidarity and urges his tormentors to turn upon his beloved (Orwell 1950). Ultimately, the struggle for human rights seeks self-determination to realize our full capacities: for sustenance, public action, expression, and compassion alike (Nussbaum 1997).

The communication strategy of human rights claims can greatly influence which forms of suffering receive attention, recognition, solidarity, and response. Although the geopolitics, economic exploitation, power elites, and cultural prejudices that cause human rights abuse can also easily block response, sometimes a powerful message will break through and inspire mobilization. The purpose of this book is to increase our understanding of how to strengthen these messages.

Twenty years of research on six continents have shown me the power of ideas, identities, symbols, and beliefs to articulate the right to protection from coercive power and claim a right to constructive power. In Argentina during the 1980s, I saw how the charismatic voices and culturally resonant appeals of the Mothers of the Disappeared brought a measure of truth and justice in the wake of a brutal dictatorship. A decade later, my work with the indigenous peoples' rights movement in Latin America showed how scripts and symbols of indigenous identity forged a transnational network and secured lands, protection, cultural recognition, and political representation for some of the region's most marginalized citizens. In *Human Rights and Private Wrongs*, I traced the emergence of accountability for transnational violations by non-state authorities in areas like human trafficking, corporate social responsibility, and health rights. In each area, successful information campaigns promoted new norms of who is included in human rights, states' responsibility to protect non-citizens and restrain private actors, and the legitimacy of social and corporate authority. These global campaigns gained policy changes from the US Trafficking Victims' Protection Act to better rules for access to AIDS drugs in the developing world. Turning to the "supply side" of human rights promoters, my study of half a dozen *Global Good Samaritans* states showed that developed democratic countries were pulled toward global good citizenship—above the level of their more passive peers—by an ethics of recognition. Persuasive leaders linked cosmopolitan ideology to national values, and deeply democratic civil societies identified with an ethos of global connection. These global good citizen societies have provided critical resources to the international human rights regime, like crafting treaties, funding and staffing international institutions, providing humanitarian foreign aid, promoting peacekeeping, and advancing refugee protection.

This study will try to extract the lessons of the politics of persuasion from these extraordinary experiences of solidarity and social change and compare them to a variety of contemporary campaigns, to understand how we can expand the resonance of human rights in troubled times. The kinds of communication that garner political will are not just information about problems or exhortations of moral principle—though these are important—because unstructured facts and free-floating norms can be and often are ignored. Human rights campaigns succeed when they follow the same rhetorical strategies of successful political campaigns: employing charismatic or authoritative speakers, compelling narratives, plots performed in public space, well-framed messages, skillful use of appropriate media, and targeting audiences. Although not every successful campaign will have all of these elements, under comparable conditions those appeals that embody more of these qualities, will secure greater recognition of human rights.[1]

One of the more successful campaigns of the past decade, the struggle to secure access to life-saving anti-retroviral medications for HIV infection, combined several forms of communication politics. The campaign constructed political will to assist previously invisible or stigmatized victims through charismatic voice by public figures like celebrities, empathetic representation of suffering victims, information politics around the incidence and treatment of AIDS in the developing world by medical professionals, reframing of health rights as human rights by advocacy movements, international legal argumentation on intellectual property rights, protest performance, and outreach to crosscutting attentive audiences of gays, development professionals, and women's groups (Brysk 2005).

The pathways for the impact of communication politics follow closely the dynamics laid out by Keck and Sikkink (1998), Risse, Ropp, and Sikkink (1999), and deepened by this study: consciousness-raising through symbolism and information politics, shaming, leverage, and institutional legalization. These dynamics are often intertwined or overlapping; the point is that there are patterns and channels for how speaking rights gains attention and transforms policy.

Naming, Framing, and Shaming:
Human Rights Watch

Of the global human rights organizations, Human Rights Watch illustrates best the sheer power of information politics and the development of expert organizational voice. The central activity of the organization is monitoring and reporting. As Peter Bouckaert, Director of Emergency Response for Human Rights Watch put it, reflecting on decades of work in Kosovo, Darfur, and Burma, "it all comes down to notebook, pen and camera" (Remarks at UC Santa Barbara, November 5, 2011). Moreover, the organization's "brand" and effectiveness are based on the collection and projection of impartial, direct information.

Through its command of reliable information, Human Rights Watch (HRW) has gained influence on recognition and response to abuse by powerful nations and world public opinion. Human Rights Watch annual and country reports routinely help to shape the aid policies and diplomatic strategies of developed democracies relative to dictatorships and conflict zones. In a concrete example of acute leverage in a critical case, in the early days of the Egyptian Revolution, White House policy makers called HRW to ask for an accurate understanding of the nature of the repression—and what kind of statement would help to stop it. Human Rights Watch highlighted their evidence that Egyptian government security forces were using illicit violence against protesters and asked the president to call for a halt to this state-sponsored violation. Obama's naming and shaming at a critical moment is credited with saving lives and facilitating an orderly transition to democracy (Talk at UC Santa Barbara, April 27, 2012). In parallel fashion, after a HRW inspection mission revealed the extent and provenance of violations in an isolated area, the president of the Central African Republic was pressed by the French government at a donor conference to withdraw his forces from zones in which HRW had documented abuses under the responsibility of the Central African Republic military.

Naming alone—consciousness-raising and labeling—can produce behavior change if background socialization and cosmopolitan identity linkages are strong. Thus, Bouckaert recounts how a rebel commander who had been a schoolteacher in the Central African Republic demobilized some child soldiers when a Human Rights Watch representative informed him of the ban on the use of child soldiers and told him of the recent human rights prosecution in Congo. Similarly, HRW persuaded the Libyan rebels—some with a prior history as rights advocates—not to use land mines in order to meet international standards in their struggle. Once a written commitment was signed, the insurgents honored it (Peter Bouckaert, UCSB, April 27, 2012).

Framing abuses in established categories and contesting government counter-frames can also mobilize international pressure more readily. In the confusion of a civil war in Nepal, HRW documented a government strategy of forced disappearances and government forces' responsibility for missing persons, leading to the acceptance of a UN Mission that greatly increased monitoring and diminished the practice. At a global level, HRW joined with other human rights organizations to document and label the use of cluster bombs as a threat to civilians analogous to land mines and successfully pushed for a similar treaty. During the 1990s, HRW granted critical support to the international indigenous peoples' movement when it included land rights as a human rights issue. HRW also played a key role in positioning women's rights as human rights and established a thematic division for women's rights—stretching its brand of monitoring public civil liberties and war crimes to demand accountability for non-state crimes like domestic violence and honor killing.

We can look inside the black box of the classic human rights strategy of "naming and shaming" and see that in between lies attention, framing, testimonial performance, and analogy. Facts do not speak for themselves—there is a learned discursive strategy that makes information effective.

Hearts and minds: The International Campaign For Tibet

The Tibetan people have gained worldwide solidarity for an obscure struggle against a global juggernaut by articulating a unique culture. An estimated one million of Tibet's six million residents died during China's 20 years of closed occupation, from 1959–79, as over 100,000 became refugees—including the Dalai Lama, the spiritual leader of Tibetan Buddhism. Chinese rule has seen the systematic destruction of Tibetan land and religious institutions, suppression of free speech and assembly resulting in thousands of political prisoners, executions, and extrajudicial killings, and forced settlement of Chinese colonists. In response, Tibetans have engaged in constant waves of civil disobedience, and have appealed to the United Nations, democratic governments, and global civil society.

Tenzin Tethong is the founder of the International Campaign for Tibet and President of the Dalai Lama Foundation, who has served the Tibetan exile government as a Chief of Cabinet and U.S. Representative of the Dalai Lama. He describes the Tibetans' fifty-year struggle for self-determination as above all, "a contest of ideas between the Chinese state and the Tibetan people." (Talk, UCSB, January 28, 2013) Above all, he highlighted the influence of the charismatic voice of the Dalai Lama, whose universalist projection of Tibetan Buddhism and aspirations culminated in the 1988 Nobel Peace Prize. Tethong witnessed how the personal diplomacy of the Dalai Lama's visits to the U.S. during the 1980's forged unexpected bipartisan support among key members of Congress for the Tibetan cause, superseding the marginality of the Tibetan constituency and the Cold War logic of allying with China against the Soviets. By the 1990's, key celebrities like Richard Gere and Desmond Tutu also lent their charisma to the Tibetan campaign. (Interview, Jan. 28, 2013)

Tethong traced the growth in Tibetan solidarity to identity-based circuits of attention, rooted in a "fascination with Tibet in the Western psyche from the turn of the century," with successive waves of mid-century growth of Buddhism in California, 1960's contact between young travelers to India and Tibetan refugees, and subsequent scholarly, craft, and diaspora networks. By the 1980's, young Congressional staffers with histories in these communities readily transmitted appeals for Tibetan visas, Voice of America broadcasts, State Department reports, Fulbright scholarships, and funding for regional refugee reception centers. He concluded that "the power of this connection, is beyond politics—you can't buy or manufacture this." (Interview, Jan. 28, 2013)

Appeals for Tibet transcended the region's physical and political isolation through alternate spaces and repertoires of protest performance. The performance of Buddhist religious ritual resonated within the Tibetan community, but also on the global stage. Tethong served as Principal Advisor to the film *Seven Years in Tibet*. The spectacle of the 2008 Beijing Olympics created an opportunity for counter-hegemonic protest by exiles, inside Tibet, and even within China (by international student activists). Currently, the growing repertoire of self-immolation has become the dominant performance—of martyrdom.

The international campaign has situated Tibet's plight in resonant global frames: human rights, religious freedom, and self-determination. The International Campaign For Tibet has secured United Nations' resolutions, cancellation of a World Bank resettlement project, and worldwide alliances. As Tethong summarized their quest, "What we want is a say in our own narrative." (Talk, UCSB, Jan. 28, 2013)

The Case for Communication Politics

If changing hearts and minds by telling the right stories is the key to the politics of persuasion, each narrative element bears further analysis, voice, message, performance, media, and audience.

Unpacking the rhetorical dynamics of successful human rights appeals has several political implications. First, it can teach us "best practices" for emerging campaigns to draw attention to unrecognized issues, deepening the current form of inductive learning by reactive feedback. But comparative analysis may also show how the semantic circumstance of prior waves of abuse has sometimes distorted recognition—inflating some struggles while ignoring less picturesque suffering, evoking inappropriate forms of intervention for some real problems because of how they are framed, or pushing movements into resonant but ephemeral campaigns at the expense of more sustainable coalition-building. Strategic analysis of human rights rhetoric should not discredit the use of semantic appeals, which are employed by every genre of political mobilization—but are not often well acknowledged by principled activists and their supporters. Rather, the lessons of past campaigns should inspire human rights campaigns to improve their communicative strategies for effective use of limited resources, and to understand the limitations and trade-offs of short-term appeals that can be better used to catalyze more long-term dialectics. At the same time, a communication politics analysis can help us to understand some of the failures of human rights campaigns and how to improve appeals in hard cases. Thus, this book is intended as both a demonstration and a constructive critique of the power of speaking rights.

When information politics campaigns succeed, they move the world community from attention to recognition to solidarity with human rights struggles and foster political will. Political will means the propensity to mobilize to protect and empower the victims of abuse that overcomes the risks and costs of solidarity. Political will can be measured by a commitment to translate cognitive awareness and normative recognition into action, such as monitoring, lobbying, litigation, people power, institutional reform, and humanitarian or diplomatic intervention. Building political will depends upon a combination of the reception, salience, resonance, and empowering guidance of human rights appeals. Since human rights campaigns operate in a diffuse fashion that creates a new zeitgeist, the signs of political will may manifest as changes in the political consciousness and discourse of individuals, social movements, mass publics, leaders, and global institutions. Thus, there will be times we can track the specific policy impact of a rhetorical appeal through mobilizing a particular decision maker or social sector, but more often an increase in political will to address a human rights problem permeates the policy environment by shifting political discourse, placement on the political agenda, awareness of policy instruments, salience of attentive constituencies, and acceptability of trade-offs, and we can track these broader changes.

Realists and materialists of every ilk scoff at humanitarian solidarity as unlikely, insignificant, or hypocritical. Yet as Margaret Mead suggested, every day a "small committed group of people" do sacrifice their own personal and political interests to speak for strangers—and do occasionally change history, as we will see through the course of this book. If human rights campaigns and appeals were purely symbolic, or meaningless modernist myths, or false consciousness, abusive regimes worldwide would not work so hard to ban, subvert, and contest them. Like all forms of principled political action, human rights appeals may certainly be contradictory or selective, but that is a reason to improve rather than discard them—since on the whole human rights campaigns achieve more good than domination or inaction, and rights norms establish grounds for their own critique.

Communication politics is only one determinant of the success of human rights campaigns—albeit an important and understudied dimension. It does not diminish the importance of understanding the politics of persuasion to remember that in the real world, the success of human rights advocacy will be influenced by a combination of material and moral force. Broad comparative studies show that access, receptivity, or contradictions in dominant forces open a space for speaking rights. These forces include hegemonic states, international institutions, national regimes, and domestic factions that become willing to tolerate challengers, foster freedom, or protect vulnerable populations for their own reasons. Within the limits of these power configurations, civil society is most effective as an agent of human rights promotion when it works in tandem with transnational networks to frame local problems in terms of globally legitimate norms (Cardenas 2007). Human rights campaigns must sometimes triage their efforts in relation to such windows of opportunity—but at times communicative appeals can push those windows open wider.

Another standard challenge to the cosmopolitan agenda of speaking rights—by cynical elites, concerned multiculturalists, and conflicted members of cultures outside the West alike—is the belief that human rights are part of a specific modern, Western, liberal identity that should not be imposed on others. Yet even as biology, culture, and power seem to conspire to draw boundaries around solidarity with "our own kind," there is a countervailing impulse to bridge every form of difference. Somewhere in every society and every era there is a quest for cosmopolitanism—and an urge to find one's own voice, from Tiananmen Square to the Arab Spring. Although many specific forms of human rights may be modern and Western, the animating spirit of connection with all that is human is universal, and just as authentic and legitimate as any other element of the world's range of cultural norms. Far from Western modernity, medieval Persian poet Sa'adi Shirazi wrote: "Human beings are parts of a body, created from the same essence. When one part is hurt and in pain, the other parts remain restless. If the misery of others leaves you indifferent, you cannot be called a human being" (the saying known as "Bani Adam"). Speaking rights means recovering these voices, empowering the cosmopolitans in every culture against those who seek to speak boundaries in their name—and speaking rights to broader participation and broader visions in the global and local construction of human rights mechanisms.

Even all of this does not mean that human rights appeals will always be the best or the only response to every social problem or all the forms of human suffering. Human rights rhetoric may be misleading, misapplied, or hijacked to serve other ends, as we shall see. The human rights response should be preceded by a careful analysis of the context of abuse, and the motives, consequences, and alternative modes of appeal and intervention. While there are some situations in which an inappropriate human rights strategy distorts response so much that "the medicine is worse than the disease"—notably some cases of humanitarian intervention in complex conflicts—there are other cases where even a misinformed, self-serving, or contradictory humanitarian appeal can still serve as a useful catalyst for recognition and mobilization. Sometimes it is legitimate to strategically launch a lowest common-denominator appeal that has the potential to grow toward a more effective and empowering response—as appears to be the case with human trafficking campaigns as a gateway to broader concern with contemporary slavery. After careful consideration, human rights campaigns are still often the best way to enact care and alleviate suffering—and when this is the case, we must learn how to use them more effectively.

Speaking rights to power is a part of acting globally; securing universal rights in a globalized world. Globalization is a double-edged sword that slices our bonds of servitude to some forms of state power with one side of the blade—and our bonds of solidarity with the other. The need is manifest for a new social imagination to weave a safety net for constant affronts to the human condition, old and new—as one recent book puts it, *Civilising Globalisation* (Kinley 2009).

From the jungles of Ecuador to the halls of Geneva, my research has shown me that the problem is power—and so is the solution. The problem is illegitimate and unjust authority, and the violence that is used to maintain control over the many by the few, to degrade difference, and to exploit vulnerability. And the solution is to construct a different kind of empowerment, available to all: to pursue our lives freely, develop our best selves, and come together to build a caring and just society. We need a social imagination that speaks truth to power, in the famous Quaker phrase—but we also need a social imagination that speaks love to power; that shows us how to replace bonds of domination with bonds of care and connection. Various religions and ideologies that have played that role in prior eras are no longer able to mobilize cosmopolitan political will. This book will show how human rights sometimes can.

Plan of the Book

The next chapter will outline a theory of rhetoric for rights. First, we will trace how the requisites and pathways of solidarity are rooted in the human condition. Then, we will define human rights and assess their special power as a contemporary form of global social imaginary that can provide the basis for solidarity. Finally, we will analyze the politics of persuasion, which locates the transformative potential of speaking rights to power. This analysis in turn generates a narrative framework and semantic elements of communication politics to guide our interpretation and strategic guidance of human rights campaigns.

The cases are designed to investigate this surprising and unusual "weapon of the weak"—to understand better how it works when it works. The detailed discussion of cases is demonstrative and exploratory; it is a map, not a model. This exploration will show that the politics of persuasion is "necessary but not sufficient" and that the more elements of information politics are present, the better the chance of gaining recognition and response. But there are no formulas for social change, only rhetorical strategies for improving the odds.

The following chapters will examine historical and comparative cases of speaking rights to power. The unit of analysis is a human rights campaign, which may coincide with a country case, genre of violation, affected population, particular human rights movement, or type of right. So in the case of Sudan, the North–South conflict and Darfur are two different cases, but there are global patterns to campaigns against human trafficking that make it a single case despite variants in mobilization in different countries and by different movements.

The outcome to examine is the success of communication politics to secure improvements in human rights. "Success" may be more meaningfully assessed as progress along a spectrum that runs from getting attention through mobilizing solidarity to the end point: securing policy change that diminishes or ends the violation, or transforms accountability for past or future violations of this type. Thus, policy change may include international or domestic intervention, regime change, civil rights legislation, defense of dissidents, transitional justice, relief or compensation for victims, asylum, education, memorials, and/or apologies. Progress may be partial or reversible, but some change in a situation of abuse protects or empowers some victims for some period—and when such change can be linked primarily to the use of symbolic appeals in the absence of significant material leverage, it suggests a potential repertoire for similar situations.

The inputs that will be assessed are the presence and level of symbolic facets of the politics of persuasion used by a human rights campaign. These include the quality of voice, framing of claims, use of performance, mobilization of media, and audience bridging. In order to show how these processes can be generalized, I try to include cases that span from the nineteenth to the twenty-first century, cases from every major world region, appeals for both specific countries and broader issues, and cases contesting a variety of types of abuse and perpetrators.

In order to highlight the mechanisms at work, some contrasting cases are examined alongside the success stories of relative progress. These cases can begin to help us to see that information politics is necessary, even when it is not sufficient, and to identify the limits to its application and impact. Congo and Colombia are not amenable to communication politics for numerous reasons and receive little attention and less solidarity and change, contrasting with Darfur and Argentina, respectively. Communication politics are used in partial but interesting ways and bring attention and solidarity but little policy change in Iran, China, and Russia. On the other hand, changes in communication politics can transform negative cases to responsive ones. For example, symbolic campaigns were initially absent or unsuccessful, but transformed dramatically in the Holocaust and the struggle against female genital mutilation. Finally, misguided use of communication politics for competing rights claims among supporters of Israel and Palestine can backfire and lead to negative results that diminish solidarity, contrasting with the Liberian peace movement in which symbolic politics bridged the rights claims of warring communities.

In chapter 2, we will begin by mapping how the roots of global repertoires of human rights rhetoric can be traced across very different eras and regions. At the close of the nineteenth century, France's anti-Semitic persecution of Alfred Dreyfus inspired one of the first solidarity campaigns and developed the repertoire of the cause célèbre. Later in the twentieth century, the Spanish Civil War was perhaps the first modern conflict to mobilize transnational solidarity through the rhetoric of human rights. The key case of the Holocaust is ground zero for the international human rights regime—and an extensive repertoire of semantic appeals. We examine these foundational cases in Europe to complement the extensive analysis of similar transnational appeals outside the West in the trans-Atlantic antislavery campaign (Keck and Sikkink 1998), and to counter the critique that humanitarian appeals are tied up with condescending notions of rescue across cultural lines (Quirk 2011). To show what a difference the globalization of communicative appeals makes in human rights recognition in the current environment, the chapter presents a final contemporary case: the Egyptian Revolution.

The following chapters trace the arc of narrative, from voice to message to audience. Chapter 3 will map a number of forms of compelling voice. Ideal characters to mobilize political will include charismatic heroes, martyred cause célèbre, those who hold central social roles, and esteemed experts who act as messengers. Charismatic speakers may include celebrities, holders of "moral capital" like Nelson Mandela (Kane 1998)—but also embodiments of charismatic roles, like mothers and healers. Credible public intellectuals, such as Amartya Sen (Misztal 2007) or collective "epistemic communities" (Haas 1989) also play a critical role—in this case, physicians as human rights advocates.

Meanwhile, selective attention is drawn by the voice and representation of vulnerable "innocent victims" such as children (Keck and Sikkink 1998). We will also consider how voice may be weak, insufficient, or contradicted by strong counter-frames, through examining relatively unsuccessful campaigns against the death penalty in the United States.

Chapter 4 will consider the message: the politics of framing the human rights claim. Previous research suggests that the best way to deliver the message is to draw a clear causal chain (Keck and Sikkink 1998) to establish responsibility, and to link the current claim to some established genre or frame of abuse (Snow et al. 2004). Thus, the campaign against international sex trafficking prospers when it is linked to "white slavery." The most successful messages are closely connected to modern and rational norms (Boli and Thomas 1999), as we will see when campaigns against female genital mutilation shift from self-determination to health rights claims. However, the relative inefficacy of appeals for human rights in Colombia shows how frames can fail when they are a poor fit with the international human rights regime. In the twenty-first century, the neighboring horrors in Congo and Darfur received very different levels of response from the world community with different modes of political rhetoric. Successful human rights framing of the genocide in Darfur mobilized attention and some action while the agonies of Congo were met mostly with silence and neglect—until very recently.

Performance matters: certain genres, repertoires, and spaces are especially powerful for conveying empathy, contention, and empowerment. In chapter 5, we will analyze the resonance of several key performance genres across diverse cultures, from Africa to India to Russia to postmodern America. Testimonial personifies abuse as the story of a single suffering individual who is warranted as representative, while it is narrated with features that connect to mass publics. It has been employed with notable success in Latin America, the contemporary United States, and to expand consciousness of violence against women worldwide. Allegory, written or performed, taps into historic mythos to locate causal chains and repertoires of response. Most religious appeals map human rights claims onto a sacred story, but nationalist reformers can also mobilize support through a heroic tale, as we shall see in contemporary India. In a different vein, satire breaks the frame of hegemonic "common sense" and the fear of coercion. Ironic humor works to support human rights struggles when it lampoons the legitimacy claims of oppressors and suggests the counter-hegemonic power of the individual dissenter. Parody has been used to great effect in the Arab Spring and the contemporary United States. However, the use of political satire has been less effective in Russia and China, where mockery contributes to mobilization but cannot secure policy change and may even intensify repression.

The availability and use of appropriate media is also a determinant of the reception of human rights appeals, as we will explore in chapter 6. In the network society, media increasingly substitutes for the physical public sphere, and information politics are increasingly salient (Castells 2009). Benkler argues that the technological characteristics of the new information economy maximize the potential for liberal individual autonomy in a networked public sphere. Individual production and consumption of potentially diverse and universal information may empower individuals' knowledge, critique, political participation, and "weak ties" to others. While such efforts face challenges from state repression, global media industries, and a digital divide in access, the net effect is to increase the potential to pursue liberal values of freedom, participation, critical culture, and social justice (Benkler 2006). The Iranian democracy movement shows how decentralized media like Twitter can sometimes counterbalance censorship in broadcast media and permit the delivery of counter-hegemonic messages. Yang Gou Bin's research (2010) on Chinese netizens suggests a similar counter-hegemonic use of new media for "contention, carnival, and community." However, the relatively effective use of new media in the Arab Spring contrasts with the rise and fall of the Kony 2012 campaign.

Human rights rhetoric must also reach a receptive audience, and chapter 7 will analyze the final aspect of communication politics. Speaking rights constructs, bridges, and depends upon target audiences. Global professional communities have formed a new kind of global solidarity audience, especially for information processors who live by the power of the pen. Bridging existing audiences to mobilize identity as a resource for rights rhetoric, I examine the unlikely case of interethnic solidarity, like Japanese Americans speaking out against the post-9/11 detentions of Arab Americans. We will see that bridging narratives of suffering can activate coalitions connecting current victims to better-situated peers across borders. Successful experiences of interethnic solidarity in the United States, South Africa, and Darfur will be contrasted to the failure of "dueling diasporas" to bridge audiences for human rights claims in the Israel–Palestine conflict and Armenian genocide recognition. Meanwhile, communication politics has been surprisingly successful at bridging audiences across the great divide of gender to combat violence against women. Rights talk with the semantic elements of voice, frame, and media has secured recognition, solidarity, and some policy change at the micro, national, and global foreign policy levels.

The concluding chapter will summarize the lessons of our deeper investigation of this process, apply it to some path-breaking contemporary struggles, and suggest concrete implications. Understanding how to deliver the message of connection, care, and empowerment is the key to humanizing the global social order.

Table I.1 Human Rights Campaigns and Communication Politics

Case	Voice	Frame	Performance	Media	Audience	Outcome	Chapter
Tibet	*	*	*		*	*	Intro, 6
Dreyfus	*	*		*	*	*	2
Spanish Civil War	*	*		*	*	*	2
Holocaust	*	*	*	*	*	*	2
Arab Spring	*	*	*	*	*	*	2, 6
South Africa	*	*	+	*	*	*	3, 7
Burma	*	*	*	*	*	*	3
Argentina	*	*	*	*	*	*	3, 4
AIDS	*	*	*	+	*	*	3
Violence vs. Women	*	*	*	*	*	*	3, 4, 5, 7
US death penalty	+		+				3
Trafficking	*	*	*	*	*	*	4, 7
Female genital mutilation	*	*	*	+	*	*	4, 7
Colombia	-						4
Darfur	*	*	*	*	*	*	4, 7
Congo	+	-					4
US civil liberties	+	*	*	*	*	+	5, 7
India	*	+	*	*	*	*	5
Russia	*	*	*	*	+	*	5
Iran Green	*	*	*	*	*	+	6
China	+	*	*	*	*	+	6
Kony 2012	-	-		*	*		6
Academic freedom	+	*	+		*	*	7
Armenia		*	*		-		7
Israel/Palestine	-	+		*	-	-	7
Liberia	*	*	*	*	*	*	8

Table I.1 provides a guide to the pathway we will follow in analyzing how human rights campaigns speak rights to power. It displays the full roster of campaigns profiled, indicates which elements of communication power are used, and shows which chapter(s) detail that campaign's use of one kind of narrative appeal. Communicative elements are marked with * if present, - if weak, and + if strong. In the next chapter, we will provide a theoretical foundation for what it means for campaigns to speak rights, construct solidarity, and build political will.

1

SPEAKING RIGHTS

Speaking is the first political act. It is the first act of liberty,
and it always implicitly involves another. In speaking, one
recognizes, "I am and I am not alone."
—James Orbinski, President of Médecins
Sans Frontières

Under the right circumstances, the naming and framing of rights can construct political will to protect them. Speaking rights to power means gaining attention, then empathy, and then evoking a powerful norm that persuades
power-holders, allies, or fellow sufferers to mobilize. Human rights campaigns
aim to shift political will to embrace cosmopolitan care through a politics of
persuasion.

The construction and communication of identities, rights, and legitimacy is
the capital of a cosmopolitan "political economy of solidarity." As a scholar of
ethnic coalitions explains, "The 'political economy of solidarity' is defined as
the 'distribution of affections, resources, and energies' among identities, who
can make claims upon them, and who has the authority to decide" (Hollinger
2006: xvi–xvii). Cosmopolitanism "promotes broadly based, internally complex, multiple solidarities equipped to confront the large-scale dilemmas of a
'globalizing' epoch while attending to the endemic human need for intimate
belonging" (xvii). We come to care across borders as we construct common
visions of our shared humanity, common fate, and social purpose.

The content and process of claiming human rights has a unique capacity to
build solidarity and to project an ethos of mutual respect across boundaries of
geography, ideology, and social location. Human rights have come to play a
privileged role in the global social imaginary—the underlying consciousness
that shapes and bounds our visions of power, identity, and political possibility
across borders (Steger 2008). The rhetoric of human rights contains powerful
and flexible notions that locate voice, responsibility, agency, and justice for
many forms of suffering.

Human rights campaigns can be modeled as a form of communicative counter-hegemony, speaking rights to power. The power of speech has the potential to transform hearts and minds, constructing political will for social change through rhetoric. "Power is based on the control of communication and information.... the most fundamental form of power lies in the ability to shape the human mind" (Castells 2009: 3–4). In different ways, several leading social theorists argue that "all states are information societies" (Giddens 1979) and that "informational capital" (Bourdieu 1989) is a key resource for social control—and resistance (Yang 2009: 45).

Along with this persuasive impact of the message, the act of speaking—coming together in public space to articulate a critique of pathologies of power—can transform speakers and audiences. Hannah Arendt's notions of the constitution of agency in the public sphere, politics as praxis, and the liberating potential of public speech suggest that the process of speaking rights can construct positive power (Knauer 1980; Penta 1996). In this sense, the public articulation of communication campaigns moves speaking rights beyond claiming protection from wrongs to claiming voice.

In order to understand the pathway from attention to recognition to political will, we must further examine the requisites of solidarity, the content and import of rights claims, and the persuasive power of speech to transform care into action. First, we will explore solidarity—why we care about the suffering that human rights seek to address. Why we care has implications for what we care about, and what forms of human rights rhetoric will mobilize solidarity. Next, we will consider the message: the role of human rights claims as global social imaginary. Finally, we will trace the dynamics of the politics of persuasion, as a way of reconstructing power through speech.

"Why We Care": Constructing Solidarity

Can I do The Vagina Monologues, *maybe for extra credit?*
—male student in an International Human Rights course

Every time we liberate a woman, we liberate a man.
                                        —Margaret Mead

The difference between male and female is the most widespread and pervasive form of biological difference, and all cultures translate that otherness into gender roles, which usually distribute power and privilege to the masculine. Thus, solidarity across gender lines is a test and model for the dynamics of altruism and interdependence. The male student's query reflects a pure case of recognition, the kind that builds human rights campaigns and response, since by definition the sexual violence against women depicted in *The Vagina Monologues* does not affect him personally.

Why does the male student come to recognize violence against women? First of all, the dramatic performance of *The Vagina Monologues*, replete with a striking title associated with highly resonant themes of sexuality, focused his attention. As we will see, the enactment of human rights appeals raises consciousness by personifying suffering, providing information that locates the abuse, and framing it in a narrative causal arc. But once we know, why do we care about the suffering of the other? Why does speaking rights sometimes move us to solidarity and action?

The plausible range of reasons we can imagine for the male student's interest in the suffering of the opposite gender mirror the range of explanations suggested by various social scientific perspectives on cooperation and altruism: *empathy, role, relationship, socialization, persuasion, calculation,* and *responsibility*. These pathways cluster around the themes of identity, information, community, and incentives that are increasingly used to explain all domains of social behavior—from economics to international relations to marriage. They also correspond roughly to the rationalist, culturalist, and structuralist approaches to social movements that would be a natural approach to interpret human rights campaigns (Giugni and Passy 2000: 21–25).

Why do my students, and the global citizens they stand for, recognize suffering and respond with solidarity? The twenty-first-century American male student may experience a direct vicarious *empathy* with women's violation that transcends rapidly attenuating gender differences. I have noticed that during classroom discussions of FGM, the most engaged male students reflexively put their hands across their laps, indicating with their body language a felt equivalence between disparate organs. On the other hand, it may be precisely because the male student is relatively privileged and exempt from sexual violence that he feels protective of female sexual vulnerability; modern masculine *roles* involve a central and contradictory feature of cosmopolitan chivalry. In a more *relational* perspective, many males I have come to know as students or advocates of women's issues relate how they became sensitized through witnessing violence or its impact upon a woman they cared about, which they later expanded to a more generalized commitment to gender equity. It is also possible that the student has been *socialized* to believe that caring about violence against women is the mark of a good person, who will win social approval—by his family, education, religious training, political activism, or peers. Or, in the bridging frame variant, he may have enrolled in a human rights course seeking intellectual understanding of civil rights that do affect him, and become *persuaded* that this personal issue merits public common concern because "women's rights are human rights." Finally, the male student may be *strategically* seeking the concrete rewards of social approbation for his seeming sensitivity: a better grade from a feminist professor, or a competitive niche in the dating market of female human rights students—as a man who cares about vaginas. In a combined relational and strategic mode of *interdependence*, some of my male students seem to recognize the long-term benefits of a more gender-balanced world for expanding their own range of options—for example, ultimately having a stronger female partner in a dual-earner household will ease his financial career pressures.

Thinking more broadly about the range of reasons for care, we must also consider the historically common dynamic of guilt, as implied by the phrase "naming and shaming." We trust that my student does not bear any personal guilt for violence against women, but he may feel indirect guilt—like most of us in any position of privilege—for abuses he has witnessed without the power to stop, attitudes he has failed to contest, or even his own collusive thoughts in younger years or periods of stress. Every mother knows that guilt can be one of the most powerful catalysts of changes in consciousness and behavior. In *Pray the Devil Back to Hell*, the documentary about the Liberian women's peace movement, there is a striking moment when powerless religious activists have shamed rampaging warlord gangs who had committed mass rapes and amputations with impunity into disarming. As he is interviewed about his decision to lay down his weapons, one of the soldiers is the very picture of shame: he looks sideways at the activist and the camera, shrugs his shoulders, shuffles his feet, and mutters, "They are our mothers. We had to pay attention." On the other hand, every lawyer knows the world is replete with shameless miscreants completely impervious to social sanction that respond—if at all—only to coercion or strong material incentives. Thus, it seems that guilt is not an independent universal pathway to care, but rather an affective marker of the operation of some role, ideology, or socialization. You cannot persuade people to feel guilty; you can only mobilize guilt by activating some underlying identity or meaning.

Human rights campaigns can also draw upon and motivate more cognitive doctrines of *responsibility*—but we can be guilty without feeling responsible or feel responsible without guilt. We can acknowledge that we are guilty in a causal sense for someone's suffering but still fail to care, due to a parochial identity (they are not really a person like us), blame (they deserved to suffer), or some form of moral utilitarianism or competing ideology (they had to suffer for some greater good). The wrong form of guilt can even disable responsibility, such as structural guilt or survivor guilt that leave us feeling numb and powerless. Conversely, the right role, ideology, or socialization can produce both care and responsibility in the absence of guilt—as seen in the mobilization of care through professional roles in movements like Doctors Without Borders, or Global Good Samaritan states that take up the "responsibility to protect" in failed states distant from their influence (http://www.un.org/en/preventgenocide/adviser/responsibility.shtml). Doctors are not guilty of causing disease, but they are responsible for healing it. Responsibility seems to be a more robust pathway than guilt and one that empowers responders to empower victims (Kuper 2005). The Canadian doctor who came to head Médecins Sans Frontières (MSF) describes his role socialization in medical school via a Chilean professor exiled from the Pinochet dictatorship who lectured on the participation of doctors in torture and corresponding challenge to professional responsibility (Orbinski 2008: 35).

We turn now to trace each of the pathways to solidarity: identity, connection, and calculation.

The Pathway of Identity: Empathy and Care

Care rests on empathy, and empathy requires humanization. From Adam Smith's *Theory of Moral Sentiments* (2007) to historical studies of Holocaust rescuers to contemporary social psychology experiments, solidarity appears to rest in affective sympathetic identification. Adam Smith's account of moral agency is centered in an inherent and universal capacity for the development of conscience as internalized "approbation." For Smith, "sympathy" is an imaginative faculty of identification with fellow humans' agency and suffering (2007: xiii). Historians link the development of a modern notion of human rights to an expansion of empathetic identification in eighteenth-century Europe, due to new modes of communication, culture, and contact that introduced cascading rights claims (Hunt 2008). Ongoing humanization is a constant dialectical requisite for building bridges to solidarity with others—who are often chronically alienated from our cultural understanding by structures of distancing and denigration by oppressors, including the ultimate recourse of "blaming the victim" (Staub 1989). Studies of altruism suggest that the single greatest determinant of self-sacrifice is consciously identifying with the other (Monroe 1996).

Various accounts of the universal human dignity we recognize in human rights describe the core quality that justifies rights ethically as reason, agency, spirit, vulnerability, and capacity (Perry 2000; Shue 1980; Nussbaum 1997). Yet these principled grounds of moral reasoning do not map completely onto the inductive practical reasoning of recognition. Research on humanitarian philanthropy shows that a concrete suffering individual mobilizes solidarity, while an abstract statistical account numbs bystanders. A leading study cites the statement of perhaps the twentieth-century's leading humanitarian, Mother Theresa: "If I look at the mass I will never act. If I look at one, I will" (Slovic 2007: 79). Most accounts of lived experiences of empathy, including my own, focus on primordial markers of biological function. The recursive capacity for recognition is encapsulated in the trope of looking into the eyes of a stranger. In my book *From Tribal Village to Global Village*, I reflected upon the catalytic encounter that inspired that decade-long study of indigenous rights. Watching a Bolivian Indian beggar scrounge my leftovers at an outdoor restaurant, I experienced a mobilization of care: "As our eyes met, my vision of underdevelopment, human rights, and my own role in the global food chain were indelibly printed with his face" (Brysk 2000: ix). It is this capacity to recognize the victim that gives meaning to "the human in human rights."

An interesting corollary of recognizing the victim is recognizing the oppressor. While some critiqued the West's failure to respond to genocide in Rwanda because they claimed we did not recognize the African victims, others located the moral failure just as much in the distancing of tropical, tribal violence committed by African perpetrators (Gourevitch 1999)—compared to the more familiar Yugoslavian repertoire of European concentration camps unfolding at the same time, which garnered greater concern. Similarly, American antislavery activist Charles Jacobs compares US mobilization against apartheid with passivity in response to contemporary African slavery and laments:

> The human rights community consists mostly of compassionate white people. When such folks, and I include myself, see evil done by people 'like ourselves,' we feel especially animated to act. 'Not in my name!' is the slogan for that feeling. We are embarrassed to be identified with evil. We want to clear our name. This part of the human rights impulse is all about expiation....But when we see evil done by people not like ourselves—as in Sudan—we are paralyzed. We don't think we have a moral standing to criticize 'them.'...Seeking expiation instead of universal justice means ignoring the suffering of victims of non-Western aggression. It also means devaluing their oppressors. (Jacobs 2003: 14–15)

Solidarity through Connection: Community and Socialization

Connection to a collective identity, network, or practice may yield solidarity directly or through socialization to outward-oriented roles and norms. The basis of connection may be affective, relational, or reasoned. Seeking to synthesize Kantian universalism with relational solidarity, Kwame Anthony Appiah's "rooted cosmopolitanism" (2006) operates through concentric circles of concern radiating outward from a core of kin and affinity groups to affiliated identities to a final widest circle of all humanity. As we move out the circle toward more distant identities, empathy is increasingly balanced by socialization, notions of moral and strategic interdependence, and rational persuasion.

The most collective and embedded source of care, connection, and responsibility is socialization. Socialization refers to a long-term process of learning values, roles, and frames regarding social order and practices that filter new information and experiences. This is the dominant constructivist explanation for state compliance with international human rights norms and the construction of the international human rights regime itself (Wendt 1999; Finnemore and Sikkink 1998; Cardenas 2007). But it is also a powerful determinant of individual, organizational, and community consciousness and mobilization around human rights issues. Roles such as childrearing teach us to think about more long-term and collective social goods, what strategic theorists call "the shadow of the future." When I interviewed one of Argentina's Mothers of the Disappeared, a pioneering human rights movement of housewives that defied a dictatorship to demand justice, she described her decision to keep protesting despite severe threats—even when she feared her own child was already dead. "After that time, I was no longer doing it for me—I was protesting *for every mother's son*" (Brysk 1994: 12, Interview).

At a cognitive level, ideologies and belief systems promise self-realization through assuming ethical collective responsibility. As a Dutch Holocaust rescuer who saved scores of Jews and was tortured by the Gestapo five times explained his motives:

> Life is possible because there are a certain amount of people who are not selfish and who believe in sharing with others. That makes life possible. If there is no love and sacrifice, no concept of others, then maybe life would be possible in some ways but it would be a terrible tragedy....I have some privileges; we get in turn some responsibilities....I have seen in my life people who are selfish, and not happy....My ambition, my aim is to be happy. (Monroe 2004: 114–115)

Students of a wide range of altruistic social movements highlight the influence of several prominent ideologies of empathy in mobilizing care by linking identity to community. Most humanitarian campaigns have been in some sense inspired by either Christianity's message to help "the least among us," humanism's mandate of cosmopolitan liberation, or a socialist imperative of universal justice (Guigni and Passy 2000: 8).

Across an entire society, diffuse socialization about victims, harms, and social boundaries may support solidarity. The power of diffuse socialization is that once attention is focused on the social rule, role, or custom, little compassion or persuasion is necessary—responsibility flows from duty, not choice. An example of relatively rapid and strong solidarity of this type is American public response to human trafficking, especially international commercial sexual exploitation of children. Socialization about slavery, sexual abuse, and children is so strong that concern and policy response on this issue overcome relative indifference to more massive and equally harmful abuses of other kinds of migrants and other forms of contemporary slavery (Brysk 2009b).

The mobilization of conscience to foster political will in this sense is epitomized in the human rights movement rubric of "naming and shaming." Kwame Anthony Appiah has recently theorized how shifts in the notion of "honor" inspire abandonment of practices injurious to individuals in the name of some social prestige or privilege, especially for previously marginalized groups such as women and slaves. Shifts in the basis of social status and reference group—notably globalization of the "honor world" of relevant peers—motivate new standards of respect for individual human dignity (Appiah 2010; also see O'Neill 1999).

But diffuse and unarticulated socialization can also be a tremendous barrier to the mobilization of care, especially when states, elites, and other beneficiaries of abuse promote counter-frames and competing values like national insecurity or cultural pride. However, socialization can evolve via dialogic interactions, social learning, and empowerment. There is some emerging evidence that successful interventions to reduce FGM have transformed socialization in just this way (chapter 4).

The Pathway of Moral Economy: Reciprocity and Interdependence

Because we are social animals, even strategic calculation may be a pathway to compassion, via interdependence and reciprocity. Contrary to the egoistic notions of social contract theory, ancient and hunter-gatherer societies closest to the "state of nature" are collectively minded and dominated by the gift economy (Mauss 2000). Evolutionary biologists like Steven Pinker (2008) conclude that we have developed a "moral instinct" that permeates our social reasoning, rooted in universal principles functional for long-term group survival. Like our innate capacity for grammar that is filled by a variety of languages, anthropological and experimental evidence seems to converge on a set of hard-wired propensities for empathy, fairness, duty, justice, non-violence toward members of the community, and shame or taboo markers (see also Haidt 2012 for a similar though distinct rubric encompassing all moral reasoning).

The application of these grammars of care are evoked in different ways by different cultures and situations, so altruism may be increased by both the awareness of interdependence—as Pinker (2011) goes on to argue—and the practice of reciprocity. Just as rational choice models of international cooperation show that the most functional strategy to secure national interest and avoid conflict is reciprocity (Axelrod 1984), micro-level studies of marriage show that interpersonal generosity is a key component of relationship satisfaction and stability (Parker-Pope 2011). Theorists of "social capital"—the basis for the capacity for collective action of any kind—show it is composed of an amalgam of associational networks, reciprocity, and trust (Putnam 2002; Norris 2002).

Summing up: Who Cares—and Why?

In reality, we have a shifting mix of motives for care. Moreover, we do not fully understand if dynamics like empathy and rational persuasion are competitive, alternative, sequential, or cumulative pathways to solidarity. Critics of explicit sentimental appeals that personalize and locate suffering in a subaltern individual decry a "pornography of poverty" that they claim crowds out understanding of deeper structural dynamics (Bell and Coicaud 2007), while supporters of "pragmatic sentimentality" claim instead that it mobilizes unreached populations and inspires the attention that will eventually produce understanding of root causes (Rorty 1993). Haidt's most recent examination of a wide range of experimental evidence suggests a sequence of moral judgment in which "intuitions come first, strategic reasoning second" (Haidt 2012). My own work on Latin American indigenous rights movements suggests a cumulative impact of cultural, legal, relational, and interdependence appeals in forming solidarity coalitions with Northern environmentalists, missionaries, and anthropologists (Brysk 2000).

If we are seeking contingent solidarity for constructed human rights, do we really need to understand *why we care*—or just *how*? Does it matter if we care about the right things for the wrong reasons, in the spirit of Richard Rorty's model of "contingent solidarity"—a pragmatic appeal through compelling narrative to a liberal, "post-metaphysical" common ground for universal empathy? (Rorty 1989) Yet strategic or confused care may distort the mode or impact of solidarity—improperly motivated care may lead to domination, dependency, burnout, or "cures worse than the disease" (Kennedy 2004). While a socialization or persuasion approach attaches great importance to motivation and orientation, an empathetic or relational perspective is less demanding, and could argue that even misbegotten initial emotional engagement permits learning. For example, there are key historical cases like foot-binding in China or indigenous rights in Latin America in which religious groups originally inspired by paternalism or proselytizing later came to play a constructive role of partnership, and even "converted" from a rescue role to a broader notion of universal respect (Keck and Sikkink 1998; Brysk 2000).

It may depend on what work we want solidarity to do. Diverse appeals to "pragmatic sentimentality" may be good enough to spark a starter human rights campaign for a previously unpublicized issue. If the rights at issue are a conceptually simple matter of including a marginalized group in a corpus of citizenship rights and the rule of law, recognition plus rational persuasion and reputational "naming and shaming" may be readily rewarded (Burgerman 2001). But more chronic, structural, interdependent abuses seem to require more complex combinations and sequences of care. When Eyal Press (2012) examined case studies of individuals who resisted social pressure in order to follow their conscience, from a Holocaust-era Swiss border guard to an Israeli refusenik to a dissident US military prosecutor at Guantanamo, he found the critical combination to evoke solidarity with a stigmatized other was a mix of care, reasoning, and socialization. Solidarity was relational, based on a combination of empathetic proximity to victims plus an internalized idealism, which held society to its own norms—for conscientious objectors, conforming to society's values meant rebelling against its practices. If we are looking for some sort of sustainable, multifaceted global governance and cosmopolitan empowerment, we need to look for forms of transformation that combine consciousness-raising, institution and coalition-building, and practice (Giddens 1979).

We care because by caring we learn to be human, recognizing our own identity, connecting to community, and practicing interdependence. As MSF President James Orbinski puts it, "Humanitarianism is about the struggle to create the space to be fully human" (2008: 8). We can ground the notion of solidarity by reformulating the "right to have rights" as the right to care.

The Message: Human Rights as Global Social Imagination

Solidarity is based on some implicit notion of human rights, because we care if people who are like us or connected to us are suffering some abuse or deprivation that denies them *something we all deserve*—even if it is called dignity, fairness, consideration, or compassion rather than a specific set of legal entitlements. The *something* that is "just not right" or "the way you shouldn't treat people" catalyzes latent concern to situated solidarity, so it must be coherent and recognizable.

Human rights are a quest to protect and promote the necessary conditions for the development of personhood in response to contemporary forms of power. Human rights are not a sacred or natural doctrine; rights are constructed and contested political tools for emancipation (Goodhart 2012). The shifting content of rights is directed by the humanistic project of universal moral equality and emancipation (Beitz 2009).

In our age, human rights discourse is a powerful paradigm (Bobbio 1996), a "standard of civilization" (Donnelly 1998), and a form of communicative action (Li 2003). Human rights provide a multifaceted ethos of connection, protection, and entitlement that substitute for the increasingly hazy promise of citizenship in an era of shifting identities and weakening states. Rights serve as the normative basis for many forms of international institutions and global governance—the "international human rights regime" (Donnelly 2007). The practice of human rights is an applied art for healing "pathologies of power" (Farmer 2005) characteristic of our times: from abuse of state power to distortions of globalization.

Why is this particular idea of human rights so powerful at this moment in world history? Human rights works because it is the contemporary social imaginary that speaks to the issues of meaning, identity, security, and freedom that define the human condition. By telling me who is human, the social imaginary of human rights reflects back my own humanity, and proposes a social order that will honor and protect my identity, promising a global social contract to limit our vulnerability. The content of human rights works to claim care not necessarily because it provides a specific answer to the questions of legitimate authority and social order but because it insists they must be answered (Beitz 2009). Conversely, in the long run recognition of rights is blocked primarily by a counterclaim on one of these bases of legitimate requisites of the human condition; short-term appeals to individual interests and material well-being cannot usually command sustainable social support without some larger rhetorical rationale. I cannot see your suffering if and when I believe you are an existential threat to my identity, security, or freedom (Katzenstein 1996).

A social imaginary is the orienting set of ideas behind every global order and phase of history, an overarching mind-set that filters our perceptions and reactions to the world around us. For example, Manfred Steger's study of contemporary history shows how nationalism informed and filtered a whole phase of our development worldwide and has more recently been transformed into a "global imaginary." That does not mean that everyone favored or even understood it, but it means this underlying framework set the terms of debate for all social developments of that era. The constructivist approach to understanding the basis of power, social institutions, and global governance assigns an important role to such collective imaginaries. Constructivism is an interpretive branch of social science, in the tradition of Max Weber, that tries to bridge our observations of the material forces and structures that shape our reality and the power of new ideas and individual agency to reshape them. As one constructivist social theorist puts it, "ideology tells us who we are, how the world works, and how to behave" (Jepperson, Wendt, and Katzenstein 1996: 42). So, for example, the oppression of South African apartheid was constituted by a combination of economic exploitation, political domination, and racial ideology—and eventually could be transformed by new universal ideas that mobilized transnational campaigns, delegitimized the South African government in the eyes of its former allies, and harnessed the shaming power of "international society" (Klotz 1995).

Human rights can play a transformative role as an emerging social imaginary because it offers us at the same time a lingua franca, the globalization of an ethic of care, and an emancipatory script. Previous studies of the growth of human rights suggest that new human rights norms become accepted and internalized as they fulfill these functions: rights are clarified and gain historic status as universal standards (Legro 2005), connect to care as humanitarian protection from physical threat to innocent victims (Keck and Sikkink 1998), and are framed to fit with prevailing ideologies of liberal modernity that promise emancipation for individuals (Boli and Thomas 1999). In an era dominated by neoliberal globalization, human rights fit the contemporary zeitgeist as a form of "revolutionary liberalism" (Goodhart 2009), which holds the dominant liberal ideology to its own highest historic claims. Boaventura de Sousa Santos considers human rights as a potential "emancipatory script" within the dialectics of the modern regulatory state and inter-state system. He concludes that "human rights are a political Esperanto, which cosmopolitan politics must transform into a network of mutually intelligible native languages" (Santos 2002: 282).

What are the claims and norms of this cosmopolitan doctrine of human rights? The essence of human rights is the idea that all persons possess equal moral worth, that social order exists to realize the essential humanity of its members, and that therefore the exercise of all forms of authority is properly bounded by its impact on human dignity and well-being. The conceptual core of human rights standards is to provide both *protection* and *empowerment* against an evolving series of threats to our common identity and vulnerabilities as humans, starting but not ending with state power. In this way it goes beyond both earlier humanitarian traditions of protection and beyond procedural or institutional doctrines of democracy as participation. Rights reframe suffering as a modern problem, as Susan Sontag puts it, shifting our understanding of suffering beyond "a mistake or an accident or a crime. [It becomes] something to be fixed" (Sontag 2003: 99). As I have watched movements come to consciousness around the vision of human rights, from Argentina to India, I have seen the power of the human rights idea to tell us that we can be self-determining subjects, that suffering is political—caused by abuse of power and alleviated by the rule of law—and that we should "get up, stand up" for our rights.

Human rights are grounded in a vision of common human needs and possibilities, or as Nussbaum and Sen (1993) label them, "capabilities." As Donnelly puts it, "We have human rights...to those things 'needed' for a life worthy of a human being. The 'human nature' that grounds human rights is more a social project than a pre-social given.... a sort of self-fulfilling moral prophecy" (2006: 603). Beitz similarly treats human rights as "the articulation in the public morality of world politics of the idea that each person is a subject of global concern." Human rights are a form of practical reason to protect urgent individual interests against standard threats in the modern world order composed of states. They fall first on states to respect individuals and protect them from non-state authority, but secondarily on international society when states lack capacity or will to protect their subjects (Beitz 2009: 1, 109).

To meet this mandate, fundamental human rights must be *universal* and *inalienable*—immune from contingent variations in geography and political conditions. The basis of rights as legal entitlements to equal protection and participation originated as citizenship in modern states, and thinkers like Hannah Arendt (1958) challenged the viability of universal rights without state enforcement. But at the same time, modern states have often lacked the capacity or political will to provide a full range of inclusion or enforcement of citizenship rights. Thus, human rights must be enforced "from above and below" as well. The safety net for human rights is the international system: the global order that aims to improve uneven citizenship regimes, incorporate the increasing numbers of displaced persons and noncitizens, and act to check the sovereign destructive power of rogue states, through the uneven but growing exercise of global governance.

The notion of an *international human rights regime* is to diffuse and embed a consciousness, practice, and locus of accountability for human rights at the global level, supplementing and transcending the promise of citizenship. The regime is oriented by legal norms (including "soft law"), but composed of a wider ensemble of actors, institutions, and practices of global governance, including global civil society. David Kinley (2009: 215) summarizes the utility of the legal foundation for the fulfillment of human rights as providing a combination of normative principles, a universal repertoire of definitions and boundaries, a link to state enforcement, a predictable process for conflict resolution, and a doctrine of equal standing. Expanding these legal facets of the regime to other forms of governance and participation is necessary but not sufficient for instantiating care.

Recognition of human rights began over a century ago with two border-crossing forms of abuse: war crimes and the slave trade. It is no accident that both of these abuses emerged with the modern system of capitalism and the nation-state, but it is also important that the same social developments generated transnational human rights campaigns against the slave trade, international treaties on war crimes (the Geneva Conventions), and the first cultural recognition that members of other races and nations were full members of the human race.

Human rights developed further along with the modernization of the inter-state system and liberal world order. The horrors of the twentieth century, in which at least 150 million persons perished at the hands of their own governments, inspired efforts to name and criminalize genocide and the systematic use of torture. By mid-century, human rights had conceptually challenged sovereignty and expanded recognition to focus international attention on stable, peacetime governments' abuse of their own citizens. Doctrines of democratic self-determination, repertoires like the "prisoner of conscience," global norms against discrimination, and greater recognition of the universal rights of refugees all signaled the growth of new standards for the legitimate exercise of authority and the rights of the individual vis-à-vis the state.

In contemporary international society, this norm of human rights has become the theoretical basis for the legitimacy of all states. Over three-quarters of the world's states now subscribe to the foundational documents that delimit human rights in theory: the Universal Declaration and two International Covenants on Civil/Political and Social/Economic Rights. This does seem to indicate what John Rawls would call an "overlapping consensus" of common commitment in principle despite cultural and ideological variation over means to the end (Kohen 2012). Massive and gross violation of human rights is the only globally legitimate basis for violent intervention in the conduct of one state by another. Under the rules of the current international system, human rights persecution is also the only universally recognized basis for individuals to change national citizenship, as refugees—and in principle to be automatically accepted by another state.

While this first generation of human rights arose to defend the lives and physical integrity of political dissidents and religious or ethnic minorities from the malfeasance of dictatorships, its mandate has expanded in every generation since. Collective and social dimensions of rights are entailed even within the most limited conventional civil rights. For example, free speech is the ultimate negative liberty of the individual—but it is only meaningful if there is someone to communicate with. In complementary fashion, freedom of assembly is essential to defend labor rights. The full range of political, economic, and social rights and authority relations envisaged in the Universal Declaration and associated treaties is now widely acknowledged—in theory. Human rights theorists and advocates now understand social rights such as education and health care to be interdependent with civil and political rights, especially for socially marginalized groups, like land rights for indigenous peoples. International human rights organizations and campaigns attempt to secure accountability of non-state actors like multinational corporations for abuses of labor rights connected with globalization, like sweatshops or conflict minerals. Similarly, international humanitarian law is applied to guerrilla groups with the potential to abuse civilians as they exercise local authority or wage war against the state. Human rights draw attention to government negligence, as well as repression, especially states' duty to provide equal protection to the female half of the world's population from gendered violence, which is often perpetrated by private citizens (Brysk 2005; Kinley 2009).

There are still many exclusions and contradictions in the concept of human rights, and it is far too often ignored or hypocritically distorted, but an evolving, accountable notion of human rights is one of the best truly global ideas we have got. And it shows a remarkable capacity for growth. Where a crude and cynical version of human rights—or even more often, democracy—is used to mask or justify international abuse of power, it can and should be criticized and exposed by showing how it violates its own claims. The real work of human rights is to build a world in which people are conscious, protected, and empowered to contest the abuse of any idea—including human rights itself. And as Goodhart (2012) points out, "The political perspective also suggests that such misuse of human rights is actually a double-edged sword for the powerful and privileged; using human rights as rhetorical cover, or co-opting human rights discourse for the purposes of dominating or oppressing others nonetheless has the effect of reinforcing the legitimacy of the discourse itself." (40)

The gap between theory and practice is morally and politically disturbing, but it does not discredit the idea of human rights—any more than the persistence of illness, bad doctors, and side effects of drugs detracts from the idea of health and the associated practice of modern medicine. In a parallel idea, one component of the modern idea of health is the concept of "infant mortality." This notion and standard implies that children are valuable members of society deserving attention and resources (rather than disposable first drafts), that many of the conditions which threaten children's survival are preventable or treatable (rather than bad luck), and that any legitimate authority must monitor the survival of children within the community and collaborate across borders to improve it. Millions of children still die, but untold numbers have been saved by some application of these ideas; for example, in the early human rights campaign against Nestlé for inappropriate marketing of infant formula in developing countries, or international brokering of cease-fires to administer child vaccinations. Such ideas even become a template for improving the practice of global public health. A rights-based perspective shifts medical practice to reduce mortality from malaria from the historic Western preference for treatment of disease through medication to more holistic preventative practices such as the distribution of bed-nets. So we see that the idea of human rights undergirds even a seemingly apolitical or objective concept of health and modern interdependent public health practices: that health involves rights, and rights involve health.

Human rights have always touched on a broader spectrum than civil and political freedoms, and some of these fuller forms of humanism have been developed by the globalization of human rights advocacy. For example, people with AIDS in developing countries turned to a language of health rights to demand access to anti-retroviral drugs from international pharmaceutical companies, explicitly calling for "human rights not property rights." The empowerment dimension of human rights—which is the next generation after protection of life and liberty—contains the potential for its dynamism, like the recent incorporation of "rights-based development" as an orienting concept by organizations such as Oxfam that work with "partner groups" rather than by simply distributing resources (Nelson and Dorsey 2008). Human rights are far more than legal entitlements; the legal checks and balances are just the most developed expression of a vision and program of the defense and development of the flourishing of the human individual within the social world.

The globalization of human rights has also intensified its claim as a lingua franca. In previous eras, international relations consisted largely of elite diplomacy, uneven trade, episodic cross-boundary conflict, and regional or religious cultural flows. None of these modes can encompass constant, multi-level interactions that touch virtually every person on the planet in some fashion: from migration to the global information economy, from environmental interdependence to transnational terror. Human rights is perhaps the only currently available common framework for debate that has the potential to include all participants and speak to all forms of interaction because it requires only human identity and proposes a comprehensive set of social understandings on that basis. Human rights provide, in the vision of feminist poet Adrienne Rich (1993), "the dream of a common language."

There are several responses to the charge that human rights is somehow limited by its Western roots or imposed by Western elites on imagined authentic members of other cultures. Even as he rejected Western imperialism and fought for the self-determination and identity of India, Gandhi appreciated and appealed to the British notions of justice, the rule of law, and the influence of British citizens on their democratic government at home. In similar fashion, one of the Amazonian Indian leaders I interviewed about his rights campaign in the 1990s remarked that although his struggle for self-determination was robbed by Western domination followed by national exploitation, "The cure will come from the same culture as the disease." Moreover, some intercultural and multicultural theorists see the development of international human rights as the best basis for overcoming the legacies of imperialism, in a universally accessible dialogue that is the best meeting place for diverse and historically disempowered cultures (An-Na'im 1992).

The idea that people "belong" to static and unified cultures is itself an outmoded Western idea that is often absorbed or even manipulated by political or religious leaders in developing societies because it seems to offer support for their nationalist goals or personal advancement. Moreover, the traditions they seek to defend are often recently invented or at least variable over time and through different social struggles within that culture. Every culture has some notion of justice, every culture has some idea of mercy, and everyone has some idea of acceptable limits to authority. Where we differ is over where these limits fall, who is included, and which social institutions enforce these limits—not the basic idea of rights. Some rights critics and even some Western advocates fail to connect the broader human rights project with the full moral palette identified by Haidt (2012) in cross-cultural studies, falsely limiting rights claims to the basis of *liberty*—or perhaps *harm*. But a fuller understanding and historical reading of human rights draws from at least four or perhaps five of Haidt's six primary moral instincts, adding to liberty and harm, *fairness, sanctity* (appeals to "human dignity" and freedom of conscience), and at times *loyalty* to a social code or unit resisting state power. Thus, some see the empowerment dimension of rights as the best way for the most marginalized to "vernacularize" global norms and legal processes and translate them into locally meaningful practices (Engle Merry 2006).

The message of human rights as a lingua franca is a potentially universal ethic of care, responsibility, and interdependence. Feminist theory has drawn attention to the ethos of care that undergirds the liberal public sphere—meanwhile, a new wave of transnational reproductive care relationships creates new challenges for "civilizing globalization" (Held 2006; Robinson 1998). On the one hand, negative freedoms for liberal autonomy are insufficient; we have a right to receive care because "without care, we would not become liberal individuals" (West in Feder Kittay 2002: 88). In converse and complementary fashion, the development of our capabilities includes the capability and need to care for dependents, and thus a social right to give care—and to a corresponding social order that supports care-giving labor and legal entitlements (Kittay and Feder 2002). Social rights are a prerequisite and expression of care, while human rights must grapple with the globalization of the private sphere of reproduction, domestic labor, and sexuality.

Although some feminist theorists see these issues as a serious challenge to the universality of human rights, others see the ethic of care as a broader basis for realizing the core values of moral equality and empowerment that encompass but are not exhausted by the traditional "rights talk" of legal entitlements. Feminist liberal human rights theorist Martha Nussbaum has extended her capabilities approach to rights in a way that attempts to reconcile freedom and care; an ethos of "love and justice." (Nussbaum in Kittay and Feder 2002: 205) In this more radical humanism, human dignity and moral capacity are grounded in both capability and vulnerability—not abstract rationality. Nussbaum's broadened approach to the capability for care displaces the beleaguered Kantian account with an Aristotelian personhood situated in the natural world, and a Marxian recognition of practical reason and affiliation needs and vocation (Nussbaum 2002). This line of feminist theory can be further extended to provide a relational, care-based form of cosmopolitan solidarity (Robinson 1998).

Human rights as a doctrine of *responsibility* promote a world-view of moral interdependence, in which we are invested in each others' well-being. Whether for personal, religious, role-based, or ideological reasons, we come to believe we are tied in a community of fate to strangers. We are fictive kin, and I am my brother's keeper. The Universal Declaration of Human Rights arcs from a straightforward natural rights justification to demand that we act toward one another "in a spirit of brotherhood." The extension of this basis for rights is the "responsibility to protect"—a United Nations principle that empowers international intervention when states cannot or will not protect their citizens from fundamental threats. The normative implication of this international report, debate, and subsequent Security Council resolution is to shift the emphasis to the rights of the person and the responsibilities of the state and international community, reversing the traditional defense of state's sovereignty rights and insistence on citizens' duties (Dunne and Hanson 2009).

At the same time, human rights draw upon a social ethos of *strategic* interdependence, which provides an account of "instant karma." Our safety and stability are interdependent in a world of global conflict; today's refugee may become tomorrow's terrorist, and failed states are vectors for "global commons" problems—from epidemic diseases to drug trafficking. As former Amnesty International director William Schulz (2001) shows in his book arguing for human rights solidarity *In Our Own Best Interest,* more peaceful and democratic countries make better partners in trade, tourism, environmental cooperation, and health. When I studied how half a dozen states broke conventional wisdom to become international promoters of human rights, one of Costa Rica's leading diplomats was puzzled by my question about his decision to "sacrifice national interest for human rights values." He assured me that in Costa Rica's understanding of its niche as a struggling democracy in a troubled region, "human rights *is* our national interest" (Brysk 2009a).

Finally, human rights provide an emancipatory script. In an era of globalization, human rights draws on the same principles of philosophical liberalism that inspire open markets, open societies, and open borders. They check the abuses and challenge the legitimacy of the distortions of neo-liberalism—by defending the integrity of the individual and demanding the level playing field that justifies the liberal social contract. This was recognized by Adam Smith in his "prequel" to *The Wealth of Nations*, *A Theory of Moral Sentiment*, which mapped the kind of social solidarity and principled boundaries that he believed would be a necessary foundation for the liberation of exchange from ,Church and Crown. While we have learned that open markets do not necessarily foster open societies as some modernization theorists predicted, conversely it does seem that open societies do promote more accountability in markets; hence, Amartya Sen's observation (1999) that there has never been a massive famine in a poor country with a free press. Similarly, human rights campaigns thus far offer the only protection against those disadvantaged by open borders—like victims of human trafficking when it is framed as contemporary slavery—where structural efforts do not avail in a world of neo-liberalism, sovereign states, and incomplete citizenship.

As Boaventura de Sousa Santos puts it in a work critical of the oppression of economic globalization yet seeking support for the oppressed through the globalization of law: "Instead of discarding cosmopolitanism as just one more variety of global hegemony, we propose to revise the concept by shifting the focus of attention to those who currently need it. Who needs cosmopolitanism? The answer is straightforward: whoever is a victim of local intolerance and discrimination needs cross-border tolerance and support; whoever lives in misery in a world of wealth needs cosmopolitan solidarity; whoever is a non- or second-class citizen of a country or the world needs an alternative conception of national and global citizenship. In short, the large majority of the world's populace, excluded from top-down cosmopolitan projects, needs a different type of cosmopolitanism. Subaltern cosmopolitanism, with its emphasis on social inclusion, is therefore of an oppositional variety" (Santos 2002: 460).

So human rights is a universal language for mobilizing solidarity to protect our most essential identity—which is a set of capacities—through building and bounding a just social order. How can human rights help to develop those capacities—notably, the capacity to imagine a better world? Human rights articulate a collective aspiration that puts the imagination in the global social imaginary. Human rights suggest that "another world is possible," in a parallel way to the words of the World Social Forum's attempt to provide counter-hegemony to neo-liberalism. In its most basic form, this means the elaboration and dissemination of standards of entitlement, institutional forms for national and global fulfillment of these entitlements, and communication of "best practices" to attain them. Treaties, truth commissions, and Amnesty International concerts are all forms of social imagination and the construction of collective aspirations. In a critical contribution to assessing the constructive power of human rights claims, Karen Zivi interprets rights claims as performative speech. She argues that "rights claiming provides a language through which we articulate and enact, at times even transform, our understandings of whom we are as citizens and a community" (Zivi 2012: 22).

When I analyzed this process further by examining global campaigns to contest "private wrongs" generated by authorities outside of governments, I found some common conceptual components specific to human rights that build an emancipatory script—across issues, regions, and contemporary time periods. An ideology teaches us who we are, and human rights propose that we are self-determining subjects—not victims, objects, or accidents. An important part of the normative work of human rights is universalizing the subject; adding categories of excluded or marginalized biological humans to full social membership as rights-bearers: such as slaves, infidels, women, and children. A social imaginary also diagnoses "how the world works" and how to make it work better. Human rights as imagination lead us to craft new mechanisms of governance; from socially responsible investment to gender-based asylum. Beyond this, human rights as emancipatory script applies what Morton Winston (1999) calls a process of "moral induction" to discover the rights necessary to safeguard and liberate all persons under changing social conditions. "New rights" such as environmental justice, informed consent for genetic research, or same-sex marriage promote equal moral worth in the face of changing patterns of development, technology, and family life.

Human rights rhetoric can be the basis for a new social imagination in the face of global change. But for such an idea to engage care and change history, it must mobilize the politics of persuasion. In Zivi's view of human rights claims as performance practice, she builds on a rereading of Hannah Arendt and John Stuart Mill to explain the persuasive power of rights claims in terms of appeals in public space—not just rhetorical debates about abstract principles or legal norms. Both Arendt and Mill emphasize that the power of rights is that they make us visible as fellow members of the public domain, and bridge between the ideas and the sentiments of justice. Zivi (2012: 52, 57, 119) goes on to show that specific rights campaigns persuade through an appeal that goes beyond protection from suffering to an assertion of capabilities and empowerment.

The Politics of Persuasion

Persuasion links compassion to connection, engaging "hearts and minds" to mobilize action in public space (Brysk 1995). Political theater, information politics, symbolic appeals, bridging metaphors, rationalist rhetoric, and role reminders all connect witness to understanding, and understanding to responsibility. Persuasion is what makes rights make sense (Brysk 2007) and enables speaking rights to build solidarity and political will.

What is the vocation and potential of the politics of persuasion in the "information society" (Castells 2000)? Many analysts and participants look to Habermas's theory of communicative action, which lauds the power of discourse to rationally constitute democracy, and the power of democratic movements to foster an "ideal speech situation" that emancipates participants (Risse 2000; Habermas 1984, 1996; Wagner and Zipprian 1989). While multicultural and feminist critics question the inclusiveness and emancipatory potential of the ideal speech situation (Young 2000; Ashley 1982), followers of Foucault mount a deeper distrust of both rationality and discourse that makes Habermas's goal of "discourse ethics" meaningless for such critics. In this view, all knowledge and the subjective illusion of agency are constituted by power and have no potential autonomy. Moreover, power is disseminated through a "regime of truth" that permeates all micro-relations and communicative social institutions, so ethics can only be constructed in a situational practice of freedom and deconstruction of abusive power relations, not through discourses of persuasion (Flyvbjerg 1998; Fox 1998).

This impasse on the possibility of persuasion can be traversed, if not transcended, by pragmatic and dialectical approaches that reposition communication as a power-laden but multifaceted arena of contestation. Pragmatist philosophers like Richard Rorty see cosmopolitan ethics as constructed through certain forms of communication and projects of representation—rights are neither discovered nor pacted, neither precluded by power nor wholly situational (Gunn 2001). Similarly, Bryan Garsten (2006) depicts persuasion as a source of both freedom and rule, and the practice of rhetorical appeals to sentiment and rationality as a tactic of manipulation that can also become a source of democratic empowerment. He tries to rescue Habermas's ideal of "public reason" by grounding the politics of persuasion in a broader "practical wisdom" that reflects and develops citizens' judgment, rather than imposing a pre-constituted set of discourse ethics. More specifically, some scholars of human rights movements apply Gramsci's insight that hegemony blends coercion and consent—which can be contested by civil society and intellectual critics—to show how articulating rights claims can reshape power relations (Carroll et al.1994; Hunt 1990).

Like Zivi's view of the emancipatory potential of speaking rights, Garsten seeks to recover the democratic potential of recognition and communication, which does not assume deliberative space but helps to constitute it. This broader dialectic begins with recognition of communicative competence that does not depend on rationality, but instead appeals to both hearts and minds by taking others "as we find them—opinionated, self-interested, sentimental, partial to

their friends and family, and often unreasonable" (Garsten 2006: 4). The funda-
ment and promise of this politics of persuasion is the capacity for judgment,
not rationality—even deconstructive critics do not deny their own capacity for
judgment of the permeation of power they decry. The chastened, contingent
humanism of this kind of project of persuasion requires

> Not that we become brothers or comrades, nor that we befriend those with whom
> we disagree, nor even that we join them in a contract. It requires instead that we
> pay attention to our fellow citizens and to their opinions. The politics of persua-
> sion asks that we look to understand the commitments, beliefs, and passions of
> the other side if only for the purpose of trying to bring them to our side—or, more
> often, for the purpose of trying to rebut their views in front of people who have
> no settled position of their own.... Trying to persuade others requires us to step
> outside our particular perspectives without asking us to leave our particular com-
> mitments behind. (Garsten 2006: 210)

If persuasion can help construct a public sphere to speak rights and develop
our capacity for recognition of solidarity, we must then analyze its tools and
requisites. How can this kind of communication persuade? To answer this question, we must begin with the concept of rhetoric, planted by Aristotle as an
active and political process that engages the listener and moves him or her to
action through a combination of logical and emotive appeals. Aristotle tells us
that persuasion depends on a combination of truth, trust, and emotions (*logos*,
ethos, and *pathos*). Almost a millennium after Aristotle, at the dawn of modernity, Adam Smith's *Theory of Moral Sentiments* takes up related questions in
its quest for an inductive and universal social theory. Although broader in its
ambit, Smith's work also emphasizes that "the desire of being believed, the
desire of persuading, of leading and directing other people, seems to be one of
the strongest of all our virtual desires" (Smith 2007: 397).

The most powerful emotions to mobilize political judgment are anger, fear,
and pity. And pity, which would be the basis for compassion, is based on the
suffering of "one who does not deserve it and which a person might expect himself or his own to suffer, when it seems close at hand" (Kennedy 2004: 139). In
terms of modern social psychology, these features of pity would be described
as moral desert, other-identification, and proximity. Aristotle further details the
susceptibility to such appeals by particular audiences, "those who have suffered
in the past and escaped and older people ... and the weak ... and those who have
been educated.... Also those who have parents or children or wives" (139). In
chapter 7, we will see the success of targeting audiences who have suffered in
the past (interethnic solidarity), those who have been educated (transnational
academic solidarity), and family ties by male advocates for women's rights.

Moreover, Aristotle states that the sense that suffering is "near at hand" can be enhanced by gestures, signs, and the "words of those who suffer"—in our analysis, testimonial—but disabled if sufferers are shown to be "unworthy" (141).

As Aristotle outlined, persuasion to accept and mobilize for human rights claims draws directly on pathos; the emotions. It is striking that contemporary neuroscience confirms the fundamental interpretive and mobilizing role of emotions in motivating social behavior and concludes that the most salient are fear, disgust, surprise, sadness, happiness, and anger (Damasio cited in Castells 2009: ch. 3). Garsten (2006: 195–196) echoes this account of the importance of emotional mechanisms in deliberation, notably salience, connection, honor and public status, and habits of response. As Castells reminds us, "social movements are formed by communicating messages of rage and hope." He points out that political persuasion is enhanced by anger, which is based on the perception of injustice and identification of a responsible agent (2009: 301, 147). From the standpoint of social movement theory, "raising consciousness" in social movement campaigns is a sequence of focusing emotional attention, building affective ties, promoting dense interactions that raise emotional energy, displaying symbols of suffering, strength, collective identity, and past struggles, and transforming suffering into moral conviction (Collins 2001). The roots of this process will be profiled in chapter 2.

The politics of persuasion operates through narrative. Hannah Arendt pointed to the importance of storytelling as a semantic strategy for bridging bonds in situations of repression and constructing a common public sphere for self-determination (Benhabib 1996; Lukes 1986). Building on the focus of attention through imagery, Susan Sontag depicts photographs that engage empathy as complementary to narrative that explains and points out that "compassion is an unstable emotion. It needs to be translated into action, or it withers....A narrative seems likely to be more effective than an image" (2003: 101, 122). In an interesting extension of this view, Boltanski (1999) argues that even narrating the witness of suffering to oneself or in the private sphere helps recover the agency and capacity for humanitarianism of the spectator of distant suffering. Students of human rights reform processes suggest that recounting stories of suffering is beneficial for the victim and teller, as well as the listener. They show the restorative power of narrative to recover voice—but also insist that "narratives draw upon surrounding cultural and political codes and are constituted by them," so that local context is critical to assess them (Wilson and Brown 2009: 21, 25). The constitution of voice will be considered in chapter 3.

Movements and campaigns must then move beyond emotional engagement to provide diagnostic and motivational frames that interpret moral shocks, foster pride in participation that redeems lost dignity and learned helplessness, and foster affection for the group through rituals (Collins 2001). Contemporary neuroscience again provides an underpinning for this behavioral observation, as decision making is shown to operate through the dual pathways of "framed reasoning" and direct emotional "gut feelings" with somatic markers. "Frames are neural networks of association that can be accessed from language through metaphorical connections.... the most important protocols of communication are metaphors" (Castells 2009: 141–144). This framing process will be detailed in chapter 4.

We think in stories (Gottschall 2012). Social information, including appeals for protection and cooperation, is transmitted in the form of narrative. As one analyst puts it, "narrative might well be considered a solution to a problem of general human concern, namely, the problem of fashioning human experience into a form assimilable to structures of meaning that are generally human rather than culture-specific" (White 1987: 1). Modernity has shaped a view of history as a plotted sequence of events that lends these stories a social center and lays the foundation for the modern legal subject—a protagonist making, breaking, or suffering from rules. The narrative form "is intimately related to, if not a function of, the impulse to moralize reality, that is, to identify it with the social system" (White 1987: 14). For Tilly (2008), social movement claims are enacted through repertoires and performances that draw on a fixed and localized pool of scripts. The construction and performance of plot will be taken up in chapter 5.

Contemporary scholars of social psychology confirm that our moral orientations and propensities for persuasion are constructed from personal dispositions, adaptations, and life narratives—that subsequently articulate with the legitimating grand narrative of an ideological or cultural moral matrix (Haidt 2012). In the words of contemporary activist James Orbinski, former President of Médecins Sans Frontières, "Stories, we all have stories. Nature does not tell stories, we do. We find ourselves in them, make ourselves in them, choose ourselves in them. If we are the stories we tell ourselves, we had better choose them well" (Orbinski 2009: 4). More broadly, narrative is now understood as an important determinant directing social behavior and agency by social sciences that formerly stressed material resources and social structures: the study of social movements (Tilly 2008; Goodwin, Jasper and Polletta 2001) and even behavioral economics (Akerlof and Shiller 2009).

Thus, the success of mobilizing political will for social change depends on some combination of the elements of narrative: credible and charismatic speakers, resonant frames, powerful explanations of urgent problems, performance in public space, accessible and salient media, and a match with a receptive audience. In an early attempt to model the narrative struggle for "hearts and minds" in collective action campaigns, I depicted this as a struggle between established canon and counter-hegemonic stories that either reverse the canon, insert new characters, or give voice to the marginalized to tell a new story. Certain forms of social crisis or repression create anomalies in an existing paradigm that challenge the official story and inspire symbolic politics appeals. Persuasive stories that succeed in mobilizing political will are those that use affective and appropriate symbols, answer fundamental questions, diagnose suffering and prescribe action, and unfold in accessible public space (Brysk 1995). My subsequent empirical work has shown that transnational ties for human rights campaigns are constructed through the communicative processes of political performance, identification with the other, clear causal narratives of injustice and redress, and "branding" of locations and victims (Brysk 1994, 2000, 2005, 2009).

These observations on the power of naming, framing, and shaming to mobilize political will and change policy have been supported broadly. Localized case studies like Anaya's work on contemporary Mexico show that amidst a plethora of abuses from classic state repression of protest in Oaxaca to non-state violence by drug lords, the single patterned abuse that has received widespread transnational mobilization and a measure of state response is the killings of women in Ciudad Juarez. He explains the difference by information politics: "because the situation has been advocated by a very dense network and because it has been amenable to the collection of sufficient reliable evidence, it has implied extreme bodily harm to vulnerable individuals and because it clearly and soundly resonates with established and uncontested international norms" (Anaya Munoz 2011: 350). In a comparative study of the impact of human rights criticism in Latin America including seven countries, a statistical analysis shows that shaming is the most significant factor in reducing repression (Franklin 2008). Even at the widest global and historical level, a comparative study of 323 nonviolent and violent resistance campaigns from 1900 to 2006 showed that nonviolent campaigns succeeded 53 percent of the time (compared with 26 percent for violent ones). The authors' analysis and in-depth tracing shows the importance of the legitimacy and the symbolic appeal of nonviolent resistance. They argue that "a campaign's commitment to nonviolent methods enhances its domestic and international legitimacy and encourages more broad-based participation in the resistance, which translates into increased pressure being brought to bear on the target," delegitimizes regime repression, and enhances broader public recognition of grievances (Stephan and Chenoweth 2008: 9).

In a narrative theory of political rhetoric, representations, claims, information, repertoires, symbols, analogies, labels, arguments, and other forms of semantics aim to transform hearts and minds. Several functions of communication politics provide the basis for collective action and social change: placing a social phenomenon on the rights agenda, providing evidence of a wrong that fits the agenda, empowering a new population, suggesting alternative paradigms, or promoting a mechanism for change (Brysk 2005). Successful human rights campaigns deliver a message of empathy with victims, connection with suffering, a causal narrative susceptible to global intervention, and empowerment of audience response. The message of hope is also critical (Just, Crigler, and Belt 2007)—above all, the belief that "another world is possible."

Conclusion

The idea of human rights must be voiced through compelling forms of communication to construct political will for solidarity. Once we recognize suffering, we must speak rights to power. The next chapter will outline the historical emergence of the modalities of human rights appeals through the construction of grammars of solidarity, internationalism, symbolic representation of suffering, and globalization. The remainder of the book will examine the application of each facet of the politics of persuasion to a wide range of contemporary global human rights campaigns—voice, frame, performance, media, and audience.

2

HISTORICAL REPERTOIRES: ATTENTION
MUST BE PAID

Willy Loman never made a lot of money. His name was never
in the paper. He's not the finest character that ever lived. But he's a
human being, and a terrible thing is happening to him. So attention
must be paid.
—Arthur Miller, *Death of a Salesman*

The first step in recognizing human rights is recognizing fellow humans--and
their suffering. Studies of social movement campaigns show how all kinds of
social movement messages must first gain visibility, then resonance, and finally
legitimacy (Koopmans 2004: 373–375). With successive struggles, attention
reaches toward wider circles of recognition, and new waves of campaigns
build upon repertoires established in previous generations. The historical arc of
human rights campaigns establishes patterns of voice, solidarity, and symbolism that lay the groundwork for contemporary struggles.

This chapter will show some of the roots and consequences of the modern
modes of speaking rights to power. These modes perform the tasks of personifying oppression, promoting principled identification across borders, establishing
frames of abuse, and providing global grammars of awareness and intervention.
The Dreyfus Affair models a principled solidarity campaign and pioneers the cause
célèbre. The Spanish Civil War constructs new frames and grammars of internationalism. The rhetorical turn in memorializing the Holocaust transforms the international human rights regime. And the emergence of globalized communication
media and mentalities is epitomized in the 2011 Egyptian uprising, that one of its
architects labeled "Revolution 2.0," to signal its connection to the new modality.

The Dreyfus Affair: The Power of Pen and Principle

The decade-long struggle to free French military officer Alfred Dreyfus from
false charges based on prejudice marked a turning point in the country that

arguably had invented human rights a century before, through the French Revolution's Declaration of the Rights of Man and the Citizen (1793). The mobilization of intellectuals to defend a pariah and accused traitor on the basis of an appeal to legal principles set the pattern for twentieth-century human rights campaigns. The campaign's combination of symbolism and narrative focused extraordinary attention on a single case and built attentive constituencies for the French Republic, modern citizenship, and the rule of law.

In 1894, Jewish French military officer Major Alfred Dreyfus was convicted of espionage, on the basis of false evidence and an unfair military trial, rigged by an anti-Semitic ultra-nationalist military establishment. The climate of national insecurity and popular racism during a period of military defeat and social instability was captured by the leading newspaper, *La Libre Parole* when it asserted: "However painful that revelation may be…we have the one consolation of knowing that it is not a true Frenchman who committed such a crime!" (Burns 1999: 34) Dreyfus was sent to France's most brutal prison colony in French Guiana and placed in solitary confinement.

Definitive countervailing evidence surfaced two years later but was suppressed by military officials. After intense public pressure, the real author of the crime was eventually tried but acquitted—and then fled following the revelation of more forged evidence. Dreyfus himself was retried, under another extremely dubious process, but again convicted. The second verdict against Dreyfus was so suspect that it was followed by anti-French demonstrations around the world, with a number of attacks on French citizens (Hoffman 1980).

Even as Dreyfus was imprisoned on the notorious Devil's Island, intellectuals and principled defenders rallied to his defense, against the tide of nationalist public opinion. This was an early cosmopolitan effort that reached well beyond the stigmatized ethnic community—most of France's assimilated Jewish community did not join the Dreyfusards, beyond the officer's own brother who published investigative pamphlets exposing false and contradictory evidence. Rather, most of Dreyfus's defenders were liberal universalists who decried clerical and military influence on justice. Prominent authors Émile Zola and Anatole France led the Dreyfusard movement. A new French counterintelligence chief who discovered contradictory evidence was moved beyond his personal anti-Semitism, expressed openly at the trial, to later become an advocate for Dreyfus as a matter of justice—and whistleblower Georges Picquart was himself later prosecuted for his principled reversal. Similarly, an appointed Senator for Life who became persuaded of Dreyfus's innocence—despite the politician's elite conservatism—published critiques but was punished by pillory, ostracism, and eventually loss of his post. Dreyfus's lawyer, Edgar Demange, was a devout Catholic and strong supporter of the French military, who took the case only because he believed that Dreyfus was innocent (Derflier 2002).

The centerpiece of the Dreyfus campaign was French author Émile Zola's article "J'accuse," which accused the military of anti-Semitism and conspiracy to prosecute an innocent man, in order to protect the true culprit. The pamphlet "J'accuse" sold over 200,000 copies upon publication (Read 2012: 218). The article inspired a libel trial against the noted author, and anti-Semitic and anti-liberal riots in France and Algeria. Pro-Dreyfus rioters responded with the slogan, "Long live the republic!"—identifying the case with the principles of the French Revolution. Zola fled to Britain, and other prominent Dreyfus supporters lost positions, suffered legal harassment, and were sometimes physically attacked.

Numerous works of art were inspired by the Dreyfus Affair, and it was debated throughout Europe for decades (Kleeblatt 1987). "J'accuse" was sold on the streets of Amsterdam, dozens of Dreyfus support committees formed in the United States, and the verdict was criticized by international celebrities from Mark Twain to Queen Victoria (Burns 1999: Ch. 7, "The World's Affair"). As historian Ruth Harris shows, the putatively rationalist and modern Dreyfusards were heavily influenced by passions, mythologies, and webs of personal relationships—and the Dreyfusards set a romanticized template for the engaged French intellectual activism that would resurface in the anti-fascist, anti-colonial, and 1968 student movements. Historians have collected tens of thousands of letters by individuals from all levels of civil society who speak of how the Affair awakened their conscience or shifted their identity (Harris 2010). Perhaps the most famous such identity shift was cited by Theodor Herzl, the founder of modern Zionism, who covered the trial as a journalist and concluded that only Jewish nationalism could redeem the French Republic's bankrupt promise of religious freedom.

Dreyfus's sentence was commuted and he was released in 1899. But he was not fully cleared and rehabilitated until 1906. Although he returned to military service despite health problems from his years of imprisonment, Dreyfus was still a target of nationalist rancor and survived an assassination attempt. He served with distinction during World War I as a lieutenant-colonel, defending the nation that had denied him his most basic "rights of man and the citizen." The Dreyfus Affair later contributed to liberal reforms in France, such as the passage of a law separating church and state.

This early cause célèbre that opened the twentieth century contained most of the successful elements of the politics of persuasion. Voice was centered on a single figure with attractive moral qualities, with a comprehensible story of personal suffering. The message was framed as a larger indictment of military authoritarianism and a defense of highly legitimate French Revolutionary principles, as well as modernist principles of religious tolerance. Intellectuals as skilled information processors used the dominant media of the era—newspapers—and many reinforcing forms of cultural representation such as theater. Although there was no special appeal to a pre-constituted audience niche (as we will see in some later episodes), the Dreyfus campaign actually helped to constitute a new public: the "Dreyfusards," marked by a modern conception of France's identity and honor. The campaign also resonated with a transnational public of progressive modernizers; ironic because Dreyfus himself was a traditional military officer and patriot victimized almost by accident—not a dissident or iconoclast. It was this transnational solidarity that is modeled in the next wave: the Spanish Civil War.

The Spanish Civil War: Principled Solidarity across Borders

During the Spanish Civil War of the late 1930s, over 32,000 volunteers from fifty-three nations risked their lives to defend an embattled left-wing democracy under assault by its own military—and foreign fascist troops from Germany, Italy, and Portugal. Communists, anarchists, liberals, and adventurers from neutralist democratic and occupied fascist nations found common cause in halting the spread of dictatorship. The most famous single contingent, the US Abraham Lincoln Brigade, was racially mixed and was for a time commanded by an African American. It was also notable for its high level of sacrifice: around 800 of its 2,800 members were killed in the conflict (Thomas 2001). This extraordinary display of solidarity to defend the freedoms of strangers also develops important elements of the modern human rights repertoire (Beevor 2006; Preston 2012).

The Spanish Civil War began in 1936 when a restive nationalist and Catholic military, led by General Francisco Franco, rose up against a democratic republic promoting modernizing reforms such as land reform and secularization. Although the armed forces advanced rapidly to control about one-third of the nation, when the right-wing rebels stalled in the face of massive civilian resistance, they called in reinforcements from friendly fascist dictatorships.

As the Western democracies equivocated, with the Republic on the brink of collapse, international activists and Communist parties organized military brigades of volunteers to counter the coup. The international brigades helped the Republic to stave off the fascist takeover for almost two years and gave international voice to war crimes such as the 1937 German fascist firebombing of civilians at Guernica. But despite the volunteers' presence, the combination of Franco's military dominance, fascist foreign troops unbalanced by the absence of trained Western forces, and some critical divisions within the volunteer and Spanish civilian ranks led to the Republic's defeat in 1939. Thus followed four decades of iron dictatorship in the heart of Europe.

During the course of the conflict, both sides committed massacres and war crimes—though the dominant fascists abused human rights more massively and systematically. It is estimated that half a million Spaniards lost their lives directly during the conflict. In the aftermath of the war, Franco's victorious forces executed at least 30,000 Republicans (most civilians), and hundreds of thousands became refugees—primarily to France and Mexico. In a chilling precursor of the tactic later adopted in Argentina, Franco took hundreds of children away from Republican families and sent them to fascist government or Catholic orphanages (Burnett 2009). The defense of the Spanish Republic was thus experienced and depicted as a defense of human rights against rapidly unfolding brutality and tyranny.

Who would volunteer for this cosmopolitan army, risking their lives to protect strangers? Almost all of the British volunteers to around one-third of the Americans were urban working class (Baxell 2004). However, there was notable leadership by public intellectuals such as Ernest Hemingway and George Orwell, and about 500 members of the Abraham Lincoln Brigade were teachers. The brigades were largely organized by international Communist parties, and between half and two-thirds of most nations' brigades were Communist Party members inspired by ideological internationalism—but significant numbers were not, aligned with other socialist and democratic movements in their own societies. A very high proportion was Jewish, in the era of rising persecution by fascist Germany presaging the Holocaust; an estimated 30 percent of the Abraham Lincoln Brigade were Jews (Rosenstone 1967). The largest single international contingent came from neighboring, liberal France, comprising around 9,000 of the 30,000 volunteers. Smaller but strikingly active battalions were exiles from fascist Germany and Italy—the roughly 3,000 German anti-fascist volunteers were renowned for sacrifice and suffered unusually high casualties. Irish volunteers were additionally motivated by their own exile following the Irish Civil War and combating the presence of a small group of Irish fascists supporting Franco's troops. Canada contributed the largest proportion relative to the size of its population of any country involved in the struggle and its slightly older, less Communist, relatively skilled volunteers adumbrate that country's UN peacekeeping vocation—although the Canadian government officially banned its citizens from overseas service in Spain midway through the conflict (Brome 1966; Krammer 1969; Cook 1979).

The naming of brigades for national heroes of freedom and independence reflects one dimension of their symbolic appeal: the US Abraham Lincoln Brigade, Italian Garibaldi Battalion, and Canadian Mackenzie-Papineau Brigade. Most national units positioned the Spanish conflict as a principled extension of domestic struggles. For example, as Franz Borkenau observed, "The Germans have to wash away the ignominy of their defenseless retreat before the forces of Hitler" (Krammer 1969: 68). Since Franco had also recruited some right-wing Catholic ideological international volunteers alongside the preponderance of official fascist conscripts from Germany and Italy, the left-wing defenders of the Republic were inspired to counter the Catholic anti-Communist rhetoric with their own modern liberal universalism.

The Spanish Civil War was perhaps the first modern international culture war. Ernest Hemingway's internationally acclaimed novel *For Whom the Bell Tolls* positioned the Republican struggle as a courageous fight for freedom, while lamenting the ethical quandaries of war and its toll on civilians. The book lauded an American volunteer as a protagonist and detailed Franco's abuses as it personified the suffering of Spain in the tortured character Maria. Similarly, Pablo Picasso brought unprecedented attention to wartime atrocities with his painting *Guernica*, which was commissioned by the besieged Republican government for the 1937 Paris World's Fair. George Orwell's *Homage to Catalonia* combined a compelling account of his own experience as a volunteer, a principled affirmation of the Republican cause as a struggle for social democracy, and a sophisticated rejection of Stalinist manipulation and internecine violence among the defenders. International conscience was aroused by the killing of Spanish poet Federico Garcia Lorca, similar to world reaction to Latin American dictatorships' assassinations of prominent intellectuals two generations later. Another hallmark of modern international consciousness was the conflict's widespread treatment in the emerging medium of film (Rosenstone 1967; Brome 1966).

The narrative of the Spanish Civil War and the internationalist effort set a template for many subsequent struggles. The tragic results of the inaction of Western powers helped stiffen US resolve for entry into World War II. The martyrdom of the volunteers was lauded, but undercut by their partisanship, yielding a mixed message taken up by Cold War era human rights campaigns. In every Western country, there were struggles over if and when to construct memorials to the fallen, who had inarguably died defending freedom—but under the "wrong" Communist flag. Their sacrifice presaged the fascist conflagration that was to follow and the global repertoire of recognition for the horrors of state terror.

The Holocaust: The Symbolic Recognition of Suffering

Why was the Holocaust recognized as the pivotal human rights abuse of the twentieth century, inspiring a radical expansion of international accountability? And why did attention and political will lag significantly after the damage had been done, although information and appeals were presented throughout the maelstrom? The state-sponsored murder of 6 million Jews, millions of Roma, dissidents, gays, and disabled persons, and massive war crimes against European civilians was certainly among the bloodiest losses of the twentieth century. But the casualty count was probably equaled if not surpassed in Stalin's Russia and Mao's China (Rummel 1994). The nature of the abuses of ethnic persecution, forced migration, and systematic degradation had been visited upon the Armenians a generation before—with little international response to this day (Power 2002). Although some diaspora Jews campaigned on behalf of their coreligionists, the transnational ethnic response was fitful and at times chillingly indifferent, favoring denial in many quarters well through the 1950s (Novick 2000). Yet today, the Holocaust has inspired multitudinous trials, reparations, treaties, documentation, memorials, and advocacy groups worldwide.

The suffering of European Jewry at the hands of Nazi state terror was recognized when the rhetorical elements that set the template for modern human rights campaigns were engaged: voice, witness, framing, media, and audience. The personification of victimization was given voice by *The Diary of Anne Frank* (Prose 2009). Although many testimonials have been collected since, the breakthrough recognition of witness was through Eli Wiesel (1982) and his account in *Night*. Framing was achieved through the coinage of the term "genocide," while plotting received a critical boost from the legal performance of the Eichmann trial. Consciousness of this genocide was further enhanced by its coincidence with greater global diffusion of visual imagery, in photos, films, and ultimately an influential television series—"Holocaust". An ironic testimony to the power of the semantic appeal by and for Jewish victims is that the equally salient suffering of voiceless non-Jewish victims such as forced laborers, Roma, and Chinese civilian victims of parallel Japanese war crimes has received attention only recently—generations later.

Consider the symbolic construction and impact of *The Diary of Anne Frank*, which dramatized massive systematic genocide through promoting identification with a single innocent young woman, highlighting her universal family ties and coming of age as an independent voice—not a psychologically painful hapless victim. The book was edited first by her father, then the publisher, then for stage and movie scripts, in order to avoid disturbing contradictions, family resentments, budding sexuality, and blame for the oppressors—precisely to preserve its appeal to a broad audience. Otto Frank, the sole survivor of the family, carefully chose a resonant photo of his daughter to maximize the impact of the publication once he realized the potential of Anne's story to symbolize the less picturesque suffering millions had endured (he also chose to donate some of the profits to human rights organizations). The publisher of the diary secured a preface from Eleanor Roosevelt that further generalized its message and downplayed anti-Semitism; this was ironic because the Frank family had been denied refuge in the United States. *The Diary of Anne Frank* sold tens of millions of copies worldwide, in English, French, German, even Japanese—and more. The creation of the Anne Frank House as the key Holocaust Memorial in Europe, visited by millions, obscured Dutch complicity; despite unusually high solidarity and Dutch rescuers, overall the Netherlands deported the second-highest percentage of its Jewish population of any country in Europe (after the epicenter in Poland) (Kuper, S. 2005).

Above all, the *Diary* recognizes the banality of suffering, and in that strange way reverses dehumanization and connects with far-flung struggles. *The Diary of Anne Frank* was read by Nelson Mandela during his imprisonment. It has been used as a training device for police in Latin American countries recovering from dictatorship. It is estimated that about half of all American high school students have read the diary. The universalism, redemptive optimism, and individualism of Anne Frank have been fiercely criticized by some Holocaust survivors and Jewish intellectuals as trivializing and obscuring the horror. But the book follows and develops the template of speaking love to power and has done more to promote Holocaust awareness than any other communicative strategy. As Primo Levi wrote, "One single Anne Frank moves us more than countless others who suffered as she did, but whose faces have remained in the shadows. Perhaps it is better that way: If we were capable of taking in the suffering of all those people, we would not be able to live" (Prose 2009:241).

The phenomenon of the mass murder of the Jews was named and framed in both directions, as both a generalizable and a particular terminology. On the one hand, jurist Raphael Lemkin coined the term "genocide" to describe the murderous ethnic persecution and connect it to prior and parallel episodes of abuse. This term entered international law and came to frame the Genocide Convention. On the other hand, the Jewish victim community emphasized the particular historical character of this culmination of European anti-Semitism as a "shoah"—the Holocaust—and sometimes explicitly resisted comparison to other groups' suffering. Claude Lanzmann's 1985 award-winning film *Shoah* deployed nine and a half hours of witness from multiple vantage points of survivors, bystanders, and perpetrators to build this frame of a situated and particular persecution of the Jews of Europe.

The performance of plot for comprehension of the Holocaust was critically enhanced by historic legal events that spanned each postwar generation: the 1945 Nuremberg trials, 1961 Eichmann trial, and the multiple investigations and ultimate trials of Ukrainian Nazi collaborator John Demjanjuk from the late 1970s through 2011 in the United States, Israel, and Germany. Each of these trials worked to establish in different ways the storyline of agency, responsibility, and consequences from the daunting morass of suffering. The Nuremberg trials established command responsibility, demolished the obedience defense, and revealed the complicity of trusted civilians such as doctors and German firms. The Eichmann trial was particularly influential in distinguishing the story of the genocide from the overall account of the war for a new generation and in Israel, as the legal drama itself interacted with its literary representation by Hannah Arendt. Felman notes the power of this combination of legal closure and literary empathy for trauma in Arendt's *Eichmann in Jerusalem* and compares it to the Dreyfus trial and Zola's literary intervention: "Law distances the Holocaust. Art brings it closer" (Felman 2000: 3). Arendt's account contributes key elements to the understanding of responsibility for repression and intervention. On the one hand, Hannah Arendt's famous observation of the "banality of evil" in Eichmann locates and personifies the responsibility of ordinary architects of destruction (Arendt 1963). At the same time, Arendt's struggle to justify Israel's authority as collective victim to prosecute an individual perpetrator builds the vocabulary of universal jurisdiction for crimes against humanity (Benhabib 1996). A notable element of the Eichmann trial was the extensive use of victims as prosecution witnesses, their role in narrating private consequences in public space, and a consequent emergence of "semantic authority by victims" (Felman 2000: 39). In this way, the Eichmann trial becomes "the privileged text of a modern folktale of justice" (44).

The growth and dissemination of visual imagery also played a key role in recognition of the Holocaust. Although war photographers had been important in other twentieth-century conflicts, the haunting depictions of concentration camp survivors, extensive visual evidence of mass murder such as piles of skeletons, and wide distribution of newsreels and later films established a new visual repertoire of mass atrocity (Sontag 2003). The level of visual documentation, increased circulation of photographs in newspapers and journals, and growing movie audiences intensified the power of this human rights appeal to mass consciousness. Stalinist abuses were hidden, and the Armenian genocide occurred before the full development of mass production and dissemination of documentary photography and film.

The importance of visual symbolism and how "the media is the message" is highlighted by the extraordinary global impact of the television series, "Holocaust." The four-part series was broadcast in the United States in 1978 and Germany in 1979—it reached an estimated half of the American audience. The television production delivered a unique combination of mass dissemination and intimate broadcast in the private sphere of the home, paralleling other influential television accounts of historical abuses, such as the TV series "Roots" (a history of African slavery in America). "Holocaust" won multiple Golden Globes and Emmys, but the production was fiercely criticized as trivializing and commercializing the genocide by prominent survivors like Elie Wiesel (http://select.nytimes.com/gst/abstract.html?res=F10912F939551A708

DDDAF0994DC405B888BF1D3). German analysts emphasize the power of this melodrama in German consciousness beyond the dozens of documentaries, plays, and even other feature films produced in Germany, in that it is the first victim-centered production that traces the fate of a single Jewish family—but also locates and personalizes responsibility in an ordinary German family on the other side. In Germany, the show had significant audience-building effects: the series generated a week-long national discussion, percolated through civic institutions like schools, churches, and political parties, and diffused attention to previously unconsidered non-Jewish victims (Zielinski and Custance 1980; Huyssen 1980).

Awareness of the Holocaust was finally facilitated by access to an unusually receptive audience: postwar America. It has been noted that the more proximate and implicated European societies were less likely to recognize and memorialize the Jewish genocide than the distant United States (Young 1993). There are several social psychological reasons an American audience was especially attentive to the wartime suffering of European Jewry, despite previous indifference to fatal European anti-Semitism. First, the framing of America's belated entry into the costly struggle as a fight for freedom and the parallel postwar mobilization against Communist totalitarianism were bolstered by evidence of the inhuman consequences of tyranny. Second, the American Jewish community reformulated its identity in the postwar years from assimilation and cosmopolitanism to a defensive identification with worldwide anti-Semitism. Finally, the individualization of suffering and the legalization of response, including numerous dramatizations of the Nuremberg trials, resonated strongly with the individual and legalistic elements of American political culture (deemed less relevant to European understandings of violence).

The rallying cry of Holocaust awareness and education was a resolution to prevent future genocide: "Never again!" Half a century later, this notion was debated in Bosnia, ignored in Rwanda, and finally tentatively addressed in Kosovo. When it resurfaced as a full-fledged rhetorical appeal, it was in the most unlikely distant conflict: Darfur. In chapter 4, we will consider how the genocide frame established by speaking rights at mid-century laid a foundation for political will at the dawn of the next millennium. In that millennium, globalization added further elements to the repertoires of human rights attention.

Globalization: Revolution 2.0

Egypt's Wael Ghonim was an unlikely revolutionary: a religious Muslim with an MBA who grew up in Saudi Arabia, worked for a multinational in the United Arab Emirates, and married an American. Yet globalization inspired him with the global imaginary of human rights in its most liberal form, and the tools to enact it. The campaign he catalyzed in Egypt combined a cause célèbre, a nationalist frame to bridge social differences, intense use of appropriate media, and protest performance to break a culture of fear. His memoir of the 2011 regime change in Egypt, *Revolution 2.0*, illustrates how globalization has changed both the media resources and mentalities of human rights campaigns.

By the twenty-first century, under President Hosni Mubarak, Egypt's military-dominated regime had morphed into a full-fledged police state. His thirty-year state of emergency entailed systematic censorship, repression of political opposition and Islamic activists, and widespread use of torture. Amnesty International reported thousands of irregular and incommunicado detentions, unfair trials, and rigged elections (Amnesty International 2011a). Egypt was also one of the leading recipients of US aid, most granted to the unaccountable military in the interest of maintaining the US-brokered peace with Israel. Mubarak's regime was massively corrupt—during his tenure Egypt's average score on Transparency International's ten-point scale of good governance hovered near the bottom around three—while an estimated half of the population lived on less than $2/day. Egypt's poverty was endemic, but inequality and unemployment had actually increased in the past generation of uncontrolled economic opening and population growth.

Wael Ghonim was emblematic of a generation of upwardly mobile but frustrated and politically disillusioned youth, keenly aware of the gap between Egypt and world standards. He was pulled into political mobilization seeking freedom, and later solidarity. The behind-the-scenes organizer of the uprising in Egypt developed his social capital and technical skills creating an Islamic website during the 1990s; initially, he was alternative but not dissident. He tells readers that his marketing background was "vital to [his] online activism," and his work with a relatively horizontal information economy global multinational taught him "the more you can get everyone involved in trying to solve your problem, the more successful you will be. I found it natural, years later, to apply this philosophy to social and political activism" (Ghonim 2012: 27).

Ghonim states that he was inspired by and later transmitted appeals and frames from an unlikely blend of international sources: the movie *V for Vendetta* about an anonymous campaigner against a dictatorship, and Gandhi's nonviolent campaign of civil disobedience (Ghonim 2012: 102, 107). Protesters on the ground also relied heavily on globalized protest mentalities, notably the work of American peace researcher Gene Sharp (Stohlberg 2011). Similarly, Dalia Ziada, a young woman active in the international Muslim human rights youth movement Project Nur, whom I interviewed by Skype during the Egyptian

Revolution, had translated comic book biographies of Martin Luther King, Jr. and was distributing them in Tahrir Square.

Ghonim's initial foray into online activism was the creation of a Web page for international diplomat Mohamed El-Baradei, who young Egyptians saw as a legitimate and charismatic alternative to Mubarak in 2009–2010; Baradei's global background and appeal eased his entry into Egyptian politics. The young online activist felt safe anonymously posting Baradei's Web page, which his surveys showed attracted hundreds of thousands of previously unmobilized youth. When he began to contemplate the political power of media more deeply, Ghonim decided to transform El-Baradei's Facebook Group to a Facebook page to increase cross-postings on the walls of uninscribed users, stating: "This is how ideas can spread like viruses" (Ghonim 2012: 43). But Ghonim's liberal marketing orientation pushed him into deeper democratic dialogue, as he began posting "customer satisfaction surveys" in the form of on-line opinion polls—and following a government media blackout, he used Google Moderator to host a forum called "Ask El-Baradei" that was viewed by over 100,000 users (55).

The Egyptian human rights campaign added an element of cause célèbre with the police beating death of Khaled Said. The tragic and targeted death of a fellow blogger inspired Ghonim to anonymously create a wildly popular Facebook page, "We are all Khaled Said." His first post is a classic solidarity appeal: "Today they killed Khaled. If I don't act for his sake, tomorrow they will kill me." This post received 300 responses in two minutes—and 36,000 by the end of the first day (Ghonim 2012: 60). As a spillover effect, Ghonim began to post dramatic visual evidence of torture collected by Egyptian activists on the "Egyptian Conscience" blog. Eventually, he created an on-line video mixing protest footage and a nationalist soccer song, which received over 50,000 views. Ghonim explained: "It was different from the regular practice of lawyers and human rights defenders, who used facts and statistics to garner support. Instead, the video created an emotional bond between the cause and the target audience. Clearly both are needed" (Ghonim 2012: 86).

The frame for the movement became a nationalist appeal to youth to redeem their country, stressing both citizenship and transcendent appeals. When pressed on-line to reveal his identity, Ghonim posted: "My name is that of every Egyptian who has been tortured and humiliated in Egypt" and declared "I want nothing other than for our country to become ours again....I dream that the people will one day love one another again" (Ghonim 2012: 89–90). The page resolutely eschewed partisanship and reached out to the Christian minority. After an early January bombing of a Coptic church raised fears of further sectarian violence, Ghonim posted symbols of religious unity and organized Muslim youth to protect Orthodox Churches during the January 7th Orthodox

Christmas service (126). As he dialogued with a rival, more radical and partisan activist page that was initially more popular but ultimately lost support and was eventually shut down by Facebook, Ghonim explained to a competing activist: "Our brand was peaceful and inclusive; it sought justice and involved its participants in decision-making. His brand ... was rebellious, angry, sometimes ill-mannered, and often dogmatic. He agreed" (112).

With attention, voice, frame, and media established, Ghonim turned to performance and organized a public protest. He describes his strategy as a "sales tunnel marketing approach" in which he sought to get users to first join the page, then interact, next post content, and finally break through fear to engage in grassroots activism. The gateway between posting and protest was to post a photo of yourself, holding a banner supporting the campaign. But Ghonim went on to design a more public protest that was relatively safe and universalist: the Silent Stand. Activists were enjoined to dress in black for mourning, amass on the Alexandria boardwalk (and later other cities), and pray, without any political symbols, slogans, or activity. The Silent Stand was organized online in two days, and a critical symbolic element was Ghonim's invitation to the mother of victim Khaled Said to attend. Although the numbers who physically participated were a modest estimated 8,000, Ghonim's follow-up on-line poll shows the Stand played a key role in signaling public dissent and breaking fear (Ghonim 2012: 67–79).

In terms that echo Castells's analysis (2009) of the emotional base of social movement rhetoric, Ghonim concludes, " 'We can' was the critical weapon to fight 'There's no hope' and 'Nothing will ever change'" (Ghonim 2012: 81). One of his last posts before his arrest was to title the January protests that sparked Egypt's regime change—"REVOLUTION Against Torture, Poverty, Corruption, and Unemployment." When he emerged from ten days of imprisonment by Egyptian State Security, that revolution had toppled Egypt's last, latter-day Pharaoh. While the long-term results of Egypt's democratization are a work in progress, information politics clearly contributed to moving that country from a generation of dictatorship to an opportunity for citizenship. Globalization of human rights vocabulary, media, and social movement strategies provided the final layer for speaking rights to power, even power imposed partly by the dark side of globalization itself.

Conclusion

To construct political will, first attention must be paid. We have seen how the Dreyfus Affair established a grammar of solidarity, and the Spanish Civil War a cosmopolitan vocabulary. Even the Holocaust secured full recognition only when it was filtered through a conscious process of communicative and symbolic appeals. These elements of cause célèbre, international solidarity, and symbolic politics came together in a globalized politics of persuasion during the Egyptian revolution. We will now turn to a deeper analysis of the rhetoric of rights: voice, message, performance, media, and audience.

3

VOICES

Heroes, Martyrs, Witnesses and Experts

> If there is any significant role that I played, it was that of being
> a vessel through which the struggle was presented to the nation
> and the world. The struggle had to have a symbol to be effective.
> —Nelson Mandela (Boehmer 2010: 181)

In speaking rights to power, the messenger matters. Social change is built by speakers who gain "moral capital" from their ideas and identities (Kane 2001. Symbolic figures such as causes célèbres, public intellectuals, and heroic movement leaders have a special ability to gain attention, shape discourse, and articulate human rights claims. While the importance of moral leadership is widely recognized in empirical literature on human rights struggles, from Mahatma Gandhi to Martin Luther King, Jr., it is rarely analyzed (Ackerman and Duvall 2000). Campaigns with charismatic leadership seem to prosper "against the odds": from Nelson Mandela's South Africa to the Dalai Lama's Tibet. Similarly, human rights movements that resonate also draw on the collective charismatic leadership and credibility of highly legitimate social roles—like mothers, doctors, and priests—that decry a policy or regime as a violation of social norms. In a more rational vein, sea changes in public opinion and "norm cascades" (Finnemore and Sikkink 1998) on critical issues are often catalyzed by credible experts who create path-breaking analyses that show that a problem is more widespread, more damaging, or more threatening to core social values than previously realized.

Why are some voices especially powerful sources of recognition and mobilization of political will? Persuasive voices draw on some combination of charisma, credibility, and connection. Heroes, martyrs, and advocates embody courage, evoke compassion, and counter dehumanization by personalizing a struggle. Credible experts similarly persuade and constitute an audience of public opinion, and their analysis connects this audience with the distant or hidden victims of human rights abuse. Human rights studies often highlight the catalyzing role of "norm entrepreneurs," who introduce a new moral standard, framework, or pattern of evidence (Finnemore and Sikkink 1998). Humanitarian witness promotes indirect connection to a credible observer that may permit a different powerful position of identification with victims by the mass public or policy makers. This historical repertoire is exemplified in Henri Dunant's account of witnessing the suffering following the Battle of Solferino, which played a critical role in establishing the International Red Cross and the Geneva Conventions (Slaughter in Wilson and Brown 2009).

Social theorists Max Weber and Clifford Geertz both emphasized the importance of charismatic leadership as a kind of socially integrative personal power. For Weber, charisma was primarily a numinous personal characteristic that competes with rational-bureaucratic authority, while Geertz observed that charisma derives from proximity to the center of social reproduction and may be role-based. Shils added the "charisma of office" (Geertz 1983: 122–123; Eisenstadt 1968: xxv–xxxiii; Shils 1965). Thus, charismatic leaders of human rights struggles may be heroes with unusual interpersonal skills and courage, inhabitants of central interpretive roles such as religion, or embodiments of transferred authority—such as dynastic leaders. Sheer personal dynamism of the sort originally discussed by Weber is often associated with a translational or bridging role as a speaker for the community relative to a broader or global audience. For example, Brazilian international indigenous rights advocate Davi Yanomami started his public career as a literal translator: a government interpreter for his tribe.

Another, often overlapping form of charismatic voice is the cause célèbre, an appealing representative victim or movement leader who embodies the violation of universal principles and encourages widespread identification by national and international publics. The cause célèbre provides credibility and connection to distant suffering and often demonstrates the moral worth of a stigmatized or previously invisible class of victim through their courage. Some religious leaders or writers may combine interpretive and heroic roles as cause célèbre, layering martyrdom with witness, and framing suffering in a religious teaching or ideology. Assassinated martyrs may transfer the cause célèbre charisma to a dynastic or political successor—especially a female or youth who theoretically transcends politics and embodies a legacy of morally pure suffering. Such martyrdom may also be collective, drawing on charismatic family, religious, or cultural roles; from Uganda's Invisible Children to Burma's dissident monks.

Celebrities and cultural figures may also attempt to transfer their charisma to a political campaign or underrepresented group. This role has been formally recognized and encouraged by the United Nations through its Goodwill Ambassadors program (also see Cooper 2008) but has also been mobilized independently by a plethora of country and issue-specific campaigns. Celebrity advocacy is especially powerful for the spotlight effect of bringing international attention and recognition to a distant or hidden issue, like blood diamonds or Darfur, but generally less salient for providing elements of credibility, persuasion, local support, or policy expertise where they are lacking. Thus, the US Campaign for Burma "decided to use some of the same brand-building strategies—simplified narratives, clear-cut imagery and, of course, the most carefully selected celebrities—used by other successful aid agencies, or even consumer-goods marketers." (Williams 2008) The campaign produced thirty celebrity spots for sequential Internet posting, including ones by Ellen Page, Will Ferrell, and Jennifer Aniston. Page's spot invoked a powerful analogy: "Hitler is alive in Burma." One of the organizing celebrities, Jim Carrey, tried to boost recognition of the local cause célèbre with a familiarizing mnemonic: "Aung San, sounds like 'unsung,' as in 'unsung hero'" (Williams 2008). Celebrity campaigns, arts and literature, and media cannot create empathy or consciousness, but they can serve as a powerful vehicle to focus attention and communicate connection.

Heroism and martyrdom can also be collective, when a group of speakers mobilize a charismatic role. The most powerful roles are those that involve a relationship of trust, in situations where the form of domination has violated the integrity or functioning of individuals charged with essential and highly valued social roles: such as mothers, healers, and clergy. Martyred mothers have exercised special influence in human rights campaigns throughout Latin America, the Mideast, and Africa—from South Africa's Black Sash to the Liberian women's movement profiled below. Dissident and heroic clergy have also been central figures, from El Salvador's Archbishop Romero to South Africa's Desmond Tutu. Physicians have deployed both moral power and expertise to campaign for the Geneva Conventions and successive international law against war crimes, access to essential medicines for AIDS patients, protection of children, campaigns against corruption in India, and in favor of reproductive rights—from Africa to the contemporary United States.

Sociology points to the public intellectual as another designated interpretive role with strong potential for political influence, commanding both universalist status and socially relevant information. Since the circulation and credibility of information is a function, in part, of the credibility of the source, we would expect speakers with greater social legitimacy to succeed more often at persuading others. Such figures are assigned the social functions of arbiters of truth and universalist values, guardians of public space, resistors to repressive authority, and critics of prevailing social practice (Habermas 1990; Bourdieu 1989; Weber 1964). Public intellectuals use expertise and analytically framed appeals to discover patterns, provide evidence, or suggest solutions (Misztal 2007).

The collective organization of intellectuals in "epistemic communities" can also serve as a source of issue advocacy (Haas 1989)—including human rights. Epistemic communities of experts are defined by shared beliefs about principle, causality, and knowledge criteria, and may constitute a transnational interest group to lobby for issue-related policies or a designated role in global governance. While most epistemic communities are scientific, economic, or technical, parallel medical, legal, and informational epistemic communities may promote a human rights agenda in areas like global public health, humanitarian intervention, universal jurisdiction, or freedom of information. Doctors Without Borders combine charismatic roles, credibility, and expertise; they represent a growing genre of transnational human rights advocacy based on an ethos of professional responsibility. In similar fashion, analysts of the global spread of legal reforms in civil liberties and improvements in international accountability for human rights abuse chart the influence of knowledge and professional networks of lawyers and judges (Langer 2007).

All of these forms of resonant voice interact with each other, and with the other elements of communicative appeals: plot, message, media, and audience. The more compelling voices, persuasive plots, and open channels of communication are present in a human rights campaign, the better the chance that rights will be recognized.

Heroes and Martyrs

Nelson Mandela: Hero, Dissident, and Cause Célèbre

Nelson Mandela combines three forms of compelling voice: he was a heroic leader who spoke for a movement, a dissident who voiced a counter-hegemonic vision of South Africa, and "the world's most famous political prisoner." After spending twenty-seven years—eighteen of them on the notorious Robben Island—as a political prisoner, he became the first black African president of South Africa in 1994. Mandela led the five years of negotiations with the white minority government that ushered in the end of apartheid and was recognized for this historic role with the 1993 Nobel Prize. He is a world historic figure who has been honored with at least 250 other awards, songs, statues, the naming of streets and public spaces, and numerous biographies and films.

Nelson Mandela was a conscious agent of symbolic leadership, not an accidental figure. As one biographer explains, in the wake of the 1950s Defiance Campaign, Mandela "came to realize, as had Gandhi on his railway journeys across India, that the reach of inspirational leadership can be measured through the number and power of the symbolic goals it sets" (Boehmer 2008: 104). In

1962, he wore a traditional African leopard-skin to a white South African court to assert his identity; later, when imprisoned on Robben Island, he refused to wear the prison shorts designated for black detainees and insisted on more dignified Western dress. Mandela studied and modeled himself on the symbolic repertoires of Mahatma Gandhi, Martin Luther King, Jr., Irish nationalists, and British suffragettes. Although the African National Congress (ANC) began with staunchly collective leadership, by the late 1960s the charismatic Mandela served increasingly as the face of the movement. In 1978, he was selected by the ANC and the international antiapartheid movement to personify the struggle through the Free Mandela campaign. One indication of the success of this strategy is that the 1988 70th Birthday concert organized on Mandela's behalf in London by Amnesty International garnered 200 million viewers (Boehmer 2008: 60).

Mandela was chosen to lead his movement in part because he did possess considerable personal appeal. In some measure his charisma was clearly temperamental, as attested by his three marriages, an unusually wide circle of friendships across racial and cultural lines, and early courtroom success as a lawyer. When he worked in South Africa's first black law firm, Mandela was "well known for his assertive, theatrical performances in court" (Boehmer 2008: 40). From jailers to journalists, interlocutors often describe Mandela as personable and charming.

But Mandela's powers of persuasion and representation also derived from his heritage and were cultivated by his education. He was a classic translational figure, bridging cosmopolitan and African ethos. Mandela came from an aristocratic Thembu clan of a minority South African ethnic group, and his princely status is indicated by the moniker intoned by South African blacks—Madiba. The Xhosa personal name bestowed by his family, Rolihlahla, means "resistance." But at his British Wesleyan boarding school, he chose the English name of a military hero: Nelson (Boehmer 2008). The universalist liberal education provided at Christian schools equipped Mandela to challenge the ideology of apartheid and culminated in a university degree in "native administration" imparting leadership skills. This education was capped with a law degree, partly earned in prison, inculcating norms of justice and tactics of institutional challenge.

Mandela's message was a Gandhian non-racialism that challenged the oppressor's legitimacy within the system's own terms. In his famous and internationally circulated trial speeches in 1962 and 1964, Mandela showed that apartheid contradicted its own mandate to safeguard "Western civilization." He stated his resistance to black and white racism, support for democracy and freedom, and limitation to violence only as a last resort. Mandela also projected a doctrine of African humanism, ubuntu, that he articulated with liberal cosmopolitanism and deconstructed Western fears of "African barbarism." While in prison, he learned Afrikaans so he could better understand and persuade his Afrikaner jailers and elite political opponents within their own ethnic and historical frame of reference, and later compared African nationalism to colonial-era Afrikaner struggles against British domination. In one assessment, "his achievement has been to demonstrate how an oppressive situation can be withstood through a process of strategically repeating and exceeding the oppressor's self-justifying discourses of rationality and belonging" (Boehmer 2008: 113).

As a cause célèbre, Mandela was both an embodiment of suffering and a representative of the nation's story. His iconic image provided a personal connection for millions worldwide to the more systematic and massive suffering of South Africa's black majority. The era of his imprisonment, from the 1960s through the 1990s, coincided with the establishment of Amnesty International and the rise of the "prisoner of conscience" as a political trope. Yet Mandela also offered hope. While in prison, Mandela's activities demonstrated his transmutation of victimhood into generative connection: Mandela was a prolific writer, started a famous prison garden, and educated other prisoners.

Mandela also provided a powerful model of courage in the face of apartheid's dehumanization and particular denigration of black men. His moral qualities of perseverance, principle, and transcendence explicitly countered racist stereotypes. Mandela's charismatic agency functioned to recover the moral worth of a stigmatized population. Critically, Mandela maintained a controlled and paternal masculinity in his dress, speech, and bearing. Even before ascending to the presidency, he was widely referred to as a leader by the Xhosa word for "father" (*tata*). Above all, Mandela's dignity resonated across racial and cultural lines—his very presence declared, "I am a man."

Cause célèbre as charismatic leader: Aung San Suu Kyi

In a very different cultural context, Aung San Suu Kyi is the embodiment of the principles that she promotes--and like Mandela is an avatar of courage. Like Mandela, she was the charismatic leader of an opposition to a highly repressive military regime and was under house arrest most of the time since 1988. She too was elected as the first democratic head of state—although not allowed to take office. Suu Kyi was released in late 2010 after decades of imprisonment, and swiftly elected to Parliament. She continues to lead a democracy movement calling for non-violence and the respect of universal human rights, and to serve as the international face of Burma's resistance. She anchors her appeal in both the language of liberal democracy and in Burma's Buddhist traditions. Her international recognition has been especially important for a country whose dictatorship consciously isolated the society and closed it to most foreign scrutiny.

Like Mandela, Suu Kyi is a bridging figure. She is the daughter of an assassinated Burmese national hero and of a prominent female politician and diplomat. Yet she lived outside Burma for decades and received a Western education. A Buddhist like most Burmese, she attended Christian schools in Burma and India before university at Oxford. She eventually married a British academic. On a visit to her native country in 1988 at age 43, to see her sick mother, she was quickly caught up in the exploding political turmoil between the military regime and a growing democracy movement—and instantly became its leader. Initially, she rose on the strength and under the burden of being her father's daughter. "I could not as my father's daughter remain indifferent" (quoted in Hasday 2007: 75), she said in her first political address. As a former Burmese Army captain who became her assistant described Suu Kyi's emergence, "Wherever she went, people came to her like bees coming to a flower. At first, everybody was interested in her because she was the daughter of General Aung San, but when they approached her and asked questions, and she answered them patiently and correctly, you could see that she had a real ability to connect with people" (Hammer 2011: 27).

During the two decades since Aung San Suu Kyi's initial arrest, most of that time confined to her house with little or no contact with the outside, she acquired a transnational aura of sainthood. Her self-discipline, political restraint, and steadfastness in meeting the hardships of her confinement made her a veritable sacrificial icon, on a par with Nelson Mandela. Despite constant threats to her safety and freedom, she first ran an electoral campaign under a state of emergency in the immediate aftermath of a military coup, exhorting her supporters and soldiers alike to refrain from violence. Soon confined to house arrest, she maintained her call for non-violence and the respect of human rights. As Philip Kreager has written, it was Aung San Suu Kyi who "first introduced the issue of human rights into Burmese political discussion" (Kreager 1991: 287). The Nobel Committee announced the 1991 Prize recipient with the statement that "Aung San Suu Kyi's struggle is one of the most extraordinary examples of civil courage in Asia in recent decades. She has become an important symbol in the struggle against oppression" (quoted in Aung San Suu Kyi 1991: 236).

When viewed in the Burmese context and, somewhat more broadly, an Asian context where human rights have come under attack as a Western imposition, Aung San Suu Kyi's advocacy should be seen in an additional light. While conversant with the liberal democratic language of the Universal Declaration of Human Rights, she has recast rights in the language of Burmese nationhood—in which Buddhism plays a central role. As Ingrid Jordt has written, "Buddhism and politics in Burma constitute a shared social field" (2007: 11). Aung San Suu Kyi contested the military regime's attempt to build its legitimacy with massive patronage of Burmese Buddhism. She has absorbed the ideas of human rights into Buddhist categories that all Burmese can understand spontaneously and has channeled them into the democratic struggle (see "In Quest of Democracy," included in her collection *Freedom from Fear* (1991)). Her constant denunciations of corruption, for instance, can be seen in this light.

Suu Kyi's essay "Freedom from Fear" is a prime example of her synthetic vision. Published on the occasion of her award of the 1991 Sakharov Prize for Freedom of Thought by the European Parliament, its title is at once a canonical human rights formulation and a strictly Buddhist call—to spiritual, psychological, and sociopolitical liberation. "It is not power that corrupts, but fear," she begins (1991: 181). She continues by listing the four kinds of corruption, with which "most Burmese are familiar."

Her early political speeches, in 1988 and 1989, had three key elements. First, she saluted not only her supporters and, broadly, the Burmese people, but also specifically monks; this anchored her message in the national culture and language. Second, she declared her nationalist faith, often including praise of and identification with the army (which was founded by her father). Third, she affirmed her human rights, democratic, and non-violent credo, in formulations infused with Buddhist thought. It is the combination of these three elements that made her early success in Burma. Internationally, the timing of Burma's democratic movement and its repression—in the same years as the post-communist peaceful revolutions in Eastern Europe and the Tiananmen movement and repression in China—multiplied Aung San Suu Kyi's audience, grounded in her mobilization of the global language of human rights.

Suu Kyi also manifests a gendered quality to her charismatic agency: as a martyred woman who transcends politics. Her ethereal physical presence signals vulnerability and shamed the regime, while her grace and elegance command visual attention. Like Mandela, her bearing is regal and transcendent, yet unmistakably feminine and compassionate. As a cofounder of her opposition party expressed it: "At the very instant I saw her, I knew, 'She is my leader'" (Hammer 2011: 27).

Suu Kyi's release was widely hailed in Burma and abroad, and she remains a beloved figure. Yet her charismatic appeal seems to have diminished slightly in the vagaries of normal politics, as multiple opposition factions now contend for influence in a still-restricted Burmese transition, and Western attention has diffused. Aung San Suu Kyi's heroism will be challenged to transmute into leadership in a new era she helped to create.

Mothers as Heroes and Martyrs

Social movements of mothers draw on charismatic roles, strong socialization, and universalizing empathy. Mobilization of mothers is especially relevant to human rights movements, since mothers are the designated protectors of vulnerable children and the private sphere. Mothers are feminine, innocent, and counterpoise compassion to the repressive state. They are guardians of social reproduction at the center of the social order. Mothers rehumanize invisible or stigmatized victims with the universal trope of "every mother's son." And mothers command a deep legitimacy as providers of primal security that contests state violence enacted in the name of national security. Mothers' movements have been important collective voices in struggles for human rights, non-violence, development, and environment worldwide—and have played key cultural roles in specific campaigns like temperance and antislavery in the United States.

Argentina's Mothers of the Disappeared were the first, sweepingly successful contemporary human rights movement based on the collective charisma of motherhood. Under Argentina's military dictatorship of 1976–83, tens of thousands of citizens "disappeared"—abducted, tortured, and murdered by their own government. With the quiescence or complicity of major social institutions such as the Church, only a tiny human rights movement publicized and challenged state terror. The movement was spearheaded by a handful of grieving mothers, demanding information on their missing (young adult) children through public vigils in the central square of the capitol—the Plaza de Mayo—in front of the Presidential Palace. The movement grew to thousands, coalesced civil libertarian and religious activists, and attained wide international recognition. Although some activists were themselves victimized, most survived, and the Mothers played a role in bringing down the military government. They went on to demand and shape a truth commission, path-breaking human rights trials, and the tracing of missing children—their illicitly adopted grandchildren, whose pregnant mothers had been kidnapped by the government and murdered after giving birth (Brysk 1994).

The Mothers of the Disappeared were heroes and martyrs who transformed Argentina and set a new model of human rights activism through a situated use of charismatic voice. The Mothers signaled their collective identity by wearing a distinctive white headscarf embroidered with the name of their missing children. Individual pain and family disorientation was transformed into a new internal bond as a social movement and a socially valued identity. Their testimonials dramatized their suffering and inspired external connection—including the formation of international solidarity groups of mothers protesting on their behalf in Sweden, France, and beyond.

The Mothers of the Disappeared rescued their lost kin from oblivion and dehumanization. They marched carrying poster-size photos of their disappeared children, with their names and dates of disappearance, and published details of their identities that the military denied. At every Thursday afternoon vigil, the Madres would read out the names of each of the missing, following the roll call of each name with the affirmation: "Presente!" Because the military claimed the missing were subversives who had gone underground, and many alienated and terrorized citizens rationalized that "they must have done something," the Mothers' affirmation of their children's presence, individual identity, and innocence was critical for establishing empathy. Many of the Mothers had witnessed their children's midnight kidnappings by armed paramilitaries from the family homes, and their testimonials countered the military's claim that missing persons were guerrillas who had been killed in armed confrontations with police.

The Mothers occupied public space through their weekly vigils. Their emergence from the private sphere of the home defied military control and also shamed the government for its inability to fulfill its duty of protection—much like the housewives beating empty pots-and-pans as a protest against government failure to provide sustenance in neighboring Chile. One of the Madres' slogans emphasized this powerful disruption of social order, "de la casa a la plaza." The movement later added other forms of public presence as protest: petitions, pilgrimages to religious sites, and paid newspaper announcements with photos of the disappeared. In the midst of severe repression, one of their petitions gained 24,000 signatures. Several campaigns posted "reappearance" photos or graphic representations of the disappeared throughout the city; a notable universal symbol was the traced outlines of bodies chalked throughout Buenos Aires.

Like Mandela's African paternalism and Suu Kyi's Buddhism, the Mothers drew from a cultural vocabulary that resonated with their society but bridged beyond. The pilgrimages to sites of Marian devotion consciously evoked images of the Madonna suffering for her lost son and contested the military's own use of Marian imagery. The Mothers challenged the military's "official story" of a nation rescued from chaos and subversion by warrior-heroes, and positioned themselves as the true soul of the society. In their first newsletter, the Madres framed their demand for truth and against torture, "Could there be any plea more elemental, more correct, more human, more Christian?" (Brysk 1994: 48).

The charismatic voice of the Mothers carried a new message of universal justice, freedom of information, and the rule of law, linking local suffering with global human rights norms. The first published advertisement stated, "We do not ask for anything more than the truth," challenging military President Jorge Videla's statement on a visit to the United States that "Nobody who tells the truth will suffer reprisals." The Madres constantly emphasized the universal right to life, demanded fair trials for political prisoners, and challenged the military to bring alleged subversives before the courts. During and after the transition to democracy, the Mothers marched at the front of multi-sectoral protests carrying banners with slogans demanding accountability: "Where are they?" and "No impunity."

The Madres provided an archetype of courage, like other causes célèbres. The Mothers defied the military's creation of a "culture of fear," as the strategy of disappearances was a deliberate attempt to demobilize and atomize Argentine civil society to allow military dominance (Corradi 1987). They manifested persistence, dignity, and sacrifice, and inspired hope. They have been compared to Antigone as heroines defying tyranny to defend primal family ties. Like Mandela, their struggle was depicted in books and films, inspired the composition of songs, and received scores of international awards.

The Mothers of the Disappeared created a repertoire of family-based human rights protest that diffused to dozens of countries, culminating in Latin America's regional confederation of such groups: FEDEFAM. For over a generation now, women around the world have been marching slowly in circles, carrying life-sized photos of their disappeared, from Lebanon to Soviet Georgia. The Madres also helped to frame a new genre of abuse—parallel to the labeling of genocide—as the United Nations created a Working Group, Special Rapporteur, and finally a binding Treaty on Forced Disappearance as a Crime Against Humanity, with strong impetus from the international human rights movement.

Witnesses and Experts

Public intellectuals, witnesses like journalists, and epistemic communities can also be a critical source of voice for human rights appeals. In a case study of Nobel laureates, Misztal assesses the broader social impact of public intellectuals in terms of the archetypes of pioneer, dissident, hero, and champion (Misztal 2007 105).[1] These witnesses, experts, and interpreters of social problems use social authority, role charisma, and the power of information to mobilize solidarity and shift the rights agenda.

Expert as Pioneer: Amartya Sen

Global economist Amartya Sen has redefined development, systematically exposed patterns of patriarchal oppression, and connected both to human rights. Public intellectuals like Sen advance human rights as they label problems, build

agendas, and help to mobilize policy responses by states and international organizations through their expertise. They provide evidence of wrongs and place
new issues on the rights agenda, using rational and principled appeals.

Using the power of the pen rather than any formal resources or position, the
Indian-born Nobel Laureate Amartya Sen has contributed greatly to drawing
attention to the interdependence of civil and economic rights, the reach and
range of gender inequity, as well as specific abuses of reproductive rights like
sex-selective abortion. Sen has used his training as an economist to reshape the
modernist master narrative of development into a vision of empowerment that
holds liberalism to its highest potential. His "capacities" approach to human
rights repositions rights from the liberal baseline of negative freedoms from
state oppression to active empowerment and agency. Moreover, his findings on
the relationship between state censorship and famine undercut developmental-
ist dictatorships' claims that civil liberties could be suspended in the interest of
advancing social rights. Sen's normative shift helped to inspire numerous gen-
der-sensitive initiatives of the UN agencies, as well as NGOs like the Grameen
Bank, with its focus on micro-enterprise loans directed to women.

In Sen's magnum opus *Development as Freedom* (1999b), a chapter on
"Women's Agency and Social Change" exposes patterns of gender inequity and
advocates for gender-specific development programs. Moving beyond the conventional approach to development as improvement in accumulation and well-
being, Sen argues that improving women's agency will have a ripple effect on
other aspects of underdevelopment. For example, Sen establishes that literacy
and employment for women is linked positively to child survival and reduction in fertility (189). Improving women's agency includes a range of civil,
social, and reproductive rights: earning independent income, working outside
the home, ownership rights, literacy, and participation in decision making both
within the home/family and in society (191).

In a foundational 1990 article, "More than 100 Million Women are Missing"
and a 2003 follow-up article, Sen shows that over 100 million projected female
births are statistically unaccounted for in parts of India, East Asia, and North
Africa. He traces the loss of these lives to unequal access to medicine and
nutrition for girls and women, the use of sex-selective abortion to abort female
fetuses based on cultural preferences for males, and lack of educational and
income opportunities (later linked to greater vulnerability to domestic violence). He compares these outcomes with those of countries that are poor but
do not practice medical bias, where women are healthier and are a slight majority of the population. This work shows how a complex of structural inequities,
private decisions, and falsely gender-neutral public policy produces a massive,
passive violation of the right to life, belying the promises of public sphere modernization. His analysis builds a bridge from a modernist agenda to promote

economic development to an empowerment frame, in which inequity helps to explain development problems. Deepening the interdependence argument for social responsibility, Sen argues that neglecting women's interests impacts the whole society negatively (Brookings Institute 2006).

Sen was inspired by his own principled identity as a liberal humanist with a professional mandate to foster development and freedom. Early on, he witnessed the ethnic violence of India's 1948 partition from Pakistan and a 1950s famine (Steele 2001). He was further sensitized to the specific dynamics of gender inequity through personal experiences and relationships, such as travel, fieldwork, and marriage. Sen (1998) has mentioned the influence of his late wife, Eva Colorni, in pushing him to characterize gender disparities and the relative disadvantage of women. Sen has also discussed how his work on women and poverty was influenced by his 1960s encounters with inequities in hunger, education, and resources in Indian households (The Atlantic Online 1999).

Sen has used his professional status, credibility, and legitimacy to "speak for the voiceless," the global poor and especially disadvantaged women. Sen's trajectory combined virtually every social resource of a public intellectual. He is a well-respected expert in his field, having received the 1998 Nobel Prize in Economics. He deployed that expertise to shift both tools of knowledge and conceptual frames in his field: from his contribution to the creation of the United Nations' Human Development Index to his path-breaking notion of "development as freedom." He secured and diffused maximal professional prestige within an influential network, as the Master of Trinity College, Cambridge, professor at Harvard, and recipient of fifty-three honorary degrees at leading academic institutions throughout the world. His creativity is apparent in applying a social justice perspective to the micro-level household. While remaining resolutely outside of governmental or political party roles, Sen displayed Misztal's kind of "civic courage" when he intervened in the "Asian values" debate arguing for a reconstructed version of universal human rights.

Expert as Champion: Paul Farmer

Paul Farmer is a Harvard-trained physician and activist who revolutionized the concept and practice of public health and human rights. Farmer's book *Pathologies of Power* (2005) frames diverse public health crises as consequences of political abuse, assigns responsibility to power-holders for structural conditions that cause disease, and fosters a global "responsibility to protect" the sick across borders. The medical organization he started in Haiti, Partners in Health, pioneered engaged grassroots treatment for HIV in isolated poor populations previously deemed unreachable. His work in Russia, Peru, and Africa revealed new patterns of epidemic and drug-resistant diseases like TB, and their relationship to distortions of globalization.

Paul Farmer grew up with a sense of social justice based in religious belief. In his biography, Farmer cites Rudolf Virchow—the "father of modern pathology" as his main source of inspiration. Virchow was conscious of social conditions and said, "If disease is an expression of individual life under unfavorable conditions, then epidemics must be indicative of mass disturbances of mass life" (Kidder 2003: 61). As a youth, Farmer was affected by the assassination of El Salvador's Archbishop Oscar Romero, and he focused increasingly on liberation theology; later, Gutierrez's "preferential option for the poor" became the motto of Partners in Health. After graduation from Duke University, Farmer volunteered in Haiti with a small medical assistance program, and his consciousness was raised by the horrors of illness and poverty he saw there. In Haiti, endemic poverty and brutal repression under US-sponsored dictatorships resulted in stunning levels of malnutrition, infant mortality, AIDS, cholera, and tuberculosis. In 1987, Farmer and half a dozen colleagues in the public health field founded the organization Partners in Health, with the explicit aim of fostering a more engaged and grassroots model of community health development.

Farmer became an expert to further his advocacy. In 1984, he entered graduate education as training for larger-scale intervention. At Harvard, he pursued a Ph.D. in Anthropology and an M.D., while simultaneously running the Zanmi Lasante clinic in Cange, a depressed neighborhood outside of Mirebalais, Haiti. He would fly back to the United States for labs and exams. In 1990, he received his Ph.D. and M.D. with a dissertation presaging his orientation: "AIDS and Accusation." "AIDS and Accusation" was an "interpretive anthropology of affliction" on the arrival of AIDS, and the belief that AIDS had started in Africa, then traveled to Haiti, then to the United States. He demonstrates that blaming Haiti and classifying Haitians as a "risk group" damaged the Haitian economy and deepened the social conditions that fuel the epidemic (Kidder 2003).

When Farmer returned to Haiti in 1992, he deepened his political framework and engagement. After witnessing a patient's husband being beaten to death for making a comment about the condition of the road, Farmer wrote an article called "A Death in Haiti" about the event. It was published in the *Boston Globe* under a pseudonym. Consequently, in 1993 Farmer received a prestigious MacArthur grant and wrote *The Uses of Haiti*—a critical account of US foreign policy toward Haiti and the School of the Americas. After its publication in 1994, Farmer was formally expelled from Haiti.

Farmer returned to Haiti the day liberationist President Bertrand Aristide was reinstated as president in 1994. Partners in Health focused on treating and preventing transmission of HIV/AIDS, TB, women's issues, and the linkage between community health and social conditions. As a physician and advocate,

Farmer would often take day-long hikes to remote areas to ensure that patients were taking their TB medications and to check on them. He married a Haitian woman and raised his children in Haiti for over a decade. In 2002, he received a $14 million Sachs' Global Fund grant for his work in Haiti to prevent HIV transmission.

Farmer's framing, advocacy, and treatment efforts quickly expanded to other venues and issues. Partners in Health established programs in half a dozen countries. Farmer's organization also extended his expansion of treatment modalities from HIV to TB, and concluded that pharmaceutical companies must be pressured to produce generic second line TB medication. This reframing was controversial because the drugs needed to be classified as essential before generic companies would produce them. Partners in Health eventually persuaded the WHO to add the medication to the list of essential drugs. After learning that TB was the leading cause of death in Russian prisons, Farmer used the platform of an interview on "60 Minutes" to state that TB was a global public health emergency. Because of this reframing, Farmer was recruited to work on the terms of a World Bank loan to staunch the epidemic in Russia (Farmer 2005).

Paul Farmer is currently based in Rwanda. He founded a new academic journal, *Health and Human Rights*, that sets a new agenda and provides ongoing analysis of the linkages between the fields. Farmer now holds the highest level of professorship at Harvard and directs institutes and programs on global health and social responsibility.

Epistemic Community as Norm Entrepreneur: Doctors Without Borders

Like Paul Farmer, decades earlier Bernard Kouchner used the legitimacy of his expertise to bring attention and shift resources to a voiceless population: sick and injured civilians subject to conflict and political repression. But Kouchner's contribution was not his individual expert knowledge, but rather his legitimate role as a physician, and the organization of collective expertise, Médecins Sans Frontières (MSF; Doctors Without Borders). Doctors Without Borders is based on the principled universalism of medical ethics. Moreover, this work as a norm entrepreneur extended the long-standing humanitarian mandate of the International Committee of the Red Cross to internal, as well as international, armed conflict, to chronic repression, and toward a vision of health rights beyond medical succor. MSF forged a new link between medical ethics, traditionally seen as an individual concern, and international humanitarian law, that proposes universal rights and responsibilities to basic human needs such as health care.

As the head of Canada's branch of Médecins Sans Frontières/Doctors Without Borders, James Orbinski described his shift in consciousness after a visit to Rwanda in the aftermath of the 1994 genocide. His call for collective voice is emblematic of the organization's mobilization of communication politics: "Doctors cannot stop this crime. But the little girl in the latrine [a survivor who witnessed the murder of her family] had no voice, and as doctors we had a responsibility to speak out against what we knew.... We spoke with a clear intent to rouse the outrage of public consciousness around the world and to demand a UN intervention to stop this criminal politics" (Orbinski 2008: 10).

MSF founder Bernard Kouchner's commitment to human rights was forged during the 1960s era of student militancy, but he linked this commitment with his medical role while working with the Red Cross as a doctor during the 1968 Biafra war. In this war the Nigerian government induced a famine against secessionists, and the Red Cross and major powers maintained a putative neutrality that effectively favored the government's campaign. Thus, in 1971 Kouchner and others established MSF to bring a universalist and politically engaged defense of health rights to conflict zones. Meanwhile, a parallel group of French doctors, headed by Raymond Borel, had experienced similar frustrations in the aftermath of a 1970 cyclone in Bangladesh (then East Pakistan) that killed half a million people—while medical aid had been delayed due to border disputes. Médecins Sans Frontières/Doctors Without Borders deepened the principle of the Geneva Conventions and the Nuremberg Principles (of the World Medical Association): that the individual's right to health care supersedes sovereignty, and the responsibility to provide care rests with physicians as a call beyond their national identities.

The organization split in 1980, with Kouchner leading Médecins du Monde (Doctors of the World) for the first half of the decade. Influenced by the Lebanese Civil War in the 1970s, Kouchner and his colleagues emphasized witness and critique, as well as medical relief, and sought to promote more active intervention by humanitarian professionals. Médecins du Monde was also catalyzed by Kouchner's single-handed relief voyage to Vietnamese refugee camps in Southeast Asia when official aid lagged. Doctors of the World has gone on to work on thousands of projects in over eighty countries: from emergency relief to post-conflict reconstruction to long-term development.

The original Médecins Sans Frontières/Doctors Without Borders also persists as a separate organization, with an even more active relief operation and increasing monitoring and advocacy role. MSF highlighted the Ethiopian government's role in forced displacement of civilians in 1985. Both organizations called for international intervention in Rwanda in 1994, more active international involvement in Sudan's multiple conflicts throughout the 2000s, and international protection for civilians in Congo and Somalia in 2008.

Médecins Sans Frontières/Doctors Without Borders now encompasses over 27,000 physicians operating in over sixty countries and in 1999 received the Nobel Peace Prize. The organization went on to play a path-breaking role in advocating for AIDS patients' access to anti-retroviral medications over the patent rights of multinational pharmaceutical companies. This campaign brought the price of AIDS treatment from around $15,000 a year to around $200 via access to generic versions of the patented drugs. The AIDS drugs struggle culminated in a broader Access to Essential Medicines campaign, in which the physicians' organization serves as a voice for health rights above the interests of capital, as well as states. In the twenty-first century, MSF has gone on to play a notable role in advocating for women's access to health care impeded by turmoil and cultural oppression in Afghanistan and Pakistan, and decrying and treating sexual violence in Congo.

Médecins Sans Frontières, like the Mothers of the Disappeared, established a new niche in global civil society: in this case, the humanitarian professional transnational advocacy group, with parallels among lawyers, journalists, writers, and others. They bridged the older tradition of humanitarian succor with the modern mode of analysis and advocacy. Their power was based on a combination of a role-based ethos of social responsibility, role status and expertise, and perhaps the oldest universal—healing.

"The Dog That Didn't Bark":
American Campaigns Against the Death Penalty

Voice is powerful, but it is not always present in significant measure—and credible, charismatic personification and witness is necessary (though not sufficient) for human rights campaigns. The lack of compelling voice for certain kinds of human rights claims can help explain the relative inefficacy of campaigns against capital punishment in the United States.

Even though the death penalty is considered a violation of international human rights standards and the United States has a strong "rights culture" for civil and political freedoms, mobilization against capital punishment in the United States has been episodic and based more on rational argumentation than communication politics. Most Americans across the political spectrum treasure the individual citizen's freedom from state intrusion in religious belief, property ownership, and privacy, yet most also believe the government has the right to deny individuals their most basic right to life—as long as they have been convicted of a serious crime. In terms of communication politics, the articulation of rights claims against capital punishment in the United States has been limited by the lack of "innocent victims," the presence of strong counter-frames, and the audience filter of American exceptionalism that blocks public receptivity to cosmopolitan values.

The United States is one of the leading users of the death penalty in the world and a rare case among developed democracies, as over two-thirds of the world's states have abolished or suspended the practice. Since the reinstatement of the death penalty in the United States in 1976 (following a technical suspension from 1972), there have been over 1,300 executions. An April 2012 NAACP report states that there are currently over 3,000 inmates on death row; over one-third of these are in California, Florida, and Texas. In every state that uses the death penalty, the proportion of minorities sentenced to death vastly exceeds their proportion in the general population, criminal population, and convicted felon population—in California and Texas, over two-thirds of the inmates on death row are minorities (Criminal Justice Project 2012). A 2010 Pew Research Center survey found that most Americans (62 percent) continue to express support for the death penalty for persons convicted of murder, while only 30 percent oppose it. (This is nearly unchanged for the past five years, although it has declined slightly over the decade.) (Pew Research Center 2010) Several states have recently suspended their use of capital punishment, but it has been untouched in the half dozen states that drive the majority of executions and is still available at the federal level.

The death penalty is condemned as an inherent violation of human rights by an ensemble of international treaties, including Protocols to the International Convention on Civil and Political Rights, the American Convention on Human Rights, and the European Convention on Human Rights. The UN General Assembly has passed several resolutions calling for a worldwide moratorium on its use, and in 2006 the UN Human Rights Committee specifically condemned the United States for use of the death penalty. Amnesty International issues regular reports and campaigns constantly against capital punishment worldwide (Amnesty International, n.d.). Human Rights Watch also makes a principled, cosmopolitan human rights claim against the death penalty. In their unsuccessful campaign against the execution of an intellectually disabled man in Texas in 2012, the organization stated: "Human Rights Watch opposes capital punishment in all circumstances because the inherent dignity of the person is inconsistent with the death penalty. This form of punishment is unique in its cruelty and finality, and it is inevitably and universally plagued with arbitrariness, prejudice, and error" (Human Rights Watch 2012).

But most campaigns against the death penalty in the United States contend that it is biased, inefficient, inhumanely administered, or mistaken—not an inherent violation of a principled right to life. For example, in 2007, the

American Bar Association called for a nationwide moratorium on capital punishment, "based on a detailed analysis of death penalty systems in eight sample states, the ABA Death Penalty Moratorium Implementation Project identified key problems common to the states studied, including major racial disparities, inadequate indigent defense services and irregular clemency review processes—making their death penalty systems operate unfairly" (ABA 2007). The chair of the ABA Moratorium Implementation Project went on to state "the death penalty system is rife with irregularity—supporting the need for a moratorium until states can ensure fairness and accuracy" (ABA 2007). The American Civil Liberties Union states as its points of opposition:

—The death penalty system in the US is applied in an unfair and unjust manner against people, largely dependent on how much money they have, the skill of their attorneys, race of the victim and where the crime took place.

—The death penalty violates the constitutional guarantee of equal protection.

—Capital punishment denies due process of law.

—The death penalty is a waste of taxpayers money and has no public safety benefit. The vast majority of law enforcement professionals surveyed agree that capital punishment does not deter violent crime; a survey of police chiefs nationwide found they rank the death penalty lowest among ways to reduce violent crime.

—Innocent people are too often sentenced to death. Since 1973, over 138 people have been released from death rows in 26 states because of innocence.

(ACLU 2001)

State moratoriums, like that recently adopted in New Mexico, have correspondingly been based on unfairness—and some states have resumed the death penalty after reforming procedures, justifying a more even-handed deprivation of the right to life.

Some experts who oppose the practice defend this pragmatic argumentation as the best way to overcome Americans' emotional defensiveness regarding the issue.

It is difficult, in my opinion, to defend capital punishment today as necessary to make society safer or more generally as an effective crime control policy. Its value, it seems, is primarily symbolic—particularly in helping assuage the fear and anger that accompany criminal violence. This symbolism is best perpetuated in abstractions: in good triumphing over evil, in a righteous and benevolent state responding to wrongs, promoting justice, and protecting decent citizens. It becomes vulnerable when abstractions yield to a countervailing reality in which errors, unfairness and awkward banalities such as confronting how best to kill those under sentence of death (three drugs or one in the lethal cocktail?) come to the surface. I think we've reached a tipping point where the abstract and symbolic benefits that some perceive in capital punishment are giving way to its many practical foibles. (Acker cited in Sullivan 2010: 480–481)

But rational challenge has produced little change in policy or public opinion, and widely publicized executions contested as wrongful or inhumane proceeded in 2011 and 2012 following this statement.

Another option for framing human rights claims is linkage to cosmopolitan standards as a "mark of civilization," and this has tremendously enhanced many dimensions of human rights policy in "global Good Samaritan" democracies that position themselves as moral exemplars, such as Canada and Sweden (Brysk 2009). Yet the United States has been notoriously impervious and even resistant to international human rights law. The closest thing to a cosmopolitan rights challenge to the US use of the death penalty was the case brought to the Inter-American Human Rights Commission for Juan Raul Garza, who had been extradited from Mexico for drug-related murders in Texas in 1993. Six individual human rights professionals and international law professors appealed to the Inter-American Commission of Human Rights for Garza, asserting that his death sentence violated Articles I (Right to Life), XVIII (Right to a Fair Trial), and XXVI (Right to Due Process of Law) of the American Declaration of Human Rights, signed by the United States. The international court duly published a decision in favor of Garza (Inter-American Court of Human Rights 2001), but the United States responded that the death penalty does not violate the right to life, and the other allegations were unsupported (US Department of State 2001). Moreover, the IACHR decision was rejected in US courts on grounds that the American Declaration is "non-binding," and therefore does not influence US policy ("The Case of Juan Garza," n.d.). Garza was executed in 2001.

Some limited social movement campaigns against the death penalty have developed in waves around cause célèbre, such as condemned prisoners who were political activists or vulnerable figures—but contemporary cases have served as rallying points for rational argument rather than systematic personification of voice. Of the over a thousand contemporary executions, only a handful have generated individual campaigns. Mumia Abu-Jamal was an African American activist who was said to be a political prisoner and was ultimately removed from Death Row. Karla Faye Tucker, one of the few women executed, had committed her crimes in youth and spectacularly converted to Christianity, winning public sympathy but no reprieve. Vulnerable individuals like Marvin Wilson, with an IQ of 61, was personified in a *New York Times* editorial when he was put to death by the state of Texas ("Mentally Retarded and on Death

Row" 2012). With these handful of exceptions, the victims of the death penalty are rarely seen as heroes or martyrs within the United States, although they are often internationally defended as such.

The closest we come to true charismatic voice on the death penalty is the presence in some campaigns against capital punishment of celebrities and religious figures. Hollywood figures have weighed in from time to time, peaking with the 1995 film *Dead Man Walking*—a cinematic treatment of the Death Row ministry of a Catholic nun. The movie was adapted from Sister Helen Prejean's book of the same name and brought attention to her decades of campaigning against the death penalty. The film, starring human rights activist actors Susan Sarandon and Sean Penn and directed by Tim Robbins, presents a humanizing view of a convicted criminal and suggests the futility of capital punishment. African American actors like Danny Glover have shown special concern in campaigns for black prisoners deemed to suffer discrimination in their trials or sentencing. Bruce Springsteen devotes regular benefit concerts to organizations that oppose the death penalty. Actors like Alec Baldwin and Morgan Fairchild have been regular organizers of anti–death penalty initiatives.

The US Conference of Catholic Bishops has consistently opposed the death penalty on principled religious grounds, through public statements, ministry, and at times participation by Catholic figures in public protests at executions. Following the execution of Troy Davis and Lawrence Brewer on September 21, 2011, 150 Catholic theologians signed a widely disseminated statement calling for a repeal of the death penalty (McElwee 2011; Winright 2011). The US Conference of Catholic Bishops stated that "the sanction of death, when it is not necessary to protect society, violates respect for human life and dignity....Its application is deeply flawed and can be irreversibly wrong, is prone to errors, and is biased by factors such as race, the quality of legal representation, and where the crime was committed. We have other ways to punish criminals and protect society" (Winright 2011). However, the Catholic leadership has devoted relatively little messaging space to this issue compared to other dimensions of the right to life, such as Church positions on abortion and euthanasia.

The Quaker community has also been a long-standing voice opposing the death penalty, mainly through legislative lobbying via the Friends Committee on National Legislation. The Friends Committee on Legislation of California helped to put an unsuccessful Proposition on the California 2012 ballot to abolish the death penalty in that state (FCLCA 2012; SAFE California 2011). Since the Quaker community is so small, Quaker voice is more important as a personified representation of principle than the mobilization of a conscience constituency.

But such efforts of charismatic voice have been relatively unavailing to date; we may say that when occasionally the dog did bark, it was a dog that couldn't hunt. According to the 2010 Pew Research survey, "About one-third (32%) of those who oppose capital punishment cite religion, compared with 13% among those who favor it.... among opponents of the death penalty, 31% of Catholics cite religion as the top influence. [But] Most regular churchgoers do not report hearing about the death penalty from their clergy; just 24% say that their clergy speak out about the issue." So of the roughly one-third of Americans who oppose the death penalty, about one-third were moved by religious values, translating to about a 10 percent potential shift in public opinion. But even of those, only around one-quarter even registered the charismatic voice of clergy on the issue, so the true resonance of religious voice (as compared to diffuse religious teachings) may only reach a few percent of the public. It is also noteworthy that there are numerous pro–death penalty organizations and Web sites, and some of these cite Christian doctrine as support for their position, so religious voice on the issue is contested.

The 2011 execution of Troy Davis brought together all of these forms of protest, without result. In the run-up to his execution, Amnesty International reported that "Approximately 300 rallies, vigils and other events are occurring across the United States and the globe, including in New York City, Washington D.C., San Diego, Boulder, Peru, Berlin, Paris and Oslo, among others" (Amnesty International USA 2011b). Facebook and Twitter campaigns were strong. Charismatic figures spoke out, from former President Jimmy Carter to Archbishop Desmond Tutu to Pope Benedict XVI. Supporters claimed the case against Davis was both weak and biased. Nevertheless, he was put to death on September 21, 2011, in Georgia. Principled charismatic voice around the protection of the fundamental right to life has been too weak in the United States to overcome the powerful symbolic politics of security and parochial defensiveness of American political culture.

Conclusion

Charismatic voices can bring connection, credibility, and compassionate consciousness to human rights struggles. The archetypes of heroes, martyrs, and experts have special resonance in the global arena, and translate between local and universal problems and rights claims. While appealing individuals have a special psychological power to personify persuasion, the collective mobilization of charismatic roles also plays an increasing role in rights campaigns. Table 3.1 shows the elements of voice used by the full range of campaigns profiled throughout the book, summarizing this chapter and projecting its analysis of voice to the campaigns that will be discussed below.

Table 3.1 Human Rights Campaigns: Voice

Case	Voice
Tibet	Dalai Lama
Dreyfus	Cause célèbre
Spanish Civil War	Writers
Holocaust	Anne Frank, Elie Wiesel
Arab Spring	Khaled Said
South Africa	Nelson Mandela
Burma	Aung San Suu Kyi
Argentina	Mothers of the Disappeared
AIDS	Doctors, Victims Movement
Violence vs. Women	Amartya Sen
US death penalty	Weak celebrities
Trafficking	Child victims
Female genital mutilation	Child victims, doctors
Colombia	
Darfur	Celebrities
Congo	Weak Celebrities
US civil liberties	Stephen Colbert
India	Anna Hazare
Russia	Pussy Riot
Iran Green	Neda Agha-Soltan
China	Cause célèbre
Kony 2012	Invisible Children
Academic freedom	Limited cause célèbre
Armenia	
Israel/Palestine	
Liberia	Mothers

The messenger matters—and so does the articulation of the message. We turn now to this dimension of speaking rights: framing the claim.

4

THE MESSAGE MATTERS
Framing the Claim

If language is not correct, then what is said is not what is meant; if what is said is not
what is meant, then what must be done remains undone; if this remains undone, morals
and art will deteriorate; if justice goes astray, the people will stand about in helpless
confusion. Hence, there must be no arbitrariness in what is said.

—Confucius

The narrative of human rights violations fosters or hinders civil society in framing, claiming, and forming collective identities around human rights. A cognitive frame identifies a social problem, directs blame, proposes solutions, and thus makes a claim to motivate action (Gamson 1995). Compelling frames "define problems—determine what a causal agent is doing with what costs and benefits, usually measured in terms of common cultural values; diagnose causes—identify the forces creating the problem; make more judgments—evaluate causal agents and their effects; and suggest remedies—offer and justify treatments for the problems and predict their likely effects" (Entman 1993: 52). A human rights frame tells a story that characterizes the victims, labels the genre of abuse, locates the perpetrators, and suggests a response.

The content of the message delivered by the frame is also significant. The most successful rights claims are closely connected to modern and rational norms that resonate with cosmopolitan consciousness (Boli and Thomas 1999). The most effective representations involve physical harm to "innocent" victims (Keck and Sikkink 1998), clear perpetrators, and linkage of the current claim to some established genre of abuse (Snow and Benford 1988). Violations against women and children—who are presumed "innocent"—are prosecuted more vigorously than similar behavior against male victims (Carpenter 2006).

The character and location of the perpetrator also matters for labeling the abuse. "Private wrongs" by non-state actors stretch the human rights frame developed for government and political dissidents—the Amnesty International "prisoner of conscience" model that established the human rights regime (Brysk

2005). Non-governmental human rights abuse by employers, families, or ethnic authorities may complicate location of responsibility and leverage and evoke counterclaims, but this type of non-state violations by civil society does not involve conceptual problems in the causal chain. On the other hand, abuses by paramilitary or criminal forces, outsourced security contractors, or international coalitions with unclear relations to state command muddy attribution, as well as responsibility for redress.

The nature of the violations may facilitate or impede recognition, framing of the genre of abuse, linkage to existing frames, and mobilization. Historically recognized violations such as genocide carry moral authority, international legal traction, specialized international institutions and NGOs, and leverage against the sovereignty defense. The United Nations' mandate for humanitarian intervention, the International Criminal Court, and many bilateral mechanisms specify "genocide, war crimes, and crimes against humanity." In contrast, chronic violations of social and economic rights are more controversial, difficult to measure, and lack issue-oriented networks (Felice 2003).

Framing is a characteristic of human rights claims, carried by and filtered through human rights advocates and organizations. Charismatic speakers gain attention space for a frame, norm entrepreneurs may craft a new frame or adapt an older one, and frames identify the nature of victims and voice to attend. Social movements and advocacy campaigns develop around and sometimes construct characteristic frames (Tarrow 1998). Amnesty International established its niche of non-partisan monitoring and advocacy for prisoners of conscience. Yet Amnesty has faced struggles of organizational loyalty and external reception every time it has switched or expanded this civil liberties frame to social and economic rights, and more structural critique (Hopgood 2006). *The Economist*, the classically liberal journal that has approvingly cited the organization's condemnations of dictatorships for holding political prisoners (even business-friendly dictatorships), queried Amnesty's newer campaigns on globalization and Guantanamo with the header, "The World's Biggest Human-Rights Organization Stretches Its Brand" ("Amnesty International: Many Rights, Some Wrong" 2007). For Clifford Bob, domestic human rights organizations' ability to "pitch" their cause to international gatekeepers makes the difference in bringing attention and ultimate success to an issue—so a good frame is one which already has an established organizational advocate (Bob 2001).

Frames fail when critical semantic elements are lacking or contradict powerful pre-existing social stories. Human rights are a counter-hegemonic claim (Brysk 1995) that must contest and deconstruct reigning paradigms. "Rights talk" of universality, indivisibility, and inalienability can fail to overcome the dominant discourses of dehumanization of victims, blurring of responsibility, and national insecurity. Many authors trace limitations of human rights campaigns to the strength of counter-narratives of state sovereignty, moral panic, and legitimate authority claims (Brysk and Shafir 2007). The politics of fear operates through the authorities' perception and manipulation of threats to national security, use of rules of exception that frame rights violations as the exercise of legitimate authority, and the consequent mobilization of a pro-violation constituency (Cardenas 2007). For "private wrongs," counter-frames of cultural autonomy, religious freedom, or self-determination are often the barriers to acceptance of the human rights frame.

Framing is both contested and dynamic, and human rights campaigns often shift or multiply frames over time. Rights movements that experience complex forms of persecution may frame their claims under an initial rubric, or launch diffuse appeals, and learn to concentrate on the frame that works best from the response of transnational networks and world public opinion. In this way, Latin American indigenous communities facing impoverishment, displacement, physical abuse, identity crisis, and environmental destruction moved from cultural appeals to rights campaigns to environmental frames, with increasing success at gaining international attention and solidarity (Brysk 2000).

We will trace the differential operation of frames through contrasting issues that evoke different levels of international response. For the issue of human trafficking, a highly conducive frame of sex slavery brings substantial policy response, but the frame's simplifications and silences distort that response and later require revision. By contrast, feminist campaigns against female genital mutilation initially stalled due to problems with leverage and counter-frames. Yet a shift to a different frame of health rights appeals gained greater resonance and a match with a different set of transnational allies. In a contrasting case, the failure of framing can explain the slow and limited response to assassinations and disappearances in Colombia compared to more successful human rights campaigns elsewhere in Latin America. Comparing public attention to mass killings in Congo and Darfur highlights the power of framing, as similarly horrific events with some overlapping features evoke different responses depending in part on how they are named.

Poster Children and Sex Slavery: Framing Human Trafficking

The problem of human trafficking is one of the best cases of gaining significant international response by framing a complex human rights issue that affects an especially powerless population in simple and powerful rhetoric. It is an issue that literally provides poster children; archetypal innocent victims invoking humanitarian protection. Moreover, attention and policy increased vastly when advocates linked the growing problem to the well-established, powerful frame of slavery. Framing was slightly slowed because trafficking is perpetrated predominantly by non-state actors, but the malefactors are usually identifiable and the causal chain is not complex. Although there are a variety of perpetrators, framing as sex slavery concentrated attention on pariah criminal networks rather than complicit kin. Similarly, the solution component of the frame was sufficient because while leverage over non-state perpetrators is more limited than freeing political prisoners held by a government, states do have a responsibility and theoretical capacity to protect the victims, and are charged with negligence rather than covert sponsorship of the abuse. Finally, the sex slavery frame provides a match with an unusual coalition of relatively well-positioned transnational religious, feminist, and human rights organizations, bypassing weaker advocates for other kinds of migrants. But the cost of this effective frame was to selectively emphasize those aspects of the problem that fit—coercive cross-border sexual exploitation of children and chaste women—diminishing attention and response to other affected populations and interrelated abuses.

Since the end of the Cold War, there has been a surge of attention to human trafficking of all kinds. The phenomenon is widespread and growing. Many advocacy groups cite figures of more than 27 million people worldwide exploited in contemporary forms of slavery, with several million of those forced or tricked across borders (based on Bales 2004). The US State Department estimates that up to 820,000 men, women, and children are trafficked internationally each year, while the International Organization for Migration cites a rough figure of 800,000 (US Department of State 2009; International Organization for Migration, http://www.iom.int/cms/countertrafficking). The International Labor Organization (ILO) estimates that at least 1.39 million people are victims of commercial sexual servitude worldwide, though this includes both transnational and domestic exploitation. The US data suggest that about two-thirds of trafficking victims are women and girls. Much of this traffic is from East to West (Europe) or South to North (Latin America–United States, Southeast Asia–Europe and United States) (Attorney General 2006, 2008; Ribando 2007). Organized, lucrative, and brutal transnational criminal networks have developed, subjecting Mexican girls to sexual slavery and physical abuse across the US border, as well as selling children from Eastern Europe via Mexico (Landesman 2004). Various forms of international child trafficking are common in poverty-stricken Bangladesh: boys as young as 4 are shipped to the Persian Gulf for hazardous work as camel jockeys, while girls are sold to India and Pakistan to work as prostitutes and maids (Sengupta 2003).

Like other forms of labor migration, sex trafficking follows dual market and organizational logics: supply and demand plus availability of smuggling and receiving networks. A supply of desperate and vulnerable women (and families, in the case of children) is generated by the collapse of local economies, due to endemic poverty, political conflict, and/or pressures of globalization. Conversely, demand is highest in areas that have benefited from globalization, with high flows of tourism and migration. Smuggling and receiving networks often developed around other illicit flows, such as drugs or weapons, but flourish in weak states and articulate with local institutions of gender inequity. It is also important to recognize that in many cases trafficking is deliberately promoted by children's families from some combination of ignorance, desperation, exploitation, or even custom (Kane 1998; Levesque 1999).

International abuse of women grows from preexisting domestic practices of commodification of female reproductive labor, such as prostitution, forced marriage, and domestic service, and patriarchal control of women's movement, education, and employment—enforced by gendered violence. A study by La Strada International, a coalition of nine NGOs in Eastern Europe, shows how trafficking is both a cause and a consequence of violations of women's human rights in that region. Higher rates and harms of trafficking in each country are linked to the national incidence of patriarchal stereotypes, domestic violence, domestic employment inequity, informalization of female-typed labor in both sending and receiving countries, feminization of poverty in transitional economies, and shortfalls in social support services that differentially affect women (La Strada International 2008). Women are especially vulnerable to the sex trade—but they are also vulnerable to exploitation in the "maid trade," and any other traditional role where domestic disempowerment meets globalized displacement.

International recognition of trafficking as a form of contemporary slavery has been swift and relatively influential in inspiring policy change, although insufficient to stem the problem as root causes continue. International treaty standards are strong; Optional Protocols to the Convention on the Rights of the Child address Child Prostitution and Child Soldiers, while a separate 2000 Protocol to Prevent, Suppress, and Punish Trafficking in Persons, Especially Women and Children has been signed by over eighty-eight countries. The United Nations has hosted annual conferences since a landmark 1996 Stockholm World Congress Against Commercial and Sexual Exploitation of Children and sponsored multiple programs under the ILO, UN Development Program, UNICEF, and other agencies. The Stockholm conference involved not only 122 countries but also 105 representatives of international organizations and 471 nongovernmental organizations (Kane 1998). Sex trafficking is uncontroversially recognized as a violation of rights of physical integrity; in 1990, the United Nations Human Rights Commission appointed a Special Rapporteur on Traffic in Children and Child Prostitution. Regional intergovernmental coordination initiatives have been launched with UN backing in Southeastern Europe, West Africa, the

Mekong Delta (UNICEF 2001) and North America. In addition, the European Union funds special programs, including victim reintegration by the seventy-six-state International Organization for Migration (Kyle and Koslowski 2001).

Half a dozen leading NGOs have formed with wide public support and frequent program collaboration with international and government agencies; including ECPAT (End Child Prostitution and Trafficking), the Polaris Project, and Captive Daughters. Meanwhile, long-standing children's rights organizations like Save the Children have incorporated anti-trafficking initiatives. For victim support in host countries, a US NGO founded in 2002 has established a National Trafficking Alert System hotline (in several languages) and worked to train US law enforcement to work more effectively with victims (Polaris Project, http://www.polarisproject.org/). One sign of the relative strength of civil society advocates in this issue area is that the US State Department's Ambassador who heads the Office to Monitor and Combat Trafficking in Persons was appointed at the behest of feminist and religious groups (Brinkley 2006).

The United States has the most comprehensive policy and has devoted the most bureaucratic and financial resources to the issue of any single receiving country—averaging around $80 million/year over the past decade. The US now states that people who have been trafficked to the United States, even if they have entered illegally and participated in crimes such as prostitution, should be seen as victims and not criminals—and they are mandated assistance from the US Departments of State, Justice, Labor, and Health and Human Services (http://www.acf.hhs.gov/programs/orr/resource/federal-government-efforts-to-combat-human-trafficking). In October 2000, the United States passed the Trafficking Victims Protection Act, which increases penalties, protects witnesses, and provides immigration relief for victims. A 2003 Reauthorization strengthened the US measure by permitting prosecution of sex traffickers under racketeering legislation and allowing victims to bring civil suits. Special visas for trafficking victims were enhanced further in a 2005 amended bill. In addition, the United States has begun to issue an annual report on human trafficking, and countries deemed to make insufficient efforts to stop trafficking face the threat of a US aid cut. Twenty-three countries were designated as trafficking source countries eligible for sanctions in 2011 ("US Expands Trafficking Black List to 23" 2011). However, in 2010, economic sanctions were imposed only on Cuba, North Korea, and Myanmar (Sisken and Wyler 2010).

Similarly, Britain has legislation to penalize trafficking for the sexual exploitation of minors; Germany has also criminalized trafficking. Sweden has begun to prosecute customers of minor prostitutes, under its Violence Against Women Act. Interpol has a Standing Working Party on Offenses Against Minors, which has promoted police cooperation between Britain and the Philippines, as well as Sweden and Thailand. In addition, by 1997 a dozen countries had passed legislation mandating extraterritorial accountability for sexual abuse of minors by their citizens, including France, Germany, the Nordic countries, Australia, and the United States (Kane 1998). Under strong international pressure, Japan has drastically reduced the number of international "entertainer" visas that were notoriously abused by traffickers to import women from neighboring countries into the sex industry; for the Philippines, from 80,000 to 5,000 (Brinkley 2006).

On the source country side, Albania, Bangladesh, Costa Rica, and the Dominican Republic have sharpened legal accountability, heightened penalties, and increased enforcement for trafficking and child prostitution. Thailand significantly tightened legislation and increased enforcement in 1996 (Kane 1998). Similarly, the Philippines reclassified child prostitutes as victims and increased prosecutions and penalties for foreign offenders (Levesque 1999).

Why has policy seized so strongly on trafficking, but adopted such a partial perspective on the nature and sources of the phenomenon? The frame of transnational sexual labor exploitation was initially established as "white slavery" (Kempadoo and Doezema 1998). It thus taps into the moral capital of the antislavery campaign, often deemed the first modern human rights movement. One indicator of this linkage is the US Trafficking Office creation of an award for the "abolitionist of the year" to reward State Department representatives attentive to the issue in their embassies (Brinkley 2006).

In a morally regrettable yet politically powerful semantic move, white slavery emphasizes the "unnatural" threat of enslavement to a portion of a population generally exempted from this peril. Differential attention to Eastern European women promotes ready identification by Western publics with the subset of victims who are culturally and racially similar. Talk of slavery taps into Judeo-Christian religious imagery that appears to transcend ideology, avoiding more challenging sociological frames of labor exploitation or the highly contested issue of immigration rights. But this frame is historically associated with prohibition of prostitution and draws some religious advocates who also view voluntary sex work as a form of enslavement and accordingly campaign to ban it.

The trafficking frame also draws on the most palatable form of feminism: the struggle to end violence against women. Internationally, the humanitarian protection rubric and transnational networks combating violence against women have succeeded in gaining much greater response than equally costly but chronic or contested economic, cultural, or social rights struggles (Keck and Sikkink 1998). Trafficked women, as "people out of place" (Brysk and Shafir 2007) bridge the universal individual claims of displaced persons and the claims of traditional family values—as they are uprooted from the ascribed protection of home and family. Moreover, even within the violence against women frame, sexual violence receives greater recognition and priority. The blurring of these frames is apparent in the US State Department's sanction of Sudan in the 2005 Trafficking Report to pressure Khartoum over rapes in Darfur. Wartime rape is a horrific crime--but that distinct crime is acute, stationary, and state-sponsored, and does not fit the definition of trafficking, which is ongoing, mobile, non-state, and profit-motivated—and has different sources and solutions (Brinkley 2006).

As with the issues profiled in the last chapter, charismatic voice—in this case, *New York Times* columnist Nicholas Kristof—played a singular role in framing and publicizing human trafficking. While his persistent depictions and impassioned advocacy brought critical assistance to numerous victims and helped to catalyze US response, the limitations of the sex slavery frame embroiled even this principled cosmopolitan journalist in contradictions. In an interview called "Giving Voice to the World's Voiceless" (Academy of Achievement 2008). Kristof explains how his decision in 2004 to buy two girls from their brothels in Cambodia was influenced by an earlier trip to Cambodia that challenged his professional ethos. While researching an article in Cambodia in 1996, Kristof was observing two teenage prostitutes when he witnessed the mother of one girl arrive at the brothel and try to take the girl home. The brothel owner demanded that the mother buy the girl from him, which she could not afford. Kristof felt guilty that he had gotten a front-page story out of the experience, while these two girls "were going to stay behind and die of AIDS" as slaves. He felt "kind of exploitative" of these and other girls whom he met on this trip and resolved to prevent this dynamic in 2004 by becoming more engaged rather than merely chronicling. Thus, Kristof controversially bought the freedom of two teenage prostitutes in a brothel in Cambodia in 2004 and helped return them to their families, which he documented in his op-ed series (see Kristof 2004).

The trafficking frame has bought attention and mobilization, but at a price. What has been the cost of this powerful frame of sex slavery for the victims of transnational exploitation? First, anti-trafficking policies framed to protect "innocent" women from sexual slavery ignore or slight prior sex workers or other women who migrate voluntarily to engage in sex work but are subsequently exploited. Second, international policy and especially American policy focuses disproportionately on East–West traffic, culturally recognizable European victims, and youth, when the vast majority of victims are interregional in the global South. Third, policies often aim to stop commercial sex rather than the violence, exploitation, and other harms associated with it—and slight the sexual abuse occurring within other forms of labor and migration (Brysk and Choi-Fitzpatrick 2012).

The sex slavery frame privileges protection over empowerment and rescue over rights. A report by the Global Alliance Against Trafficking shows that anti-trafficking programs too often impinge the rights of the people they are supposed to help. Based on research in a range of sending and receiving countries—Australia, Bosnia and Herzegovina, Brazil, India, Nigeria, Thailand, the United Kingdom, and the United States—the report shows that women who are "rescued" from trafficking may be indefinitely detained against their will in police facilities or shelters, involuntarily deported, forced to provide evidence which puts them and their families at risk, or even abused or harassed by law enforcement officials. In other cases, young female migrants and potential border-crossers are profiled and subjected to preemptive scrutiny and interdiction that impinges their freedom of movement in the name of protecting them from trafficking (GAATW et al. 2009). Thus, some argue more broadly that a "rescue industry" undercuts the rights of migrant sex workers when it types them as "innocent victims" in need of humanitarian protection rather than displaced agents in need of migration rights (Agustin 2007). Under the terms of 2003 legislation, renewed in 2005, US policy has even gone so far as to deny funding to health, migration, and sex worker assistance organizations for anti-trafficking and HIV prevention programs if such NGOs tolerate or advocate decriminalization of commercial sex work, unless the agencies explicitly condemn all prostitution (Pisani 2008).

The "white slavery" frame also leaves out the largest group of the most vulnerable victims in the global South. Moreover, trafficking in Africa and the Middle East is more likely to involve children and to mix sexual exploitation with other forms of forced labor and even institutionalized slavery (United Nations Office on Drugs and Crime 2006). But both positive aid and legal assistance and negative US sanctions have been focused by cultural construction and geopolitics, not need. For example, almost half of US anti-trafficking funding went to East Asia or the Western Hemisphere and only 26 percent to Africa (US Department of State 2010).

Consider India, where tens of millions of women and children suffer contemporary slavery and sexual exploitation that does not fit the "white slavery" model. First, India's Ministry of Home Affairs estimates that 90 percent of sex trafficking in India is internal, intrastate (from rural to urban centers) and interstate (from poor to rich states within the country). The "international" component is not South to North, but rather South–South; the Global Alliance Against Trafficking in Women and the United Nations Economic and Social Commission for the Asia and Pacific estimate 300,000 Bangladeshi women to have been trafficked to India, and 200,000 to Pakistan (Brysk and Maskey 2012). According to ILO estimates, there are 21.6 million child laborers aged from 5 to 14 years in South Asia (India, Bangladesh, Nepal, Pakistan, and Sri Lanka). India, with an estimated 12.6 million working children, has the third largest labor force of children in the world. (http://www.ilo.org/legacy/english/regions/asro/newdelhi/ipec/responses/index.htm)

Trafficking and sexual exploitation in South Asia are clearly driven by the structural vulnerability of poverty, patriarchy, and discrimination—not smuggling or coercion. Three-fourths of Indian women are illiterate. Some 90 percent of rural and 70 percent of urban women are unskilled (ADB 2003). As home and farm-based subsistence opportunities are on the decline, more and more women have had to leave their traditional spheres of life and migrate to urban centers or foreign countries to work as unskilled laborers. These uneducated women lack basic information about employee rights, let alone bargaining power, and are often duped by fraudulent agencies, charged exorbitantly, and remain in bondage-like situations to pay off their recruitment debts. This is compounded by the vulnerability of outcastes; a study commissioned by the National Commission for Women in India found that 62 percent of women in commercial sex work were from scheduled castes (NCW 1996 cited in Nair and Sen 2005). Patriarchal norms deepen the damage through child marriage, arranged marriage, dowry, and sexual violence that serve as trafficking vehicles or precursors. The National Human Rights Commission of India found that 71.8 percent of survivors of sex trafficking had married when they were below 18 years of age, a quarter of the married respondents were sexually assaulted by persons other than their husbands (mostly by extended family members and neighbors), and 41.35 percent were abused when they were less than 16 years of age (Nair and Sen 2005).

The disproportionate emphasis on trafficking within migration policy also slights the wider set of persons exploited and abused across borders. Although international sex trafficking is an especially egregious violation of almost every fundamental freedom, enacted on especially vulnerable populations, other forms of labor exploitation and abuse are even more widespread and affect greater numbers of people. For example, the ILO estimates there are nearly 700,000 child domestic workers in Indonesia alone, and Human Rights Watch has identified that country as one in which a large number of such workers face "slave-like conditions," including frequent physical and sexual abuse (Human Rights Watch 2006b). This is a far larger (and more vulnerable) affected population in one country than the maximal estimates of Eastern European women trafficked to the West for sexual exploitation. The numerical preponderance of people trafficked domestically are men indentured for debt slavery in rural areas of developing countries or forced labor in dictatorial regimes and war zones. Significant numbers of male and female children are also enslaved on plantations, in informal factories, as domestic servants, as beggars, and as child soldiers. The largest flows of domestic labor trafficking are within the poorest countries and regions: Africa, South Asia, and the Middle East.

The recognition of contemporary slavery and sexual violence is a necessary but not sufficient response to trafficking. But successful frames can sometimes be widened to permit a broader vision; academics and advocates have been arguing for a decade for a human rights approach to trafficking and contemporary slavery (Brysk and Choi-Fitzpatrick 2012). Under the direction of Secretary of State Hillary Clinton, the 2009 US State Department Annual Report on Trafficking shows signs of a modest conceptual breakthrough in the understanding of trafficking. The report now begins with a broader discussion of forced labor that frames transnational prostitution as one facet of trafficking, and the 2008 legislation encompasses fraud and exploitation following voluntary migration. The US report explicitly states that prior employment in sex work for adults or parental consent to exploitation of children should not diminish accountability for forced labor. The new report also highlights the emerging US practice of forcing traffickers to pay restitution to victims, which has the potential to increase the effectiveness of enforcement by diminishing the profit motive of traffickers. The dynamic evolution of frames can build communication politics from recognition to response to learning, and a human rights campaign from protection toward empowerment.

Reframing Female Genital Mutilation: "Our Bodies, Our Selves"

Female genital mutilation (FGM) has different characteristics than trafficking that complicate framing as a human rights abuse that can be used to shame or pressure controlling agents. Like sex trafficking, FGM affects women and children who are innocent victims of physical coercion. But because the abuse is perpetrated by legitimate non-state actors—families and social authorities—it is more difficult to shame governments to enforce global norms. Unlike the match between trafficking and a preexisting frame of sex slavery, advocates contesting FGM had to search for a fit between the harms of the practice and a variety of broader rubrics, including children's rights, individual self-determination, health, and gender discrimination. Campaigns against FGM were met with counterclaims of cultural rights, unlike trafficking, but the shift from humanitarian health to women's rights to health rights eventually enabled the most universal claim to modernizing norms. Finally, unlike the fortuitous match between trafficking and a diverse coalition, FGM initially drew upon the relatively weak sector of global civil society concerned with gender issues in developing countries—but the widening of the appeal to health brought in charismatic health professionals with greater leverage on enforcing states and global institutions.

FGM is one of the terms used to describe a variety of practices that involve the partial or complete removal or cutting of the female external genitalia for the fulfillment of cultural, religious, or other nonmedically therapeutic purposes.[2] The World Health Organization (WHO) estimates that 100–140 million living women and girls have undergone some form of the procedure, while an additional 2 million girls are at risk each year (World Health Organization et al. 1997). FGM is practiced primarily by certain cultures in twenty-eight sub-Saharan and northeast African countries but also occurs in parts of Asia and the Middle East. It also is practiced among migrants from these areas now living elsewhere. Short-term consequences can include extreme pain, shock, bleeding, tetanus or sepsis, and infection. Long-term complications can include scarring, damage to the urethra, chronic infections, infertility, and infant and maternal mortality during childbirth. In recent decades, the procedures have become a conduit for the transmission of HIV from unsanitary instruments used on multiple girls.

African states and local elites initially resisted colonial and later modernizing attempts to legislate against FGM, citing cultural relativism, a spurious religious basis in Islam, and national self-determination over "their" female citizenry. Efforts by Westerners to prevent FGM began in the 1920s, with Protestant missionaries in Kenya prohibiting the custom among their converts. For the missionaries, the practice was unchristian and unhealthy (Keck and Sikkink 1998). For Kenyans, however, the missionaries' campaign quickly came to symbolize the imposition of outside values on their communities. Thus, FGM became associated with nationalism, particularly among Kenya's dominant Kikuyu ethnic group among whom the anti-FGM campaign was centered (Keck and Sikkink 1998). For example, Jomo Kenyatta, Kenya's anticolonial leader and first president, defended the practice in his 1938 book, *Facing Mount Kenya*. Kenyatta described FGM as an initiation custom that helped maintain Kikuyu identity (Kenyatta 1938). Similarly in colonial Sudan, a 1943 British policy to outlaw infibulation (the most severe form of FGM) was deeply resented and led to the secret and rapid circumcision of some girls (Dorkenoo 1995).

By the 1970s, however, there was broad consensus within the international rights community that FGM violated a number of core human rights: the right of women to be free from discrimination on the basis of gender, the right to life and physical integrity including freedom from violence, the rights of the child, and the right to health (Rahman and Toubia 2000; Skaine 2005). Heightened international awareness around FGM in the 1970s mobilized one important audience, the burgeoning women's movement in Western countries, particularly the United States. For feminist leaders, FGM was a "tool of patriarchy and a symbol of women's subordination" (Skaine 2005: 46). In the name of women's rights, according to these Western activists, the practice must be ended everywhere. Thus, in the 1970s and 1980s, Gloria Steinem, Mary Daly, Fran Hosken, and other feminist leaders condemned FGM and urged international organizations and NGOs to take up the cause (Walley 1997). As an important step toward globalizing the issue, feminist organizations renamed the issue, from the relatively neutral "genital cutting" or "female circumcision" to the far more emotive "female genital mutilation" (Keck and Sikkink 1998: 20).

Robin Morgan and Gloria Steinem's article, "The International Crime of Genital Mutilation" published in *Ms. Magazine* in 1980 was an early example of Western campaigning against FGM. Later *The Hosken Report: Genital and Sexual Mutilation of Females* (1982) educated many Westerners about the practice, while Hosken's rhetoric sparked debate over the appropriate way to approach the issue. Similarly, the documentary film *Warrior Marks* (Walker and Parmar 1993) by Pratibha Parmar and Alice Walker also brought the issue to American audiences, as did Walker's 1992 fictional account of the life of a genitally mutilated woman, *Possessing the Secret of Joy* (Walker 1992).

During this time, women's rights were increasingly becoming accepted as human rights, which opened space for the discussion of FGM as a rights issue on the international level (Bunch 1995; Charlesworth 1994; Smith 2000). For example, the creation of the UN Convention for the Elimination of All Forms of Discrimination Against Women (CEDAW), adopted by General Assembly Resolution 34/180, December 18, 1979, was a critical step toward international recognition of human rights abuses taking place within the private realm such as FGM. CEDAW incorporated feminist arguments about state obligations to protect women and girls from private abuse of human rights.

However, at one stage the human rights campaign was derailed when feminist groups, international organizations, and human rights NGOs encountered unexpected resistance to perceived imposition of inappropriate norms from the very people they aimed to assist—African women, including many who opposed the practice but resisted the intervention. While rights-based feminist mobilizing scored some successes internationally, for many years this framing was handicapped by the emphasis on national sovereignty within international organizations. International organizations such as UNICEF and WHO struggled to reach consensus on how to approach FGM in the 1980s due to the diversity of member states' positions on the subject (Boulware-Miller 1985: 162–163). Some African states resisted international pressure to eradicate FGM and objected to women's rights framing. African leaders cited higher national priorities, such as dealing with underdevelopment, as reasons not to embark on FGM eradication campaigns (163).

This international reluctance to view FGM as a rights issue began to change in the 1990s, with the post–Cold War strengthening of human rights discourse (Boyle 2002). By the mid-1990s international bodies had shifted from an emphasis only on the medical consequences of FGM to a model based on human rights (Boulware-Miller 1985). In 1990, the Committee on the Elimination of Discrimination against Women adopted General Recommendation No. 14, which expressed the Committee's concern over the continued practice of FGM and urged governments to support efforts to eradicate the custom (United Nations 1990). A 1993 UN Declaration on the Elimination of Violence Against Women explicitly included FGM within the category of violence against women, which also includes marital rape, dowry-related violence, and sexual abuse of female children (United Nations General Assembly 1993: Article 2). The 1993 UN World Conference on Human Rights in Vienna, a milestone in making FGM a human rights issue, called for the elimination of violence against women including traditional practices that take place in the private sphere ("Vienna Declaration and Programme of Action" 1993). The International Conference on Population and Development (ICPD) held in Cairo in 1994 also highlighted the interconnections between women's health and human rights regarding FGM. These international declarations placed FGM squarely within the rights framework, while previous international attention to FGM had focused on the medical aspects of the practice.

Since about 2000, the tensions among African women, Western feminists, African leaders, health and development NGOs, and international organizations have been reduced through the rise of a new and less controversial combined "health rights" framing for the issue, which appeals internationally but does not alienate locally. A critical component in the next phase reframing was the entry of highly legitimate and "neutral," non-feminist professionals as interlocutors between the rights community and national sensibilities: doctors and humanitarians. As a result, dozens of African countries outlawed the practice during the 1990s and 2000s, but perhaps just as important for implementation, African states have begun to encourage holistic attention to women's health rights and transnational support for some humanitarian programs of local women's empowerment. The health rights frame brought in additional allies and broadened solidarity.

The charismatic authority and problem-solving modernity of medical professionals has played a critical role in delegitimizing FGM as a threat to health rights, with a joint effort above and below the state from health IGOs and NGOs. To assess this change, it is useful to recall that when the Economic and Social Council of the United Nations asked the WHO to study FGM in 1958, WHO leadership refused because FGM was seen as a cultural matter, not as an international medical issue (Boyle, 2002: 41). But by the late 1970s and early 1980s, UN subcommittees began to study FGM and began providing outlets for national governments and NGOs to discuss the health issues related to FGM (Boyle 2002: 48). One such forum was the WHO-sponsored Seminar on Harmful Traditional Practices Affecting the Health of Women and Children in Sudan in 1979. After another generation of feminist consciousness-raising, in 1998 the WHO, UNICEF, and the United Nations Population Fund issued a strong and influential joint statement against FGM, calling FGM a violation of the rights of women and girls to the highest attainable standard of health (World Health Organization et al. 1997). This represents a breakthrough from the communicable disease model of public health to a rights-based perspective, and in a 2008 update of the joint statement, the WHO goes on to assert universal reproductive rights. The 2008 norm-setting standard calls FGM a practice with "no known health benefits" that reflects "deep-rooted inequality between the sexes" and is an "extreme form of discrimination against women" (World Health Organization 2008a).

The WHO has a Department of Reproductive Health and Research (RHR), which is a joint endeavor with several other UN agencies to "strengthen the capacity of countries to enable people to promote and protect their own sexual and reproductive health and that of their partners, and to have access to, and receive, high-quality sexual and reproductive health services when needed" (World Health Organization 2008b: 5). The WHO now uses its legitimacy as a public health organization and source of knowledge to promote attention to issues of sexual and reproductive health (also manifest during the AIDS crisis and struggle for access to generic anti-retroviral medications). A study sponsored by the WHO was published in *The Lancet* in 2006 on the links between FGM and maternal and infant mortality and health consequences (World Health Organization 2006). The WHO provides training manuals for nurses, midwives, and other health professionals on how to prevent FGM and how to provide health care to girls and women with FGM-related complications. The manuals also provide strategies for involving families, communities, and political leaders in preventing FGM (World Health Organization 2001a, b). Finally, the WHO has reviewed anti-FGM programs by other agencies to assess the effectiveness of public health interventions in this area (World Health Organization 1999).

At the level of global civil society, the World Medical Association (WMA), an independent confederation of about eighty national medical associations, condemns the participation of physicians in any form of female genital circumcision and encourages national medical associations to oppose the practice (World Medical Association 2003). Formed in the wake of the Nuremberg trials to oppose unethical medical experimentation, the organization has played a broader role in opposing physicians' participation in torture, as well as drafting guidelines on emerging ethical issues such as new genetic technologies. The WMA offers specific "best practice" guidelines for physicians in environments where women and girls are at risk of cutting and states: "Regardless of the extent of the circumcision, FGM affects the health of women and girls. Research evidence shows the grave permanent damage to health." In terms of concrete policy work, in the late 1990s the WMA publicly encouraged the Egyptian Minister of Health to continue working to ban female circumcision in Egypt (World Medical Association 1997). The WMA has also extended its opposition to the transnational medicalization of the procedure in immigrant communities, especially in Western Europe. In a press release from 2003, Dr. James Appleyard, incoming president of the WMA, specifically mentioned FGM as a rights issue: "One form of a gross breach of the rights of young girls is female genital mutilation. Even in the UK where the practice is outlawed it is widely alleged that FGM continues to be practiced in private hospitals" (World Medical Association 2003).

Similarly, humanitarian service providers have reframed medical, development, and missionary identities to adopt and transmit a rights-based perspective on FGM. Doctors Without Borders strongly opposes FGM as a human rights violation and a threat to health, and identifies medical staff involvement in the practice as a breach of ethical and professional standards. In addition, Doctors Without Borders attempts to ensure that the practice is not performed in facilities where the agency works and that instruments provided by Doctors Without Borders are not used for the procedure (Médecins Sans Frontières, "Female Genital Mutilation," n.d.). At the local level, CARE found that Somalis living in Kenyan refugee camps who had been exposed to the human rights dialogue used by international aid workers were open to rights-based discussions of FGM and health consequences, which led many people in the camps to abandon the practice (DeVoe, n.d.; Majtenyi 2009).

Amidst the spectrum of such abuses occurring in very poor and patriarchal countries, FGM stood out for its senselessness and threat to innocent mothers and children. The harms of FGM also helped to explain or contribute to a range of health and development problems, from fistulas to AIDS. The practice is a dramatic visual representation of sexual violence against women that registers viscerally with Western men taught to identify the clitoris with the penis. Physicians have an additional ethos and social role as defenders of the body, which is violated by FGM.

While at least fourteen African countries have outlawed the practice, estimated prevalence remains stubbornly high at over 90 percent in half a dozen core countries such as Somalia and Egypt. However, high prevalence countries are highly concentrated in the Sahel region and the Horn of Africa; even in Western Africa and certainly in the South, FGM is generally restricted to certain ethnic groups in isolated rural areas. Many immigration-receiving countries have also banned FGM, including Canada, Sweden, the United Kingdom, and the United States, and many European countries such as France and Spain lack specific legislation but have prosecuted the practice in immigrant communities under child protection and assault laws (Baer and Brysk 2009).

A comprehensive 2010 report by the Population Reference Bureau shows some encouraging trends in the wake of reframing and more collaborative networks.

One indicator is a significant intergenerational reduction in younger women affected even within some high-prevalence countries. There has also been such significant reduction in several lower incidence countries like Kenya and some West African states (Benin, Liberia, and Togo) that they now fall in the range of a possible emergence of a "tipping point." Similarly, FGM has become much less common in urban areas in countries like Kenya, Liberia, and Mauritania, suggesting increasing decline with the general modernizing trends of urbanization, education, and media exposure. Although data is quite incomplete and uneven on forms and harms of FGM within these countries, there is also some evidence that the most harmful form of infibulation is increasingly concentrated as a widespread practice only in a few core countries such as Somalia, while a few other countries such as Eritrea have shifted significant numbers of practitioners to a symbolic nick which does not involve the removal of flesh or impairment of future function (Innocenti Research Centre/UNICEF 2010). Reframing FGM has been dialectical in a double sense: shifting frames with learning over time and fostering an evolving dialogue among victims, advocates, and governments across cultures and layers of the global governance system.

Human Rights Claims in Colombia:
When Frames Fail

In the twenty-first century, violent government-sponsored human rights abuse in Latin America has declined greatly, and when it does occur is generally challenged by international advocates and met with some response by accused states. Yet in Colombia, continuing assassinations, kidnappings, forced displacement, and torture through the late 2000s received limited attention and only checkered state response. In 2006 alone, more than 770 civilians were assassinated or disappeared, while over 200,000 were forcibly displaced. A portion of US aid, temporarily suspended due to human rights concerns, including paramilitary links with public officials, was quickly restored (Amnesty International 2007). The Colombian government, while disbanding paramilitary groups and initiating limited prosecutions against military and civil leaders implicated in the killings, failed to significantly prevent impunity or provide sustainable security in rural areas—or to stem the remobilization of an estimated 3,000 to 9,000 paramilitary fighters (International Crisis Group—"New Armed Actors in Colombia," 2007). Moreover, dozens of members of the Colombian Congress were in jail or indicted for links to the paramilitary groups (Romero 2008b).

Yet Colombia possessed all of the ingredients for change predicted by comparative study of human rights reform and the democratizing experience of its neighbors in the 1980s. Colombia is a democratic regime, relatively visible to international media, and sufficiently developed to generate a stable civil society, with the potential leverage point of US aid. While Colombia is a US ally and trade partner, the US hegemonic power benefited less from repression in Colombia than Cold War support for repressive Central American dictatorships during the 1980s, where human rights protest was ironically more effective. Conversely, the United States has had a positive interest in suppressing violent actors linked to the drug trade who are responsible for some measure of the violations; cleaning up crime and strengthening the rule of law in Colombia is a US national interest. A plethora of human rights organizations eventually formed in Colombia, including transnational coalitions, and the United Nations has had a strong presence via the High Commission on Refugees, the High Commission on Human Rights, UNICEF, and other programs since the early 1990s. But human rights mobilization has been less effective than in peer states such as the Southern Cone or even Andean neighbors like Peru—where violence was framed as political rather than criminal. In fact, the Colombian government has tried to restrict civil society organizations and successive regimes have attempted to depoliticize the violence.

What distinguished Colombia from similarly situated zones of insecurity that received greater response was a question of hearts and minds, not guns and butter. The human rights problems in Colombia are difficult to frame as such. Colombia is a sovereign state that resists intervention, yet the state eschews responsibility for the violence. The perpetrators are often unclear, and the alleged and actual guerrillas do not fit the profile of "innocent victims." Some of the forms of abuse, like internal displacement and socioeconomic land rights struggles, do not map onto preexisting frames like cross-border refugees and ethnic cleansing. Moreover, human rights advocacy groups inside Colombia initially used a weak frame of Marxist social struggle and imperialism, with limited outreach, that received little support from more cosmopolitan transnational organizations. Conversely, the limited areas of success in protecting some indigenous peoples and internally displaced people in Colombia reflect shifts in the dominant frames for those subpopulations. Tate shows that even international agencies responded to Colombia only after they adopted a frame change, from drug-related to political violence, to show how the UN High Commission on Human Rights was finally persuaded to appoint a Permanent Representative for Colombia (Tate 2007).

The Colombian state claims sovereignty and resists being labeled as a failed state or a war zone. Since the international human rights regime—like all international law—operates when "domestic remedies have been exhausted," the presumption of sovereignty sets the bar for intervention high. The Colombian government claimed to be both too strong to warrant international intervention and too weak to exercise full control over paramilitary and guerrilla violence.

Thus, President Uribe downplayed human rights conditions and used continuing violence to argue for more US aid, even though an investigation of a 2007 wave of civilian killings showed that almost half of the military units involved were financed by the United States. Uribe stated, "We need association with the United States, not to hide our problems, but to help us in solving them" (Romero 2008b). While the free trade agreement with the United States was postponed as trade unionists decried the assassination of their peers, there were no significant long-term cuts in US military aid, and the trade accord was approved in 2011.

The predominance of non-state actors in the Colombian conflict blurred the boundaries between counterinsurgency, drug trafficking, law enforcement, and vigilante frames. In Colombia, over 130,000 legal private security contractors patrol urban streets, rural lands, and multinational facilities, exceeding the official armed forces of around 100,000 (Garay 2003). A majority of massacres of civilians have been committed by paramilitary groups and most kidnappings by guerrillas; despite involvement and some abuses by the official military forces, most violators do not wear uniforms.

As a democratic sovereign state, Colombia is shielded from pariah status or from being pressured for regime change. The international human rights regime is backstopped by a transnational network for democracy promotion, with its own cross-cutting NGOs, international institutions, stalwart support from strong states, and reinforcing regional nodes in Latin America (Santa Cruz 2005). As Tate (2007) notes, even symbolic UN sanctions are usually used on a country-specific basis—and only against dictatorships. Southern Cone human rights movements of the 1980s faced illegitimate military dictatorships, while ethno-cratic countries like South Africa or Serbia that systematically disenfranchised identity-based groups are generally stigmatized. By contrast, Colombia's free elections, impressive Constitution, and well-developed judicial system have generated admiration, confusion, and "plausible deniability" from a variety of international observers. Colombia's citizens have strong rights in a weak state—somewhat like receiving an impressive settlement of a lawsuit drawn on a bankrupt account.

Moreover, recent Colombian governments learned to semantically manipulate and diminish human rights accountability by taking advantage of these features of the Colombian experience (Tate 2007). Responding to the United States' concern with continuing killings of union members and the arrest of his cousin and political confidante on charges of sponsoring paramilitaries, President Uribe responded that "Colombia is not in the time of crisis, but in the time of remedies" (Romero 2008b). Since the Colombia trade pact with the United States hinged in part on the international public perception of Colombia's human rights record, the Colombian government invested millions of dollars in US public relations firms and congressional trips to promote its image (Lipton and Weisman 2008).

Within this political environment, the kinds of violations in Colombia are difficult to capture in a human rights narrative. Despite the equal moral worth of all victims and types of suffering, we can easily observe that some kinds of victims and violations receive greater political attention and generate a more emphatic response from concerned audiences. "Innocent victims" are more difficult to identify in a chronic and diffuse civil war characterized by significant concurrent criminal activity. Colombian elites consciously manipulated these frames; Uribe claimed that "in Colombia, we have not insurgents against dictators.... We have terrorists against democracy" (Romero 2008b). In Colombia, hundreds of marginalized civilians each year have been murdered by troops and falsely claimed as combat casualties (Romero 2008a). The large numbers of internally displaced persons are by definition less visible than international refugees, and transnational middle-class Colombian migrants usually do not publicize the political factors that pushed them to exile. Tate describes a breakthrough 1997 incident in which internally displaced persons (IDPs) finally received recognition, in the words of a foreign diplomat who registered the African-looking waves of tattered families fleeing the conflict in terms that this group "really looked like refugees" (Tate 2007).

As far as root causes, the narrative of long-term social injustice is trumped by a story of immediate national insecurity that articulates well with dominant narratives generated by the hegemonic United States: the conflict in Colombia has been framed from the Cold War to the War on Drugs to the War on Terror. The perennially problematic interpenetration of social and political rights struggles is much more difficult to articulate in democratic, developed Colombia than it was in dictatorial and impoverished Central America. The social roots of Colombia's conflict are much more about inequity than absolute poverty—resource-rich, middle-income Colombia has one of the highest levels of inequality in the Western hemisphere, with a GINI Index of 58.6 (World Bank, World Development Indicators). The "just resistance" frame was further belied by the violent tactics of guerrillas such as assassinating the peasants that they claimed to represent, killing journalists and aid workers, and kidnapping for ransom. Solidarity was slowed when some advocates failed to distinguish themselves clearly from violent militants; this early distinction was one of the fundamental elements that mobilized international support for South Africa's antiapartheid movement.

While more fitting frames were articulated by charismatic and legitimate voices for issues such as trafficking, FGM, and Darfur, Colombia also lacked compelling voices to deliver information and interpretation. First of all, all parties to the conflict literally killed the messenger, targeting journalists. In a

2005 report, Reporters Without Borders concluded that in areas of persecution, threats and killings produce a climate of "anxiety and circumspection among the remaining journalists.... 'We are very passive in our work,' several have said." Within Colombia, journalists were further hindered by government persecution and military influence over mainstream outlets (Brittain 2006). Violence was directed at foreigners at a relatively high rate, which discourages direct monitoring and exchanges of solidarity, while foreign journalists reporting on chronic conflict did not benefit from the protection of being embedded with an international military force.

On the international level, stories of suffering are assessed by referencing to regional and historical baselines (Brysk 1994)—tragically, the world has learned to depreciate violations from perpetually troubled or exceptionally brutal zones. An abuse that would generate headlines in a neighboring or peer country may not even be reported when coming from Colombia. If it is reported, political violence in Colombia is more frequently described by dominant international media as war, crime, or terror—rather than a violation of citizens' rights by political authorities, or their delegated surrogates. As one small illustration of this trend, a search of the *New York Times* index since 1981 showed ninety-nine stories using the term "human rights" in Colombia—compared with 140 labeled as "human rights" regarding Colombia's much more tranquil neighbor Ecuador.

It is these semantic factors that seem to make the difference in recognition and political will in objectively similar situations of human rights abuse, such as forced disappearances in Argentina during the 1970s and Colombia during the 1990s. Argentina benefited from the charismatic advocacy of the Mothers of the Disappeared as speakers, while the high prevalence of abuse by non-state guerrillas and paramilitaries in Colombia muddied public understanding and framing. The Argentine regime as responsible agent was discredited as a military dictatorship, while equally abusive Colombian governments could defend themselves and stand on sovereignty as electoral democracies. In terms of audiences and outreach, Argentine exiles in Europe and the United States used universalist campaigns and later appealed to international law to gain response. But Colombian civil society was until recently more partisan and embroiled in a national frame of social struggle rather than a cosmopolitan social imagination of human rights. The speakers and frame were conducive to human rights campaigns in Argentina and inhospitable to them in Colombia— the result has been a generation of justice in Argentina and a lamentably tardy and scant response to the crisis in Colombia. A similar contrast can be seen in the neighboring horrors of another continent: successful framing of genocide in Darfur, coupled with ignorance, denial, and confusion in Congo.

Story vs. Silence: Darfur and Congo

During the first decade of the new millennium, at least half a dozen conflicts unfolded involving mass killings, torture, rape, war crimes, and associated civilian deaths from hunger and disease. While the suffering in Darfur certainly merited attention and response, the more sustained and bloodier crisis in Congo received minimal recognition. The conflict in Congo was estimated to kill 3.9 million people from the late 1990s through the mid-2000s, while the fighting in Darfur was variously reported to slaughter from 70,000 to 400,000 during the same period. While some differences in geopolitical factors and perceived leverage informed international response, there were resource conflicts in both areas, and the apparent anarchy of Congo was belied by the many abuses perpetrated by militias sponsored by neighboring states—potentially just as amenable to pressure as the Sudanese regime. Although some Western observers contrasted racial and religious war in Darfur with more indiscriminate violence and noncombat deaths in Congo, detailed reports show more similarities on the ground: some of the violence in Darfur was non-ideological resource competition and many deaths there were also from hunger, while much of the violence in Congo also had an ethnic component. Virtually ignored by the world, Pygmies within the Congo have in fact been the targets of ethnic genocide; hunted for sport by virtually all the combatant parties, targeted for extermination by some groups, and sometimes even victims of cannibalism (BBC 2003). An important determinant of the difference in monitoring and mobilization for Darfur and Congo was not the reality, but the representation.

The Congo was planted in Western consciousness as the original Heart of Darkness, and the site of King Leopold's colonial depredations. Throughout the Cold War, the country was further exploited and oppressed by the US-installed kleptocrat Joseph Mobutu. The DRC entered the 1990s heartbreakingly poor, ethnically fractured, stunningly corrupt, and ill-governed. The current cycle of epochal violence has its roots in the aftermath of the Rwandan genocide of 1994, which led to a succession crisis, civil war, and invasions by neighboring regimes, and heightened several simmering regional insurgencies.

Following the end of the Rwandan genocide, 2 million Rwandan Hutus sought refuge from retaliation in the Kivu region of the DRC. While many of the refugees were civilians, some were genocidal members of the Interhamwe Hutu militia and Hutu-era Rwandan Armed Forces. Two years later, the now Tutsi-led Rwandan army of the new regime invaded to dismantle the refugee camps that had become a site of incursions into Rwanda. The Rwandan military was accompanied by Congolese rebels, who overthrew the government of Joseph Mobutu. The new government, headed by Laurent Kabila, was widely viewed as corrupt and foreign-dominated, and further alienated his former allies by dismissing the Rwandan military. When a sector of the Congolese army rebelled in turn against Kabila, the Rwandan and Ugandan governments sent troops to aid the revolt. Meanwhile, Zimbabwe, Angola, and Namibia entered the country to aid the sitting Kabila government, and a continental war based in the Congo erupted, officially lasting until 2003. Estimated casualties for this period alone range from 3 to 5 million; the deadliest war since the Holocaust (International Rescue Committee 2007).

But after the official war ended, civilian suffering and war crimes continued as rebel groups remained in the region, including the Rwandan Hutu FDLR (Democratic Forces for the Liberation of Rwanda), domestic militias such as the Movement for the Liberation of Congo, and the Ugandan Lord's Resistance Army. While a free election was held in July 2006, the government has been unable to establish authority in rebel held provinces and has been unable to control its own national army. This ineffective and rampaging national army has clashed with the CNDP (National Congress for the Defense of the People), a Tutsi-led political military movement led by Laurent Nkunda and supported by Rwanda. In addition, the national military has carried out a series of attacks on civilian camps in the Kivu region ("DR Congo: Conflict History" 2011). In 2008, the DRC accepted a joint military operation to suppress the predations of the Hutu FDLR, to be carried out in collaboration with Uganda, Rwanda, and South Sudan (Doyle 2011). But the January 2009 effort was ineffective, and in its wake the FDLR regrouped and began a series of retaliations against civilians who they deemed had collaborated with the military ("Congo-Kinshasa: FDLR Threat Continues in Kivus" 2011). A renewed operation by the national army later that year met with some modest success, but was heavily criticized for causing massive civilian casualties and suffering, and for failing to dismantle the rebel movements ("DRC: MONUC Sticks to its Guns" 2009). A third attempt in 2010, with greater emphasis on civilian protection ("DR Congo Releases 'Amani Leo'" 2011) also resulted in ferocious backlash and a campaign of terror by rebel forces—including the massacre of entire villages and mass rapes.

The abuses in the Congo wars are mind-boggling and complicated, but they were not completely unknown or incomprehensible—a few journalists, some international organizations, and human rights groups have been documenting the occurrence and origins of the violations throughout the conflict, but without achieving widespread awareness or mobilization. The World Health Organization, UNICEF, and International Rescue Committee each issued detailed mortality assessments in 2004–2006 demonstrating the magnitude of the millions of deaths, and showing the linkage between combat casualties, forced displacement, hunger, and disease. Human rights groups such as Human

Rights Watch and Oxfam have linked the ill-trained, often unpaid, and corrupt Congolese national military (FARDC, Armed Forces of Congo) to killings of civilians and refugees, rapes, kidnapping of child soldiers, and illegal resource exploitation ("Democratic Republic of Congo—Children and Armed Conflict" 2012).

The bewildering number of rebel forces, shifting alliances, and unclear motivations for their actions have shaped coverage of the conflict, and shaped a perception that UN peacekeeping efforts are doomed to fail (Loyn 2008). Yet the most abusive paramilitaries have often been recruited, mobilized, or sponsored by neighboring states. A leading source of rebel abuses that morphed into a source of state abuses, for example, is an armed Tutsi militia established inside Congo in 2006 commanded by Laurent Nkunda, the CNDP. After the CNDP was decapitated by its Rwandan sponsor—in part due to international pressure and publicity of the militia's abuses—it was incorporated in the Congolese government forces in 2009. Yet the CNDP reportedly continues to operate as a criminal network within the FARDC national army for resource exploitation and to prey upon civilians in its zone of operation ("UN Report: CNDP Congolese Soldiers Involved in Illegal Mining Operations" 2010).

The official militaries of neighboring powers are also culpable, and their abuses have also been documented, but downplayed by the media in favor of militia war crimes. One plausible explanation for Western media's inattention to Congo atrocities generated or sponsored by the neighboring states of Rwanda and Uganda is that these states are US allies; in fact, the Congolese government approved the joint military operations within their borders under considerable US pressure (Doyle 2009). The Tutsi-dominated Rwandan army first entered the DRC after the Rwandan genocide to pursue former Hutu genocidaires, which tends to blunt Western perception of their subsequent abuses—in the Western imagination, since the Tutsis were the victims in 1994, they are marked forever as victims. After the end of the first Congo war and expulsion of Rwanda's forces, the Rwandan army allied with Congolese ethnic Tutsi rebels and again invaded the DRC, remaining until 2003 (Faul 2011). In early 2009, Rwandan soldiers were invited to help deal with the rebels still operating within the DRC (Doyle 2009). Currently, Rwandan soldiers operate within the Kivu region. In late 2010, the UN released a report implicating the Rwandan army in committing genocide against Hutu refugees in the Congo. The Rwandan government vehemently denounced these charges, and the Ugandan and Rwandan governments both threatened to withdraw their forces from UN peacekeeping missions. This threat forced the UN to moderate its report on possible Rwandan atrocities ("UN tones Down Congo 'Genocide' Report" 2010).

The Ugandan army also originally invaded the Congo during the 1990s to uproot one of it own rebel groups. In 2008, Uganda re-entered the DRC to hunt the cultish Lord's Resistance Army (LRA), which had escaped Uganda and found refuge there (Doyle 2011)—again the legitimacy of the original mission has diminished international ability to perceive abuses and unintended consequences. After being pushed out of Uganda, the Ugandan LRA increased its activities in the DRC—maintaining a campaign of terror and abductions inside the DRC; committing massacres every few weeks (Rice 2011). Of all the rebel forces in the DRC, the LRA has killed the most civilians, and is notorious for its mass kidnappings, torture, and rape of child soldiers—and the LRA is the most truly autonomous from state control. But Ugandan attempts to expel the LRA have only resulted in failure and violent backlashes against civilians. In March 2009, the Ugandan army withdrew from the DRC. In late 2010, a UN report also accused the Ugandan army of committing genocide in the DRC during its military operations in the 1990s. Like the Rwandan government, the Ugandans threatened to withdraw their peacekeeping forces in response.

Finally, the most long-standing foreign rebel force in the region, the Hutu FDLR has committed massive abuses and carved out a regional base in the Kivu region of Congo, with the complicity of transnational supporters and a different set of regional neighbors. The FDLR are led by an international chain of command, with leaders residing in Europe and North America. The FDLR have been involved in illegal mining operations, as well as campaigns of rape, mass killings, and abduction of children ("FDLR Arming for War with Congolese Children" 2010). Despite estimations that the membership of the FDLR has fallen in recent years, the FDLR has increased the frequency and intensity of attacks against civilians since 2008, as well as forced recruitment of child soldiers ("DR Congo: Top UN Humanitarian" 2009). In October 2010, the leader of the FDLR, Callixte Mbarushimana was at long last arrested in France for war crimes and crimes against humanity (International Criminal Court 2010).

In sum, more than a decade after the most massive suffering since World War II, there is only scattered recognition and fitful policy response to the Congo's ongoing atrocities. The faint voice of independent activism is provided by the Congo Coalition and Friends of the Congo, and these groups generally focus simply on raising awareness rather than full-fledged campaigns. A handful of celebrities have tried to draw attention and foster humanitarian relief, usually "serious" rather than headliner figures with a track record of humanitarian involvement: Ben Affleck, Mia Farrow, Javier Bardem, Julianne Moore, and Emannuelle Chriqui ("Celebrities Raise Hopes for Congo" 2009). But for most Western public and policy makers, the story is too distant, numbingly massive, with complex causality, shifting relations between victims and perpetrators, few communicative links to transnational communities, and reinforcing tropes of tribal African barbarism.

By contrast, the more articulate tragedy of Darfur garnered widespread and rapid recognition and an energetic campaign, which did generate a meaningful international response. A key element in this campaign was the genocide frame. In contrast to the Francophone Belgian Congo, Sudan was an English-speaking British colony and heavily influenced by Arabic culture, so more accessible to international awareness via these transnational circuits. Sudan was also relatively more urban and modern during the postcolonial period, shaping media access, the locus of repression, and international expectations. The Islamist dictatorship that pursued the North–South genocide and later sponsored the paramilitaries in Darfur was more coherent than Congo's kleptocracy, and conveniently already a US enemy post-9/11, as well as an ally of human rights pariah and strategic rival China (Goodman 2011).

Like the millennial violence in Congo, Sudan's mid-2000s persecution was linked to an earlier genocide—in this case, the Khartoum regime's brutal twenty-year campaign to suppress a secession movement of southern Sudanese who were racially and religiously distinct, and inhabited the richest oil-producing region of the country. The roots of Darfur's violence lie in the racial tensions between Arab Muslims in the north and black Africans in Southern Sudan, as well as more mixed-motive divisions in western Sudan (Knickmeyer 2011). Although the 1983–2005 North–South civil war killed an estimated 2 million civilians, international awareness was limited to sporadic famine relief efforts for almost a generation. Around the turn of the millennium, international religious and human rights activists did spark attention to a renewal of the slave trade in the South as a weapon of war, and engendered labeling of the conflict as genocide by the United States in 2002. One notable element of this belated movement against the North–South violence that resurfaced in the Darfur campaign was the mobilization of previously isolationist US evangelical Christians on behalf of beleaguered Southern Sudanese Christians suffering religious, as well as racial, persecution.

Meanwhile, Khartoum's hardening militarization, government land grabs, and forced migration from the war also affected other regions of Sudan beyond the South, and exacerbated desertification and associated resource conflicts between villagers and nomads over water and fuel (Muhammad 2010). In several regions, such as Darfur, these local conflicts contributed to insurgent movements, and the Sudanese government responded with various forms and levels of counterinsurgency violence. In early 2003, the JEM and SLA rebel groups attacked and captured the capital of Darfur. Alarmed at the threat of secession, the Sudanese government responded by arming Arab militias traditionally hostile toward the African tribal groups of Darfur (Reeves 2005). Armed and occasionally logistically supported by the Sudanese military, the Arab militias known as janjaweed wreaked havoc across Darfur, destroying villages and massacring civilians on the pretense of their alleged association with the JEM and SLA. Some hundreds of thousands were killed by a combination of direct conflict, scorched earth policies creating drought and famine, and forced displacement—and perhaps a million survivors of the fighting were also displaced, impoverished, and brutalized. Although the Sudanese state clearly exploited ethnic tensions to commit horrific war crimes, it does not appear to have pursued a systematic program of cultural eradication in Darfur, and many of the abuses were intra-ethnic; the reality in Darfur was more like the ethnic-tinged counterinsurgency of Guatemala than the ethnic cleansing of Bosnia.

Yet the Darfur movement's consciousness-raising efforts benefited from a triple analogy of that conflict to the Holocaust, the Rwandan genocide, and Sudan's own North–South civil war—each a massive genocide marked by a failure of Western response (Mamdani 2009). Journalist Nicholas Kristof, who advocated intervention in Darfur, explicitly compares, "Congo is essentially a tale of chaos and poverty and civil war. Militias slaughter each other, but it's not about an ethnic group in the government using its military force to kill other groups. And that is what Darfur has been about: An Arab government in Khartoum arming Arab militias to kill members of black African tribes" (Kristof, "Darfur and Congo" 2007) and adds, "We have a moral compass within us and its needle is moved not only by human suffering but also by human evil. That's what makes genocide special—not just the number of deaths but the government policy behind them" (Kristof 2007). Reports of the abuses in Darfur definitively place blame on the Sudanese government for militia abuses, label the conflict as genocide, and call for international intervention (Booker and Colgan 2011). The genocide frame was spearheaded by public intellectuals, as well as journalists; Samantha Power's *A Problem From Hell: America in the Age of Genocide* is described by a leading advocate as "the key text, bible if you will" of the movement (Budabin 2012).

Also contrasting with Congo, this powerful frame was given voice by a highly legitimate advocacy coalition. The Darfur movement was organized by the Holocaust Museum and catalyzed by Holocaust witness Nobel Laureate Eli Wiesel. Recognition diffused through student activism on hundreds of US campuses and created an interfaith coalition of hundreds of religious groups. Extensive involvement by public intellectuals and high-profile celebrities also played a special role in giving this crisis voice and visibility. A plethora of youth groups mobilized; their action-oriented and idealistic names bespeak their appeal: Save Darfur, STAND, Darfurian Voices, Dream for Darfur, and Help Darfur Now. The vocabulary of responsibility is further illustrated by the labeling of one campaign and publication: Not On Our Watch. Among the celebrities advocating for humanitarian intervention are Meryl Streep, George Clooney, Don Cheadle, Angelina Jolie, Mia Farrow, and Brad Pitt ("Celebrities,

Activists Rally for Darfur" 2011). Some of the celebrity activism and documentation came from a parallel campaign by John Prendergast, a long-standing African human rights advocate who wrote two books with Don Cheadle and later founded a Web-based celebrity pressure group called the Enough Project. The Darfur campaign rallied 70,000 people in Washington, DC, in 2006 (Bergner 2010).

The Enough campaign built on the consciousness raised in Darfur to focus President Obama's long-standing interest in Africa on the next chapter of Sudan's conflict: the North–South peace accord. After a series of full-page ads in the *New York Times*, celebrity fact-finding tours of the region followed by appeals on television talk shows, and direct celebrity lobbying of the president, Obama appointed a special envoy and linked respect for the referendum to US sanctions on Khartoum. As the National Security Council's senior human rights figure Samantha Power describes the impact of John Prendergast's charismatic advocacy, "He's elevated Sudan to Himalayan proportions on the mattering map in Washington" (Bergner 2010).

As a result of this earlier recognition, charismatic voice, successful framing, and good fit with a receptive audience, the Darfur crisis mobilized more timely international efforts. In 2004, the conflict in Darfur was recognized as genocide by the US government, and the UN and AU sought to introduce peacekeepers in the region. The United States passed sanctions, increased humanitarian aid, and introduced a no-fly zone. Although the effectiveness of these interventions was incomplete, for a variety of reasons violence in the region declined significantly by 2006 and slowly deescalated, with periodic resurgences punctuating a gradual decline. In 2009, the ICC issued an arrest warrant for Sudanese president Omar Al-Bashir on charges of genocide (Al Jazeera, "ICC Charges Bashir with Genocide" 2010). The dictator responded by expelling aid agencies from Darfur (Rice 2010). Under continuing international pressure, the Sudanese government signed a peace accord with the main rebel group in Darfur in 2011, which will be implemented with international support.

Conclusion

The framing of human rights claims in a narrative that is a good match for international standards and networks is a key element for securing recognition and mobilization. The most evocative frames tell a story of innocent victims abused by identifiable perpetrators in a familiar repertoire that violates widely shared norms. Although some problems lend themselves to resonant frames more than others, advocates can strategically reframe violations and learn from the relative success of their appeals to different norms. Table 4.1 shows the

Table 4.1 Human Rights Campaigns: Frames

Case	Voice	Frame
Tibet	Dalai Lama	Self-Determination
Dreyfus	Cause célèbre	Democracy, citizenship
Spanish Civil War	Writers	Democracy
Holocaust	Anne Frank, Elie Wiesel	Genocide
Arab Spring	Khaled Said	Democracy, citizenship
South Africa	Nelson Mandela	Discrimination
Burma	Aung San Suu Kyi	Democracy
Argentina	Mothers of the Disappeared	Torture, disappearances
AIDS	Doctors, Victims Movement	Health rights
Violence vs. women	Amartya Sen	Violence
US death penalty	Weak celebrities	
Trafficking	Child victims	Sex slavery
Female genital mutilation	Child victims, doctors	Violence, health rights
Colombia		Crime
Darfur	Celebrities	Genocide
Congo	Weak celebrities	Barbarism
US civil liberties	Stephen Colbert	Democracy, discrimination, detention
India	Anna Hazare	Citizenship
Russia	Pussy Riot	Democracy, citizenship
Iran Green	Neda Agha-Soltan	Democracy, torture
China	Cause célèbre	Democracy, civil rights
Kony 2012	Invisible Children	Child soldiers
Academic freedom	Limited cause célèbre	Civil rights
Armenia		Genocide
Israel/Palestine		Genocide, refugees
Liberia	Mothers	War crimes

frames employed by the campaigns studied throughout this book, adding to the elements of voice.

Communication politics appeals may be informational or representational, but the politics of persuasion often involves a performance. Messages do not deliver themselves—they must be articulated in testimony, protest, theaters, and courts. Thus, we turn to analyze the power and structure of human rights performances.

5

PLOTTING RIGHTS

The Power of Performance

[The 1968 Prague Spring uprising] was merely the final act and the inevitable consequence of a long drama originally played out in the theatre of the spirit and conscience of society.
—Vaclav Havel, *Power of the Powerless* (Havel and Keane 1985: 43)

Vaclav Havel was a Czech playwright and political dissident, imprisoned for scripting resistance to Soviet rule. The words above were published in 1985, reflecting on the unsuccessful uprising that he narrated on the radio. Cultural politics laid the groundwork for continuing human rights appeals in Eastern Europe—including the formation of Helsinki Watch, that became Human Rights Watch—one of the pillars of the international human rights movement. Four years later, the goals of the Prague Spring uprising were finally realized, and Havel became the first democratic president of his liberated country.

We have seen that human rights appeals must convey the humanization of victims, connect the audience with their suffering, decry the violation of norms, and offer a grammar for response. While the speakers, message, and media are important components of communication, there are also structured narrative forms that enhance the salience of appeals and the ability to perform them in public space. Leading human rights theorist Martha Nussbaum develops an overall linkage between literary imagination and the capacity for justice, while historian Lynn Hunt empirically links the rise of the notion of human rights to the emergence of the novel in modern Europe (Nussbaum 1995; Hunt 2007).

Neuroscience now confirms the relationship between narrative forms and recognition. The introduction or diffusion of any form of sustained narrative depicting diverse individuals models empathetic connection and engagement with others (Paul 2012). As cognitive researchers summarized their observations, "Engaging in the simulative experiences of fiction literature can facilitate the understanding of others who are different from ourselves and can augment our capacity for empathy and social inference" (Mar and Oatley 2008: 173). The mechanism is that "some of the same neural structure in the brain that is used when we live out a narrative is also used when we see someone else living out that narrative" (Lakoff 2008: 40, cited in Castells 2009).

Narrative forms help construct the social imaginary of human rights. Beyond this, the power of narrative is influenced by its packaging in specific linguistic formats. "Genres consist of orienting frameworks, interpretive procedures, and sets of expectations," which become communicative resources for conveying meaning and constituting social relationships (Hanks 1987). Thus, the narrative genres based on performance seem to have the greatest power to communicate norms and evoke response—whether the narrative is actually performed, posted, or disseminated in written form. This notion is an amalgam of Tilly's notion (2008) of political protest as a contentious performance in causally and symbolically coherent repertoires, the performance approach to the influence of folklore (Bauman 1992), and a dramaturgical analysis of social interaction.

Literature stimulates the moral imagination; that is why oppressive regimes ban it. Literature expands our consciousness of "who is human, what is right, and who is responsible"—the conceptual foundations for human rights mobilization identified in a previous study of campaigns against private and transnational abuses (Brysk 2005). In *Reading Lolita in Tehran,* we see the liberating power of the narrative form in a contemporary authoritarian setting, through humanizing identification with individuals, depictions of agency and transformation, and alternatives to limiting social codes. As the teacher leading the women's reading group says, "That room, for all of us, became a place of transgression" (Nafisi 2003: 8). Similarly, a study of the role of literature in Central American revolutionary movements describes narratives as a form of ideology, that provide "a structure of experience that enables them to recognize themselves in the world, to see the world as in some way created for them, to feel they have a place and identity in it" (Beverly and Zimmerman 1990: 2).

The politics of persuasion have an affinity to theater. Theater has been a privileged site of human rights critique since Antigone, while the key "secular" human rights vehicles of trials, truth commissions, and public protest all take theatrical forms. Theatrical treatments of human rights include documentary or historical theater, testimonial theater, participatory "street" or community theater, allegories and politicized restagings of classical tales, and psychodramas like *Death and the Maiden* (Rae 2009). Legal performances plot the story of violations and the restoration of voice and social order, embodying the relationship in "human rights culture" between "law in its relationship to narratives of suffering" (Laqueur in Wilson and Brown 2009: 36).

We can further extend these converging understandings of politically signifi-cant performance genres to the power of specific forms, following Castells's observations about the emotional pathway of decision making that operates through direct signaling of somatic markers (Castells 2009: 144). Hare and Blumberg begin this analysis inductively with the historic dramatic genres of comedy, tragedy, melodrama, and farce, but ultimately expand to seven social situation types. For human rights, the most relevant of these genre types are "crime and punishment," search, and self-sacrifice (Hare and Blumberg 1988: 16-18). The most emotionally resonant formats seem to be testimonial, quest, allegory, satire, and ballads. Each of these formats draws on affective brain pathways deeply rooted in our collective consciousness--and historically often salient to our survival: personal witness of danger, a search for refuge or lost kin, cultural myths embodying key norms of social conduct, laughter break-ing fear and bonding audiences, culturally coded transgression of dominance, and the comfort, mnemonic function, and emotive-cognitive bridge of music.

In this chapter, we will trace some representative uses of these performance-based genres across diverse settings. Testimonial personifies abuse as the story of a single suffering individual. Human rights testimonials are labeled as tragedies in common consciousness, but technically they are melodramas, in which bad outcomes are caused by a situation—not personal behavior or character, and often reflect the transformation of personal tragedy to a case of wider social drama. Allegory is a didactic mode depicting struggle that provides heroes and martyrs, locates causal chains, and suggests repertoires of response. Allegory is linked to both melodrama and folklore, and often incorporates plot types of "crime and punishment," search, and self-sacrifice (Hare and Blumberg 1988: 18). Satire breaks the fear of coercion, challenges the legitimacy of authority, and creates common consciousness among the audience. It is distinct from comedy, which generally resolves social order after contradiction, and more like farce—which exaggerates and often reverses social codes and relationships. Each of these genres shows a performance pathway for constructing a human rights imaginary.

From Tragedy to Testimonial

Life narratives of human rights abuse have become a powerful vehicle for human rights campaigns, tribunals, truth commissions, and cause célèbre literary texts. They provide witness, put a human face on massive abuse, and model the pro-tagonist's emerging awareness of causality and responsibility for their suffering. Personal accounts such as Jacobo Timerman's *Prisoner Without a Name, Cell Without a Number* and *I, Rigoberta Menchu* brought vast increases in attention and pattern recognition of forced disappearances in Argentina and the genocidal war crimes of civil conflict in Guatemala. On the basis of the circulation of her story, Rigoberta Menchu won the Nobel Peace Prize in 1992, as a symbol of the suffering of all indigenous peoples in the symbolic year of the Quincentenary of the European encounter with the Americas. Influential works in the most direct testimonial genre of theater include Chilean Ariel Dorfman's plays, *Speak Truth to Power* and *Death and the Maiden*, South African Athol Fugard's works, and the famous testimonial of sexual violence, *The Vagina Monologues* (Rae 2009: 16). This narrative form situates the individual's suffering as a symptom of a social problem and moves the story from a "case" to "a case of."

Schaffer and Sidonie Smith argue that the "narrated lives" of human rights testimonials play a privileged role in the ethics of recognition, drawing on Wilson's anthropology of truth commissions:

> Storytelling in action accumulates political import. In local contexts, life story-telling constitutes a social action on the part of individuals or communities....As stories circulate beyond local contexts through extended national and transnational communication flows, they enable claimants to "speak truth to power," to invoke Michel Foucault. The stories they tell can intervene in the public sphere, contesting social norms, exposing the fictions of official history, and prompting resistance beyond the provenance of the story within and beyond the borders of the nation (Schaffer and Smith 2004: 4).

Voices of Witness

The Voices of Witness human rights campaign uses the testimonial repertoire to build a narrative channel for solidarity. Following the success of American author Dave Eggers's novel *What is the What?*, a chronicle based on the life of a Sudanese refugee, his publishing house McSweeney's launched a project to collect and disseminate human rights testimonials around underpublicized human rights problems. As the Web site's mission statement proclaims: "The books in the Voice of Witness series seek to illuminate human rights crises by humanizing the victims. Using oral history as foundation, the series explores social justice issues through the stories of men and women who experience them." The eight books draw attention to distant crises in Sudan, Burma, and Zimbabwe. But they also focus American audiences on "bringing rights home," with volumes on wrongfully convicted prisoners, victims of Hurricane Katrina, undocumented migrants, and post-9/11 injustice.[1] Each book contains recorded oral histories from interviewees, who are regarded as the authors. Editors' introductions provide background, context, and brief descriptions of the narrators.

The project provides training workshops for teachers and promotes the use of oral histories in public education.

The project began when human rights journalist Samantha Power invited Dave Eggers and Valentino Achek Deng, the Sudanese refugee profiled in *What is the What?*, to speak at Harvard's Carr Center for Human Rights, where they met editor Craig Walzer. The introduction by Eggers and Valentino to this first effort highlights the overall purpose of the project: "The Amplification of Seldom-Heard Voices." The book, *Out of Exile: The Abducted and Displaced People of Sudan*, carries forward the stories of abuse and forced displacement from Sudan revealed in Eggers's novel to focus wider attention on the world's contradictory treatment of refugees. It depicts violence and rape in refugee camps, denial of refugee status in host countries, and international minimization of suffering in Africa as "tribal."

In another vein, *Nowhere to be Home: Narratives from Survivors of Burma's Military Regime* provides a full arc of twenty-two stories from Burma that include victims still in Burma, refugees in Thailand, Malaysia, Bangladesh, the United States, and even one child soldier. The book provides basic background on the abuses of Burma's military regime: forced labor, arbitrary arrest, physical and sexual violence, torture, censorship, and forced military conscription. But the focus of this volume also includes the victims' hopes and best memories, to recover and communicate their humanity. It quotes British novelist Ian McEwan: "Imagining what it is like to be someone other than oneself is at the core of our humanity. It is the essence of compassion, and it is the beginning of morality" (Lemere and West 2011: 19).

The Voices of Witness series also turns the lens back on the United States, as it seeks to reveal unrecognized patterns of human rights abuse and shortfalls at home. *Surviving Justice: America's Wrongfully Convicted and Exonerated* and *Voices from the Storm* both question the American public's assumption that their government operates fairly and offers equal protection to all citizens. The story of thirteen exonerated Americans calls into question trust in the judicial system and documents the extent of witness misidentification, forced confession, and prosecutorial misconduct. The testimonials from Hurricane Katrina show how the victims of a natural disaster are then victimized again by their own government; revealing racial and economic rifts in citizenship. Telling tales include a twenty-two-member family seeking help together from the Superdome, a grandmother who rescued her grandchildren by floating them in buckets, and model Muslim migrant Zeitoun, a New Orleans house painter who traveled the city in a canoe to rescue his neighbors—only to be falsely arrested on terrorism charges. The message of these volumes is twofold: it does happen here, and it could happen to you.

A different strand of the Witness series chronicles American abuse of non-citizens, showing the contradiction between the universal standards we promote but do not internalize. *Underground America: Narratives of Undocumented Lives* profiles far-flung individuals from Mexico, China, South Africa, Colombia, Peru, Pakistan, Guatemala, and Cameroon. Many of their tales meet the international standard for asylum, though none are recognized here as refugees. Instead, the testimonies show how they suffer in the United States from exploitation, unsafe working conditions, separation of families, arbitrary detention, forced labor, harassment, and violence. *Patriot Acts: Narratives of Post-9/11 Injustice* adds the testimony of eighteen direct victims of illicit detentions, hate crimes, forced renditions, surveillance, and harassment to institutional and policy critiques of US domestic counter-terror initiatives. Perhaps the poster child of this collection is a 16-year-old Muslim girl from Guinea who was arrested with her father due to immigration status, falsely accused of a link to suicide bombing, and eventually granted asylum on the basis that she would be subject to forced circumcision if deported.

The introduction to the Voice of Witness volume on Zimbabwe is titled, "History by Ordinary People." The testimonial genre fosters human rights at every point in the communicative arc. Life narratives restore the humanity of their narrators, giving voice to the voiceless. They frame suffering as a social problem, not just a personal tragedy. And they manifest a unique power to reach the consciousness of listeners across the globe, with the deep grammar of a fireside tale.

The Vagina Monologues

The Vagina Monologues is a path-breaking work of testimonial theater by US feminist Eve Ensler that chronicles the impact of gender discrimination and sexual violence through the voices of representative characters. The overall theme is women's survival and empowerment through reclaiming their sexual and reproductive voice. Originally composed in 1996, the play has been translated into over twenty languages and performed worldwide in thousands of locations for over a decade. The half-dozen core monologues were written based on Ensler's interviews with several hundred women about sexuality, trauma, and representation. But additional monologues are now added every year to represent a broader spectrum of experiences, including contemporary expressions of violence against women. The monologues treat issues of menstruation, childbirth, rape, sexual awakening, child abuse, FGM, women's health care, women's sexual self-image, homosexuality, and violence against transgendered people, among others. Prominent international themes have included wartime rape in Bosnia, chronic sexual suppression in Afghanistan, and sexual violence in Congo.

The Monologues have often been performed in the United States around Valentine's Day, the celebration of romance that has been extended by some feminists to inspire chivalrous concern for women' suffering, but contested by others to highlight the contradiction between sentimental depictions of hetero-sexual romance and the realities of widespread sexual assault and domestic violence. In 1998, Ensler's work catalyzed the creation of V-Day, a day of action to protest violence against women and raise funds for women's organizations through benefit performances of the play. According to the V-Day Web site, "the V stands for Victory, Valentine, and Vagina." There were almost 6,000 benefit events in 2011. Thus far, over $85 million has been raised for V-Day projects (http://www.vday.org).

The V-Day mobilizations then became a global movement to fight violence against women and girls, which has now spread to 140 countries. The campaign's Web site lists the following range of activities:

> Performance is just the beginning. V-Day stages large-scale benefits and pro-duces innovative gatherings, films and campaigns to educate and change social attitudes towards violence against women including the documentary *Until The Violence Stops*; community briefings on the missing and murdered women of Juarez, Mexico; the December 2003 V-Day delegation trip to Israel, Palestine, Egypt and Jordan; the Afghan Women's Summit; the March 2004 delegation to India; the Stop Rape Contest; the Indian Country Project; Love Your Tree; the June 2006 two-week festival of theater, spoken word, performance and commu-nity events UNTIL THE VIOLENCE STOPS: NYC; the 2008, V-Day 10-year anniversary events V TO THE TENTH at the New Orleans Arena and Louisiana Superdome; the Stop Raping Our Greatest Resource: Power To The Women and Girls of the Democratic Republic of Congo Campaign; the V-Girls Campaign, and the V-Men Campaign.

The performance of *The Vagina Monologues* has been controversial world-wide, but especially in its land of origin. Traditionalists bemoaned its negative emphasis on sexual violence in heterosexual relationships and endorsement of lesbian sexuality, while Cardinal Newman campaigned to stop performances on Catholic college campuses—resulting in some dislocations but no over-all decline in performances. But *The Vagina Monologues* has also become a weapon of contention in the US culture wars about reproductive rights.

Over the past generation, Republicans increasingly sought to limit women's access to abortion, which had been framed by the Supreme Court's *Roe v. Wade* as a privacy right. From the 2000s, some US states went beyond more passive measures such as withdrawal of funding, waiting periods, and parental con-sent to more intrusive legislative directives to doctors requiring or forbidding information and examinations—including medically unwarranted trans-vaginal ultrasounds. In 2012, during a legislative debate on such proposed new restrictions on abortion in Michigan, a male Republican lawmaker had a female Democratic representative censured and suspended from debate—because she used the word "vagina." In a sharp, ironic statement questioning his right to legislate her control of her reproductive decision making, adding the feminist pro-choice to the privacy frame and linking state intrusion to sexual violence, Rep. Lisa Brown said, "I'm flattered that you're all so interested in my vagina, but no means no." When she was evicted from the legislature, her few female colleagues followed her in protest, and she became a free speech cause célèbre. Social media slogans linked the issues: "VAGINA—can't say it, don't legislate it." Thus, the final phase of Brown's protest was to take back her voice—by staging a performance of *The Vagina Monologues* on the steps of the Michigan legislature, with ten legislators and playwright Eve Ensler, to an audience of thousands (Thistlethwaite 2012).

Allegory as Protest Performance: Indian Summer

> My life is my message.
> —Mahatma Gandhi

One influential scholar of modernity sees all narratives that succeed as history as "a kind of allegory, [that] points to a moral, or endows events, whether real or imaginary, with a significance that they do not possess as a mere sequence...to moralize the events of which it treats" (White 1987: 14). Moralized narrative appeals have a special mobilizing power to contest injustice. "At the heart of any allegory will be found this conflict of authorities....they are symbolic power struggles....When a people is being lulled into inaction by the routine of daily life, so as to forget all higher aspirations, an author [of allegory]...may arouse a general self-criticism" (Fletcher 1964: 22–23). Allegorical performances reenacting stories central to national or religious identity as a critique of current authority have been important protest repertoires for a range of human rights movements, from protest pilgrimages in Latin America to Solidarity workers' protests in Poland (Brysk 1995).

In 2011, citizens of India, Russia, Spain, and the United States took to the streets to protest rising inequality, corruption, and manipulation of the rule of law by unaccountable elites—the "citizenship gap" between formal political entitlement and social exclusion (Brysk and Shafir 2004). The political pathology of corruption violates human rights in multiple ways: corruption impedes the right to political participation, to equal protection before the law, to health and education, to freedom of speech and assembly, and to protection from police violence (International Council on Human Rights Policy 2009). Even the democracy protests of the Arab Spring itself were initially sparked by corruption—not regime change—when a Tunisian street vendor harassed and repeatedly beaten by extortionist police set himself on fire in desperation.

The universalist, nonpartisan, yet deeply contentious protest movements of Anna Hazare, opponents of Vladimir Putin, and Occupy Wall Street all sought fairness, equal access to political decision making, a restoration of social mobility, and a "level playing field." These and similar movements, from Brazil to Belarus, were usually sparked by the middle-class and youth, yet deeply concerned with increasing poverty at the grassroots. They used the informational tools of globalization and a global standard of good governance to protest what they deemed a skewed form of economic globalization. Regardless of limited policy outcomes, each of these citizenship movements succeeded in communicating a political critique of social problems that had been seen previously as a consequence of tradition, abusive individuals, self-correcting markets, or bad luck. They were all movements that relied heavily on symbolism: from the anti-Putin white ribbon to Occupy Wall Street's "99%."

In India, an unprecedented anticorruption movement mobilized the most broad-based national level protest, social awareness, and attempt at policy reform in that country's half-century of independence.[2] This is especially notable because corruption in India has achieved stunning proportions and is deeply embedded in most governmental, business, and other social institutions, entailing massive beneficiaries, while those it hurts the most are the poor and powerless. Transparency International reports that over half of Indians report paying bribes and ranks India 95th out of 175 countries surveyed (Transparency International 2010). In 2008, over 120 of 520 Members of Parliament faced criminal charges ("Democracy Tax is Rising" 2008). By 2011, even a Calcutta High Court Justice was impeached for corruption. Corruption in India degrades elections, undermines law enforcement, blocks access to justice, health care, and education, promotes unsafe construction of key infrastructure and scandalous working conditions, allows criminal exploitation of women and children, and cripples response to natural disasters and epidemics. Bribes are frequently required to transact routine forms of social life: to register a child's birth, buy property, obtain a driver's license, start a business, and even to benefit from government antipoverty assistance. During the Anna Hazare protests, participants interviewed in newspapers, broadcast media, and my own observations described their galvanizing experiences of watching a relative die because they could not afford to bribe hospitals for medical care, losing their livelihoods because they could not pay a bribe for a taxi or vendor's permit, being jailed and often beaten without cause by police seeking extortion for themselves or bribed to act as enforcers for local landlords and gangs, and being assaulted and persecuted for uncovering corruption. Numerous Indian families named babies born during the protests "Anna" in honor of the anticorruption crusader, and one exulted to the *Times of India* that things were changing so much that "this time, the doctors didn't even take a bribe to deliver the baby" (Saxena 2011).

These corrupt conditions stand as the deepest contradiction to India's status as the "world's largest democracy" and a rapidly developing rising power. Although India has the developing world's longest unbroken postcolonial democracy, secured by a nonviolent social movement and characterized by a well-established rule of law and a formal regime of multicultural membership, its public sphere is persistently undermined by the patriarchal family, caste hierarchy, and rural feudalism—which spills over to undermine urban political party machines. Dominant party hegemony of the Indian Congress Party and systematic patron–client relations throughout society further distort social relations. Like in post-revolutionary Mexico, state socialism from Independence to the 1990s created bureaucratic rent-seeking corruption (referred to as the "License Raj"). Post–Cold War globalization merely privatized the problem: auctioning off the national patrimony to predatory elites and generating a secondary layer of corruption. Despite these clear abusive effects and structural roots, corruption in India had often been excused or rationalized as a traditional alternative to inappropriate modernizing institutions, a covert mechanism of redistribution for petty civil servants, and even as a form of national resistance to global homogenization (Kumar 2011). Prior to the 2011 protests, virtually the only social force with an interest in contesting this governance structure directly had been a thin civil society, heretofore populated mostly by relatively weak urban intellectuals and professionalized NGOs. Grassroots movements of peasants and workers had focused on redistributive visions of local social justice, rising marginal groups often joined or created parallel political party machines, while burgeoning anti-globalization movements such as dam protesters were oriented toward international interlopers and corporate malfeasance more than national governance.

The rise of the 2010–11 anticorruption movement marked the culmination of a new kind of broad-based civil society coalition and consciousness that had begun since the 1990s to directly challenge governance and demand enforcement of the rights promised in India's exemplary Constitution. Media coverage of the Anna Hazare movement labeled its speakers as "the voice of civil society"—not a particular sector, or even the grassroots. The movement created a cadre of non-partisan "volunteers" highly visible in the protests, unprecedented in Indian social movements; at least 500 managed the August Delhi protests over ten days (Sodhi 2011). In a parallel move, when a mosquito-borne dengue epidemic struck the swampy poor state of Orissa during the 2011 monsoon—and it was discovered that drainage funds allocated to local officials had evaporated, even as dozens died each week—enraged local residents created neighborhood "citizen sweeping committees" (Pradham 2011). That summer, the most popular movie in India was the uncharacteristically serious drama *Arakshan*—a leading Bollywood director's powerful indictment of caste bias, corruption, and privatization of education through the story of a crusading headmaster who triumphs over racism, scheming elites, and criminal officials.

Anna Hazare was a reforming social worker of humble origins. He had participated in a series of projects to promote social welfare, human dignity, and restore "Indian values"—such as creating a Gandhian model village in his home region plagued by feudalistic exploitation and alcoholism. "Anna" is an honorific meaning "elder brother," that was bestowed in recognition of his social work, which was honored by the Indian government in 1992. From that period, he had led local campaigns against corruption in forestry, government contracts, and grain management. Anna was also connected to a grassroots organization in Rajasthan, hamstrung by local malfeasance, that fought for and won a 2005 "right to information" in India (Jenkins and Goetz 1999). In his seventies, he had turned to campaigning for the strengthening of nascent local ombudsman monitoring offices into some sort of national check on growing corruption, and working with citizens' movements proposing new forms of legislation. By 2011, the Indian Parliament had delayed treating these citizen initiatives for years and had systematically weakened the few proposals that reached the floor (Yardley 2011a).

Anna and his loose coalition of supporters were galvanized by frustration and initially launched two waves of protests in Delhi, in April and June of 2011, prior to the August surge. Anna's April public fast for an ombudsman law attracted thousands of supporters, including prominent Hindu religious leaders and civic figures such as authors and cricket stars, and led the government to promise summer treatment of an anticorruption mechanism, and to sign the United Nations Convention Against Corruption. Anna's Hindu collaborator Swami Ramdev organized another protest in June, specifically focused on money laundering and capital flight—but the Swami's more militant protest was broken by police in a midnight raid resulting in dozens of injuries and arrests, subsequently condemned by India's own courts.

Meanwhile, as the summer session of Parliament dithered through July without advancing treatment of the issue, Anna Hazare announced a culminating fast demanding direct treatment of a full alternative Lokpal [Ombudsman] proposal drafted by civil society groups, launched on the August anniversary of India's Independence. The Hazare movement's proposal demanded that the Ombudsman's oversight powers reach upwards to the level of the Prime Minister, down to the estimated 22 million grassroots civil servants, and articulate and harmonize with oversight of regional governments. Hazare announced an indefinite fast and set up a giant stage platform in Delhi's central square, the Ramlila Maidan. He dressed in Gandhian garb including the famous white toque, unfurled a giant poster of Gandhi behind him, and framed his anticorruption message as a "second freedom struggle" to liberate India from internalized domination. As he called upon his supporters and the media to bear witness to his principled sacrifice, hundreds, then thousands, then tens of thousands of supporters came to join him—this time, encompassing a widening swath of civil society. Although Anna was the charismatic embodiment of the movement, his organization was led by a cluster of activists who comprised the self-denominated "Team Anna." The movement's leadership included prominent civil society activist Arvind Kejriwal—a disillusioned former official, legal figures including a former Supreme Court Justice, Hindu reformers such as Swami Ramdev, and India's first female Police Commissioner Kiran Bedi—a "tough love" figure known for her unavailing efforts to clean up police corruption.

The protests widened to national and then international proportions. As I happened to be travelling across India during the initial week in August 2011, I personally observed the main protest in Delhi, as well as smaller marches in Jaipur, Agra, and Bhubaneshwar. In an unnamed small town in Uttar Pradesh, as I drove through I witnessed the village schoolteacher leading dozens of uniformed schoolchildren down the road waving Indian flags, bearing photos of Anna, and chanting for a new India, as stalled drivers signaled support. Significant demonstrations in the thousands were broadcast from Kolkata, Mumbai, Bangalore, and Hyderabad—the latter significant because these high-tech development poles were more globalized and less embroiled in the poverty and social rigidity of the old India. Even the legions of lunchbox messengers of Mumbai, the famous *dabbawallas*, went on strike for the first time in a century. As I interviewed participants in the Delhi protest at the Ramlila Maidan, I discovered that significant contingents, including many people of modest origins and some of advanced age, had traveled hours or even days from neighboring Punjab, Uttar Pradesh, and even Bihar to join the protest.

Overseas non-resident Indians, previously largely apolitical, mounted sympathy protests in London, several US cities, Australia, and Germany, among others. But after the government tried to delegitimize the movement as foreign-funded, the India Against Corruption campaign carefully refused financial support from any overseas entity. A representative diaspora dissident, an Indian defense researcher now resident in Brisbane who led a Facebook sympathy fast in half a dozen countries, explained that he had left India after his father was hounded out of a headmaster post by a corrupt Education Ministry and died fighting for his pension and government flat (Mukherji 2011).

After the first days of August protest and tense negotiations over the protesters' permits and demands, the government decided to arrest Anna for "violating

the conditions of protest," while government supporters critiqued the movement's "manipulation" of parliamentary due process. Anna was jailed overnight and hundreds of protesters arrested. But his supporters massed around
the prison, creating a new protest site and a secondary civil liberties grievance.
When a judge overruled the arrest and ordered Anna released, he initially refused
to leave the prison, inspiring a day of unusual political theater as the authorities
pleaded with and pressured the man they had arrested the day before to leave
prison and disperse his supporters. After Anna returned to Ramlila Maidan, still
fasting and beginning to suffer health problems, contingents of his supporters
fanned out through Delhi to direct blockades of the homes and offices of MPs,
to further highlight their demand for action and accountability from Parliament.
One supporter even immolated himself, the only recorded death in the weeks
of massive protests.

For the next week, a weakening septuagenarian Anna and his supporters
remained steadfast in the square, as political party leaders visited and tried
to negotiate partial versions of his platform. In the end, after 11 days' fast,
as Anna was being hospitalized, the government accepted the movement's
demands: immediate treatment of the civil society Ombudsman proposal. Anna
broke his fast in highly symbolic fashion: with coconut water, served to him by
minority Muslim and Dalit [Untouchable] girls. This ending was specifically
designed to echo Gandhi's outreach to Muslims and across caste lines, counter
the uneven adherence of Muslim and Dalit groups to the coalition, and blunt
criticism of the broad-spectrum Hazare movement as tinged by unsavory Hindu
nationalists. Anna announced that he would not seek political office, but would
turn his next campaign to electoral reform, contesting a key mechanism of corruption. The Indian media labeled the outcome "a victory for People Power,"
making explicit comparisons to the democracy movements of Eastern Europe
and South Africa. In neighboring rival Pakistan, in a rare instance of positive
emulation, civil society activists marched to demand their own anticorruption
crusade (Khan 2011).

The Anna Hazare movement's unusual success at shifting the agenda in India
can be traced to several elements of communicative appeals that coalesced in
the summer of 2011, organized in a coherent and culturally resonant allegorical
narrative. The movement was labeled in the most encompassing vision of the
nation possible: "India Against Corruption." The label of "Team Anna" echoed
the preceding year's World Cricket championships and the triumph of "Team
India." This was also a latent recovery of India's international prestige after
the embarrassment of hosting the Commonwealth Games, when international
athletes complained of inadequate facilities and unsafe conditions—traceable
to corrupt contracting of India's hosting venue. The movement was led by a
full spectrum of charismatic figures, from Anna himself to several Swamis,

from Bollywood stars to India's favorite "lady cop." At one point during the August protests, several Indian medical associations proudly deployed their professional legitimacy, marching as a body in support of Anna. Speaking of Anna as a transnational symbolic figure, a senior journalist at CNN.com in London told the *Times of India*, "He is old, determined, sincere, non-violent and ready to give up his life for the greater cause of the nation. He is perfect story material" (Kalla 2011). Hazare was highlighted as a person of the year or "top global thinker" by India's NDTV, *Time Magazine,* and *Foreign Policy* journal. (Sengupta 2012).

Although the protests advocated for the poor, including later peasant and labor rights, the political support base of the movement was modern, middle-class, and transnational. One *Times of India* editorial chastened the unresponsive government, "It's The Middle Class, Stupid" (Ganguly 2011). The movement engaged large swathes of politically alienated youth, both students and slightly older self-proclaimed "techies." Analysts pointed out that the prior generation of the Indian middle class were mostly civil servants—who tolerated or even benefited from corruption—but that their children, competing in a neoliberal globalized society, suffered from the lack of a level playing field (Yardley 2011b). The Indian diaspora also flocked to the movement, often recounting corruption bottlenecks that had pushed them abroad to gain an education or pursue a career blocked by favoritism at home. Ironically, the most modernizing young, foreign-educated, and middle-class Indians were the most receptive to the appeal of a grassroots village activist hearkening back to Indian communal norms and symbolism. While some local rivals, like leaders of Dalit political machines, and a few transnational left intellectuals such as Arundhati Roy criticized Anna's nativist Hindu roots and questionable alliances, the main thrust of the 2011 campaign was assiduously multicultural. I witnessed numerous chants for Hindu–Muslim unity, a large Sikh and another Christian contingent, and a Gandhian eschewal of caste distinctions in daily practice (such as eating together).[3]

Accordingly, the movement was simultaneously disseminated through the full spectrum of old and new media. Information politics were used to communicate compelling images, legislative proposals, petitions signaling the extent of support, and framing statements by key cultural figures. It was a "Facebook revolution"—but protesters also handed out grainy newsprint photos of Anna on street corners, with minimal text accessible to the illiterate. "Team Anna" took to the airwaves of India's lively and near-universal television channels but also managed extensive Twitter feeds. In one telling example of the nexus between old and new media, an elderly man at the Delhi protests, with limited education and no English, insisted that a foreign observer he mistakenly identified as a journalist (despite my disavowals) should publish the "evidence" he had carried to Delhi from his home village. That evidence was a crumpled printout of the Swiss bank holdings of Indian politicians, downloaded by his son from Wikileaks at the village cyber-cafe.

The symbolic politics and cultural repertoire of the movement were extensive and multivalent, centered on the allegory of "the second Freedom Struggle." Anna positioned himself as the embodiment of Gandhi, and in turn, the predominant slogan of the campaign was "I am Anna." Supporters often donned Gandhi-style white hats inscribed with this slogan, some in Hindi and some in English. The public fasts and sit-ins were labeled as a Gandhian "satyagraha" struggle; in an amazing transnational intergenerational feedback loop I heard 2011 anticorruption protesters in India singing (in Hindi) the 1960s American civil rights protest song used in Gandhi-inspired US sit-ins: "We Shall Overcome." The occupation of the Ramlila Maidan, Delhi's central public space, was similar to movements such as Argentina's Mothers of the Plaza de Mayo or China's Tiananmen Square protests. One of the key sites within the protest grounds further drew on international symbolism: a giant poster "Democracy Wall" with a simple anticorruption petition for protesters and visitors to sign, as thousands did (including the author).

Even as the protests drew on an international repertoire of the legitimacy of "people power," they framed corruption and distortions of democracy as an affront to national values and national dignity. Indian flags were ubiquitous during the demonstrations, and some smaller transportation strikes around half a dozen major cities aligned themselves with the protests simply by displaying Indian flags and honking horns—in the summer of 2011, the flag became a symbol of "Team Anna" instead of "Team India." At the Delhi protests, pamphleteers distributed copies of the Indian Constitution, often underlining clauses relating to "we the people." During the secondary protests following the arrest of Anna and hundreds of his supporters, signs castigated the government's suppression of civil liberties as an "Undeclared Emergency"—comparable to Indira Gandhi's now-repudiated mid-1970s State of Emergency.

The power of performance by Anna Hazare has proven somewhat ephemeral, as his movement has faced the challenges of cohesion of a diverse coalition, the fragility of the charismatic leader, and the vagaries of institutionalized politics. Anna's health has declined, forcing him to curtail a December 2011 hunger strike. But that protest also seemed to gather less popular support, in part because the Indian Parliament had already passed a partial version of the Ombudsman proposal—the classic pattern of social movement support declining once they have shifted the agenda and secured some state response to their grievance, even if inadequate. Moreover, some Hazare activists' cross-cutting participation in the BJP and Hindu nationalist groups continues to plague the movement's mandate of inclusion (Sengupta 2012).

Nevertheless, the Anna Hazare movement transformed India and helped to build a repertoire of protest and worldwide anticorruption movement. This highly globalized movement was truly comparable to Gandhi's in its reassertion of self-determination, grassroots activism, collective non-violence, and an ethical agenda for democratic politics. As one activist interviewed by NDTV in August 2011 summarized the narrative that mobilized his participation, "They sold our land, they sold our villages—now they want to sell our souls." The allegory of Anna Hazare was a rich exercise in framing and shaming. But shaming is not the only way to deflate power and restore a notion of human dignity. The other mask of drama, comedy, can also serve to speak rights to power.

The Power of Parody

Against the assault of laughter, nothing can stand. —Mark Twain

Satire is a time-honored tactic for deflating authority and empowering the *vox populi*. Its fundamental force comes from a mode of authorized transgression. Many parodies subvert canonical social discourses, whether texts, performances, politics, or religion. Grotesque theatrics insist on the material base and the body, sometimes highlighting the contradiction between the primal human needs of eating, sex, or excretion with dominant ideology or authority figures. The performance style of satire is exaggerated, confrontational, absurd, and playful—and each of these elements may play a social role. Finally, satire is the most participatory genre; it is rarely simply consumed but often expands through audience response. The contemporary apogee of the audience participation aspect of satire is the prevalence of large and engaged "fan cultures" that some theorists claim model citizenship and emotive communicative appeals in the public sphere (Burwell and Boler 2008).

But the political purposes of satire vary tremendously, from revolution to reaction, from humanism to racism. Discussing the variations and political indeterminacy of satire, Dustin Griffin reminds us that "to assess the satirist's purpose and strategy, we need to know for whom and against whom the satire is written" (Griffin 1994: 188). And satire is not a natural vehicle for the promotion of human rights because suffering is not funny—although survival may be. In similar fashion, Guobin Yang shows the shift in Chinese Internet activism from the historically dominant epic style to two "genres of digital contention": "confessional"/testimonial and counter-hegemonic humor, which he labels as a species of Bhaktin's "parodic-travestying" form (Yang 2009: 77).

Which elements of satire tend to work as counter-hegemony for human rights appeals? First, human rights satire is written for citizens and against leaders or elites. It mocks domination but not suffering. The main mechanisms of human rights parody are protesting the truth claims of authorities, unmasking contradictions in their legitimacy or behavior, and exaggerating oppressive policies to show their absurdity. While many kinds of satire contain a mock-juridical element, humanistic satire refers explicitly to universal standards for judgment. It is often playful and transgressive, but rarely absurd—there is a take-home moral. Finally, human rights satire tends to be strongly participatory and empowering. The parody is circulated and reconstructed dialectically, whether in protest or performance. Above all, human rights satire complements more expository modes because laughter breaks fear and bonds the audience in a common experience of physiological release of tension.

We will see parody play an important role in human rights campaigns as disparate as the Iranian Green Revolution (the 2009 web site watchmeconfess. com), the Chinese cyber-dissidents "grass mud horse" punning, and the Arab Spring, all profiled in the next chapter. For example, in Egypt, protest placards against Mubarak mockingly compared him to the Pharaoh, and street musicians composed satiric ballads recounting his crimes (Slackman 2011). Since the Revolution, a Cairo-based English-language "fake news" website called *El Koshary Today*—modeled on the US satirical news network *The Onion*—has attracted a dedicated and growing fan base with ironic stories such as "Egypt's National Security Agency Helps Former Torturers Find 'Inner Child'." The fake story draws attention to the real problem of lack of accountability and transitional justice for the large number of abusers linked to the dictatorship (*El Koshary Today* 2011). Satire has also given voice to Egyptian civil society and a new style of secular, globalized critique. After Dr. Bassem Youssef participated in the January 2011 Revolution and was frustrated by the media's subservience to the regime, he launched *The Bassem Youssef Show* on YouTube, which became so popular that it was quickly picked up by one of the new independent television networks. "The Show," explicitly modeled after Jon Stewart and Stephen Colbert, deconstructs the daily news and mocks political figures throughout the region (Gladstone 2011).

In this chapter, we will examine two in-depth profiles in comedic courage: the use of sarcasm in protest against Vladimir Putin and Stephen Colbert's ironic critique of US civil rights policy.

The Politics of Parody in Russia: From Putin's Penis to Pussy Riot

In Russia, a recent resurgence of a long-standing culture of political satire has both reflected and inspired the emergence of broad-based opposition to President Vladimir Putin's violations of civil liberties and electoral norms. The Russian opposition movement has been largely youth-based, middle-class, globally conscious, and centered on information politics. Their symbol has been a white ribbon, like the color revolutions in Eastern Europe, and they have crafted new symbolic protest repertoires such as forming a 35,000 person human chain encircling Moscow—organized on the Internet.

This movement has also mobilized dialectical satire to contest disparagement by authorities. When Putin compared the protesters to Jungle Book monkeys to signal that they were marginal chatterers, a popular TV show showed Putin as the boa constrictor of the tale (Yaffa 2012)—countering his dehumanized dismissal of dissidents with his own animal identity as a predator who crushes the breath from his opponents. When Putin attacked the democratic movement's use of the white ribbon to symbolize clean elections by comparing it to a condom, the movement parried with Internet postings and protest placards of photos of Putin draped in a giant condom, and protesters playfully waving condoms (Barry 2011; Ioffe 2011). The protesters thus ironically deflated Putin's hyper-masculine persona and associated his dirty politics with unsafe sex, creating an internationally salient and locally resonant image.

In a similar, even more incisive parody, a Moscow museum exhibit symbolically contested Putin's manhood. The puppet show was based on Nikolai Gogol's short story "The Nose"—the story of an official whose nose leaves his body to lead a life of its own—but the 2012 show substitutes Putin's penis as the errant organ. As Reuters reports,

> In the museum's version of the play, Russia's "alpha-dog" leader loses his genitalia, becoming an impotent "anti-Putin" until he finally rediscovers them. During his journey, Putin talks to himself, struggling with an inner conflict that reflects his own pre-Kremlin past as both KGB spy and adviser to one of Russia's liberal leaders. "There is a constant dialogue between the authoritarian Putin, the tyrant, who has a constant erection, and the more democratic (anti-Putin), who shows no aggression, no eroticism, and has no penis," Donskoy said. (Astrasheuskaya 2012)

Meanwhile, the popular weekly television show "Citizen Poet" provides an ongoing satire of the week's news in classic Russian verse style, a parody that deeply challenges the regime's monopoly on information and claim to nationalist legitimacy. Elsewhere in Russia, youthful cultural critics stage ironic protests using South Park giant dolls as participants that evade repression and associate with global imagery. Online, a viral music video called "Our Nuthouse Votes for Putin" challenges Putin's stewardship of oil revenues and shows the "crazy" questioner attacked with a needle—evoking the history of Soviet repression of dissidents through imprisonment in mental institutions (events reported in Yaffa 2012).

Political satire in Russia plays all the roles of mocking authority, contesting truth claims, and liberating protestors through laughter. One of the authors of a satiric Twitter critiquing Putin's increasing authoritarianism—"Kermlin"— affirmed the impact of his wide online following, "Putin stopped being scary. He started to become silly" (Yaffa 2012: 4). Street-level jokes question the regime's management of elections, playing with the initial claims that candidates won "146%" of the vote: "Breaking news: Vladimir Churov, head of the central elections commission of Russia, has been badly injured in a fire. He has sustained burns over 146% of his body surface." A popular joke with the common themes of sexuality and undermining the masculinity of the leadership says that "The wives of United Russia [regime] party members don't fake orgasms—they *falsify* them." In another display of humor as empowerment, at December 2011 spontaneous mass demonstrations for an opposition leader defeated in questionable elections, supporters chanted, "We joke therefore we exist!" (Kovalev 2011).

The latest chapter in the saga of sexual symbolism in Russian performance politics is the cause célèbre of the feminist punk band Pussy Riot. The collective of a dozen dissidents is famous for transgressive performances of rock music, masking and universalizing their identity in colorful balaclavas, and for their edgy name that bespeaks female sexual empowerment. Their lyrics have been especially critical of Putin, the nascent Russian elite, and traditional institutions like the Russian Orthodox Church. The band specializes in unauthorized appearances in public space such as Red Square and the Moscow Metro, and posts its performances rapidly on the Internet to wide acclaim. As the band describes its own role, "Pussy Riot's performances can either be called dissident art or political action that engages art forms. Either way, our performances are a kind of civic activity amidst the repressions of a corporate political system that directs its power against basic human rights and civil and political liberties" (Alyokhina et al. 2012).

On February 21, 2012, five members of the band staged a controversial performance in a Russian Orthodox Cathedral that resulted in their arrest and trial for hooliganism and "hate crimes" against the Church. The Russian Church is currently headed by a former KGB official, who campaigned for Putin's election in 2012, calling him "a miracle from God" who "rectified the crooked path of history" (Bennetts 2012). Pussy Riot's song lyric responds with radical feminist castigation: "The Orthodox Religion is a hardened penis / Coercing its subjects to accept conformity." The video of their protest performance in a Moscow Cathedral was labeled as a "punk prayer" called, "Mother of God, Chase Putin Away!" (Shuster 2012).

Three performers were charged and held from March to August 2012 without bail. Despite international outcry, they were sentenced to serve two years.

International human rights groups like Human Rights Watch sent observers to the trial, Amnesty International declared them prisoners of conscience, and the United States, United Kingdom, Germany, and European Union decried the charges and sentence as excessive. Transnational supporters donned balaclavas to protest—and sometimes perform—at Russian embassies and other symbolic locations in dozens of cities worldwide. Dozens of international rock stars condemned the prosecution, notably including Madonna, who wrote their name on her bare skin and called for their freedom during a packed Russian concert tour. Inside Russia, the case provided a rallying point for domestic opposition, and there were numerous protests at the trial—although grassroots public opinion was split. Former world chess champion Gary Kasparov was beaten and detained while protesting Pussy Riot's prosecution (Ryzik 2012).

Pussy Riot's only formally released song, composed as a protest to their persecution, is called, "Putin Lights Up the Fires." As Human Rights Watch explained in its analysis, Russia's prosecution of Pussy Riot was an explicit repudiation of free speech—and feminism. In the sentence, the (female) Russian judge stated,

> "Feminism is not a violation of the law and is not a crime," Judge Syrova said. "But the ideas of feminism are not in line with a number of religions, including Russian Orthodoxy, Catholicism, and Islam. Although feminism is not a religious precept, its proponents cross the line into the sphere of decency and morals" (Denbar 2012).

The closing statement of the defendants mounts a dialectical defense, citing the power and political prosecution of speech from Socrates to national heroes like Dostoevsky. Nadezhda Tolokonnikova concludes: "Allow us to enter into a dialogue, into contact with this country, which is also ours and not only the land of Putin and Patriarch. Just like Solzhenitsyn, I believe that in the end the word will break cement. Solzhenitsyn wrote: "Thus, the word is more essential than cement. Thus, the word is not a small nothing. In this manner, noble people begin to grow, and their word will break cement" (Solzhenitsyn, cited in Alyokhina et al. 2012).

Speaking "Truthiness" to Power: The Colbert Challenge

The epitome of contemporary political satire occurs ironically in the world's self-styled leading democracy, ironically speaking through the voice of a false reactionary, ironically claiming to deliver opinion as news, and ironically monitoring and advocating for rights it claims to eschew. *The Colbert Report* began in 2005 as a spin-off of the satiric fake news *Daily Show* and has gone on to win Emmy, Grammy, and Peabody awards. Host Stephen Colbert excels at disrupting the truth claims of authorities, unmasking contradictions, and exaggerating oppressive policies to the point of absurdity. This satire has crossed over to social movement mobilization, as Colbert has launched a presidential bid, ballot initiatives, a super-PAC, political rallies, and numerous fund-raising campaigns and petitions. From around 2010, the two shows have been estimated to draw over 1.5 million viewers per broadcast—almost equivalent to the Fox News pundits—with exceptionally high proportions of youth and women (Kondolojy 2012). Both politicians and products featured on the show experience a documented increase in attention and finance, the so-called "Colbert Bump."[4]

Colbert also illustrates the dialectical role of empowering satire in several dimensions. First, *The Daily Show* and subsequent *Colbert Report* arose in part as a direct response to the emergence of Fox News as a tendentious, personality driven, and tabloid conservative stream of broadcast television that cynically claimed to be "fair and balanced." Second, Colbert the provocative faux-conservative is also part of a dialogue with Jon Stewart's liberal centrist Everyman commentator. This was exemplified in their 2010 twin rallies protesting the violence and dysfunctional partisanship of American politics; Colbert's ironic March to Keep Fear Alive contrasted with Stewart's Rally to Restore Sanity—attended by over 200,000 people. The rally combined both forms of dialectic, since one of the catalysts to the rally was Fox News host Glen Beck's comparison of President Obama to Hitler (McGrath 2012).

But the most powerful dialectic of all is with the fans, "Colbert Nation." Colbert Nation is an ironically constituted audience that Colbert has encouraged to simultaneously parody celebrity culture worship of his performance and to mobilize on behalf of various causes—from apolitical charities to his super-PAC. Colbert famously directed his audience to deliver over 17 million votes to name a Hungarian bridge in his honor. This audience has taken on a life of its own as a virtual community of debate and dissemination across numerous Web sites, blogs, and Twitter feeds, and has come to serve as an emotionally invested public sphere (Burwell and Boler 2008). Above all, Colbert Nation contests the reactionary populist claim to represent "the true America," ironically positioning Colbert's self-deconstructing exclusionary bombast. This is the double message of his best-selling book: *"I Am America (and So Can You!)."*

Perhaps his most influential contribution is Colbert's coinage of "truthiness" to condemn political figures' increasing reliance on and promotion of emotional beliefs about events that stand in contrast to objective reality. On the show, this has often been combined with broadcast of footage that contradicted the politician's untrue claim. Although the "truthiness" critique is theoretically applicable across the American political spectrum, the distortion of historical events and scientific facts was especially characteristic of the Bush Administration and Tea Party politicians like Sarah Palin. But it also served to indict the manipulation of Fox News and the silence of mainstream media. Colbert's related broader critique of the decline of overseas and investigative journalism was voiced openly during his controversial speech at the 2006 White House Correspondents' Dinner, when he stepped out of character and mockingly praised the silence of the mainstream media, "Over tax cuts, W.M.D. intelligence, the effect of global warming: we Americans didn't want to know, and you had the courtesy not to try and find out" (April 29, 2006). By the next morning, a new Web site called "Thank You, Stephen Colbert" had 14,000 members. "Truthiness" is ironic, but not postmodern; the take-home message is that democratic accountability depends on the discipline of objective facts in political debates.

Colbert's stance is both interrogative and deconstructive. He engages in "satire of provocation" in confrontational interviews with legislators in "Better Know a District" and the authors of featured books. His deconstructive tactic is exemplified in "The Word," when Colbert declaims a series of falsely authoritative and usually self-contradictory conservative positions—shadowed by a side screen that exposes the untruth, illogic, or corruption of each statement of the argument. "The Word" also contributes to a more general stance of subverting canonical texts and authority figures which is pursued in other features and special reports. Perhaps the feature most directly relevant to human rights is "Threat Down," a blatant mockery of the politics of fear undergirding national security policy through a list of exaggerated threats cited by politicians alongside patently absurd concerns.

The specific messages delivered by Colbert's satire amount to a sophisticated and systematic defense of civil liberties and diversity in twenty-first-century America. Colbert has consistently criticized post-9/11 abuses overseas and at home, including the use of torture, Guantanamo, and the Patriot Act. A recent Word critique of the Obama-era extension of presidential powers to detain Americans without trial was titled, "The National Defense Authorization Act strikes at the heart of the most notorious safe haven for terrorists: the U.S. Constitution." He has given a platform to seldom-broadcast human rights activists in interviews, such as Human Rights Watch Ken Roth, war crimes monitor Michael Posner, and the gay rights Human Rights Campaign. He devotes significant attention to racial issues, does features on black history, exposes racist resurgences in his native South, and interviews a high proportion of African American guests, including community leaders and intellectuals like Henry Louis Gates, Jr. and Cornel West.

Colbert has defended the repeal of "Don't Ask, Don't Tell" and gay marriage equality in numerous segments. His scathing parodies in defense of gay rights culminated in a riposte to Rick Santorum's homophobic condemnation of gays in the military paired with his complaint of discrimination against civic celebration of Christmas with a depiction of two male Santas kissing under mistletoe. Despite Colbert and his character's avowed Catholicism, the comic has been a staunch defender of women's reproductive rights and a critic of Church attempts to influence public policy on contraception and abortion. He has interviewed Gloria Steinem and Nancy Pelosi, and mocks theocratic pretensions worldwide in an occasional feature called "Yahweh or No Way" (http://www. colbertnation.com).

Although the *Colbert Report*'s contribution to American civil liberties is indirect and progress on the issues he emphasizes has been uneven, his broad-based satiric appeal has plausibly contributed to shifting the zeitgeist on gay rights with the humanizing power of humor to break social taboos and homophobia. Colbert has even played with his ultra-straight character's "accidental" attraction to men and conversely as an interviewer projects palpable ease and respect toward gay public figures. The *Colbert/Daily Show* decade has coincided with, reflected, and perhaps shaped public opinion toward the legalization of gay marriage in a dozen states, the abandonment of the military's "Don't Ask, Don't Tell" requirement to conceal sexual orientation, and the endorsement of major hate crimes legislation in 2009. President Obama's own shift on marriage equality explicitly cites his own evolving understanding, responsiveness to public opinion, and appeal to the demographic represented by his appearances on both the *Daily Show* and "Colbert Nation."

In September 2010, Colbert participated in politics in earnest on behalf of US migrant workers. After participating in the United Farm Workers' educational "Take Our Jobs" program, where he spent a day working alongside migrants in the fields, Colbert testified before the House Judiciary Subcommittee on Immigration, Citizenship, and Border Security. At the end of his testimony, Colbert broke character and explained why he cares about the plight of migrant workers.

> I like talking about people who don't have any power, and this seems like one of the least powerful people in the United States are migrant workers who come and do our work, but don't have any rights as a result. And yet we still invite them to come here and at the same time ask them to leave. And that's an interesting contradiction to me. And, you know, "Whatsoever you do for the least of my brothers," and these seem like the least of our brothers right now.... Migrant workers suffer and have no rights. (Zak 2010)

The *Colbert Report* has operated in tandem with a wave of counter-hegemonic satire with special appeal to youth and international audiences that continually contest rising economic inequality, political disenfranchisement, and the national security state, including *The Daily Show*, *South Park*, and numerous

You-Tube channels. Like a *Jester in the King's Court* (Kuo 2010), satire at the heart of power deconstructs the verities of patriotism and neo-liberalism and breaks through apathy, as well as fear. The twenty-first-century jesters encourage their audience to question authority, deepen citizenship, and reclaim their own voice.

Table 5.1 Human Rights Campaigns: Performance

Case	Voice	Frame	Performance
Tibet	Dalai Lama	Self-determination	Protest
Dreyfus	Cause célèbre	Democracy, citizenship	
Spanish Civil War	Writers	Democracy	
Holocaust	Anne Frank, Elie Wiesel	Genocide	Testimonial
Arab Spring	Khaled Said	Democracy, citizenship	Protest, parody
South Africa	Nelson Mandela	Discrimination	Protest, testimonial
Burma	Aung San Suu Kyi	Democracy	Protest
Argentina	Mothers of the Disappeared	Torture, disappearances	Protest, testimonial
AIDS	Doctors, victims movement	Health rights	Protest
Violence vs. women	Amartya Sen	Violence	Testimonial, protest
US death penalty	Weak celebrities		Protest
Trafficking	Child victims	Sex slavery	Testimonial
FGM	Child victims, doctors	Violence, health rights	
Colombia		Crime	
Darfur	Celebrities	Genocide	Testimonial
Congo	Weak celebrities	Barbarism	
US civil liberties	Stephen Colbert	Democracy, discrimination, detention	Testimonial, parody
India	Anna Hazare	Citizenship	Protest
Russia	Pussy Riot	Democracy, citizenship	Protest, parody
Iran Green	Neda Agha-Soltan	Democracy, torture	Protest
China	Cause célèbre	Democracy, civil rights	Parody, testimonial
Kony 2012	Invisible Children	Child soldiers	
Academic freedom	Limited cause célèbre	Civil rights	Limited testimonial
Armenia		Genocide	Limited Protest
Israel/Palestine		Genocide, refugees	Protest
Liberia	Mothers	War crimes	Protest

Conclusion

The power of performance is an extension of the ability of narrative to raise consciousness of suffering, build empathetic bonds with its victims, and create understanding of its causes and consequences. This power is multiplied when specific genres provide plot vehicles for humanization, agency, transformation, and alternatives to limiting social codes. Performance genres draw on affective pathways of witness, metaphor, and laughter. Thus, testimonial turns personal tragedy to political drama, allegory models the past in order to change the present, and satire subverts oppressive authority and breaks social codes. Table 5.1 displays the range of performance modalities used by the campaigns analyzed throughout the text, combined with the elements of voice and frame.

These performances are increasingly delivered in cyberspace, along with broadcast media and public space. We turn now to examine the dynamics of these multiple and emerging media in human rights campaigns.

6

MOBILIZING MEDIA

Is There an App for That?

Electronic media have become the privileged space of politics.
—Manuel Castells

How can the use of media mobilize human rights solidarity? Can digital dissidence help to raise consciousness and empower victims? The political functions of media for human rights include monitoring state behavior, creating common identities, communicating grievances, mobilizing citizen action, and diffusing models and repertoires of rights claims and campaigns. The use of media by human rights campaigns has been a "necessary but not sufficient" source of change (Acuff 2010). "By using both horizontal communication networks and mainstream media to convey their images and messages, they increase their chances of enacting social and political change—even if they start from a subordinate position in institutional power, financial resources, or symbolic legitimacy" (Castells 2009: 302). Media are most important for human rights campaigns when they channel symbolic voices, frames, and plots to reach targeted audiences.

Scholars of communication analyze the shifting political impact of media patterns of production, reception, content, and circulation (Castells 2009). They show that media is far more than a channel of communication; it is also a source of information power, as well as a dialectical public space that is transformed by producers, broadcasters, audiences, and even states (Curtin 2003). The "communications revolution" of our times is comprised by a combination of the use of digital technology, the globalization of media production and reception, increasing scope of commercialization, diversification of media forms and markets, growth of multimedia business networks, and cultural change in use patterns and content (Castells 2009: ch. 2). The result has been a vast increase in "mass self-communication" and a related redistribution of communication power that "enhances the opportunity for social change, without however defining the content and purpose of such social change" (Castells 2009: 8).

Access to media is itself a right; the concept of open media is integral to the broader form of democracy as an ensemble of political, economic, and social institutions envisaged in the "open society" (Popper 1971). Just as Benedict Anderson linked the rise of nationalism to the development of newspapers as a forum for the communication of national identity, the existence of new, transnational spaces of communication may foster new levels of transnational solidarity and even global citizenship (Anderson 1991). In "The Media Is the Message," Marshall McLuhan (1960) optimistically contended that new forms of information technology would liberate individuals and permit the emergence of new ideas. As Todd Gitlin (2003) noted, improved access for the communication of grievances in real time may protect protest when it insures that "the whole world is watching." More broadly, social movement theorists predict that more widespread access and diffusion of knowledge of social conditions and "protest repertoires" will contribute to dissident movements' "social capital" (trust and networks). "Information politics" is one of the key mechanisms of impact identified by students of transnational issue networks (Keck and Sikkink 1998).

Information politics are channeled through overlapping layers of different media forms, local and global. Old media are characterized by physical diffusion from a central source to a mass audience. They include newspapers, television, and radio. The emergence of such media coincided with the growth and consolidation of the modern state and nationalism. Old media have grown as the privileged public sphere of the "open society"—but these media have also been used by revolutionary and totalitarian regimes alike to limit access to the public sphere, disseminate propaganda for regime legitimacy and mobilization, and construct national identity. However, even within such regimes, human rights and citizenship claims have been advanced through citizen-controlled alternative traditional media such as underground newspapers, the penetration of frame-breaking information into broadening news coverage associated with some aspects of modernization, and the globalization of some streams transcending state control (the so-called "CNN effect"). Moreover, for most of the grassroots population of the developing world, radio and television are far more accessible and influential than newer technologies.

New media, by contrast, involve digital transmission from multiple sources and may permit interactive direct communication between the user and source or among users. Such media include e-mail lists and chat rooms, Web sites and blogs, Twitter, FAX, video forums such as YouTube, and cell-phone texting and transfer of political messages and visual material. New media are predominantly commercial in control and content, diffuse in access, and often anonymous. However, the network architecture and lower capital requirements of new media permit much more individual, non-commercial, non-governmental ownership and access (Benkler 2006).

The power of new media is that they may be more accessible and more salient; opening a channel for new voices, transmitting more emotive imagery, enabling more performance genres, and permitting a more decentralized dialectic. As Yang's study of China puts it, "Internet contention is radical communicative action conducted in words, images, and sounds. Language, stories, and symbols have always been an important part of popular movements, but they have taken on new possibilities in the information age" (Yang 2009: 33).

Diffuse access should expand membership in the public sphere, for production and consumption of information. The speed of electronic communication should enhance monitoring and mobilization in real time. Broader and more rapid diffusion of identity markers should bolster the creation of community and appeals for transnational support. Social networking may serve as social capital for any political purpose, including dissidence. Moreover, the breadth and potential anonymity of new media lower the costs of mobilization and should shield protestors to some extent from repression. Unlimited bandwidth contrasts with limited newsprint or broadcast hours, permitting a wider range of voices and greater volume of information. Finally, the multiplicity of forms and modes (besides old media's text and photos, new media provide links, graphics, and video) should expand the repertoire and robustness of dissidence and citizen claims making. Twitter is especially robust, since it is a service rather than a site, which can originate from a cell phone, blog, or Facebook. The higher proportion of visual and multi-sensory material may enhance the emotional resonance of grievances, crossing language and literacy barriers. Benkler argues that the technological characteristics of the new information economy maximize the potential for liberal individual autonomy in a networked public sphere. The net effect is to increase the potential to pursue liberal values of freedom, participation, critical culture, and social justice (Benkler 2006).

While early enthusiasts of the Internet predicted an electronic global village fostering freedom without borders, latter-day naysayers minimize its effects on both rights and membership (Morozov 2010). New media may be even more vulnerable to greater surveillance by repressive states; "thought-crime" now leaves a digital footprint. Moreover, the empowering potential of the Internet may be outweighed by a Huxley-like distraction and segmentation of the body politic as consumers of infotainment. Furthermore, global corporate sponsors of new media services may collaborate with repressive governments to retain access to their markets, or distort coverage of anti-corporate initiatives and dampen mobilization potential. But Yang points out that "consumers" of the Internet are also producers and that Internet businesses have an incentive to increase traffic "by any means necessary" (Yang 2009). Finally, scattered and emotive new media may be less capable of conveying deep analysis of social structures or patterns of repression.

The effects of the increase in nonmarket production of information as a collective good are dependent on social context—just as the printing press had different impacts in Protestant and Catholic polities—and are neither automatic nor utopian. But they do represent a systematic shift in the contours of the public sphere from a mass-mediated information environment dependent on either state or centralized commercial control to a relatively more open civil society. Thus, on balance, we would expect that the diffuse access and anonymity of new media should lead to enhanced effectiveness and decreased danger of repression in environments where centralized authoritarian governments seek to control access to conventional media. Electronic dissidence is obviously dependent on a level of technological development permitting widespread access to the Internet for a range of social purposes; in Iran, about 35 percent of the country uses the Internet, while in Burma, only about 0.1 percent of the population has access (Stelter and Stone 2009: A8). New media should matter less when the source of repression or exclusion is more diffuse or structural than a single authoritarian government, or where countervailing access to conventional media is more widespread, such as in illiberal democracies rather than frank dictatorships.

Digital dissidence will also be more effective when certain critical sectors of "the whole world" are watching: transnational pressure points via diasporas, diplomatic leverage on repressive governments, or embarrassment of corporate sponsors vulnerable to consumer boycotts—and less for utter pariahs, countries with limited or passive diasporas, and corporations whose markets are relatively immune from public disapproval (like natural resource vendors). New media are less dependent on designated speakers and thus probably less amenable to charismatic leadership than direct representation or conventional media, and correspondingly less vulnerable to repression of notable movement leaders. But digital forums should be equally effective and potentially more accessible for publicizing the experiences of representative grassroots victims and emerging groups. Finally, the impact of digital dissidence will be strongest when the target government lacks the capacity, will, or legitimacy to shut down or contest the channels of electronic communication.

This chapter will chart the emergence of information politics as a tool of human rights campaigns in the information society. Then, we will consider the electronic organization and repression of dissidence against a theocratic nationalist regime in Iran during the 2009 Green Revolution. Next, we will examine contrasting dynamics of Internet use, Web-based appeals, and blogs in modernizing authoritarian China, over a longer period and by diverse groups of claimants. With different levels of capacity and legitimacy bases, both governments converge in responding to these challenges with a high level of concerted

attempts to censor their citizens' access. We will analyze the most successful use of information politics for empowerment of the current era: the Arab
Spring. And we will consider the contrasting spectacular rise and fall of the
Kony 2012 campaign, to learn why information politics can fail, in the absence
of sufficient conditions.

Human Rights Campaigns
in "the Information Society"

The use of all forms of media—old and new, national and global—for human
rights struggle has become legion in the past generation. At the dawn of the
Internet age, Mexico's Zapatistas used the Web to publicize their grievances and
mobilize transnational protection for their 1994 rebellion through a decade of
negotiations with the Mexican state and the establishment of autonomous areas
for Chiapas' indigenous peoples (Brysk 2000; Olesen 2005). In more conventional contested elections against dictators, protesters from Serbia to Zimbabwe
have organized "flash mob" protests using cell phone texts. The twenty-first-
century "color revolutions" used new media extensively to mobilize broad civil
society coalitions to peacefully overthrow authoritarian dictatorships. These so-
called "Facebook revolutions" include the 2003 Rose Revolution in Georgia,
2004 Orange Revolution in Ukraine, 2005 Tulip Revolution in Kyrgyzstan, and
perhaps the 2005 Cedar Revolution in Lebanon, protesting Syrian occupation
and the related assassination of a Lebanese political leader.

Every international human rights organization has a Web site, Facebook
page, and list-serv that seem to enhance transnational consciousness-raising,
in ways difficult to measure. Burmese monks, Nigerian environmentalists, and
Russian journalists post videos of their persecution to make claims against their
state and invoke transnational protection. As the documentary *Burma VJ* on
Burma's 2007 "saffron revolution" of monks' protests shows,

> Connected through cell phones and e-mail, shooting clandestinely on mini-cams and
> smuggling footage out of the country by courier, the Internet and satellite hookups,
> the correspondents for the Democratic Voice of Burma (a television station in exile
> based in Oslo) not only revealed the totalitarian character of the Myanmar authorities
> to world scrutiny, they revealed the future of war reporting. (Anderson 2009)

A recent analysis of Southeast Asian politics concludes that "around the region
bloggers are becoming a Fifth Estate, challenging the government's monopoly on information in Singapore, evading censors in Vietnam, and influencing
events in places like Thailand, Cambodia and China. In March, political experts

said, Malaysia's bloggers helped influence elections, contributing to the biggest upset that the governing party, the United Malays National Organization, had suffered since independence in 1957" (Mydans 2008: A8).

At the transnational level, some argue that networks and organizations dedicated to electronic exchange constitute a kind of "Fifth Estate" of new media with a specific social role and purpose (Cooper 2006; Dutton 2009). The diverse content, structure, and expressive agenda of the blogosphere make it something less than a global "republic of letters." However, there is a growing network of users, service providers, and watchdogs that struggle to shape the character of cyberspace as a public sphere and global commons, intermittently interacting with supportive and targeted states, as well as international organizations.

Moreover, within this space there is a freedom of information alliance; a cluster of information processors and social movements dedicated in some fashion to preserving the diffuse, interactive, "open society" of the web, for different reasons. At the academic level, there is the OpenNet Initiative, a partnership of universities that study Internet filtering and surveillance. The partners are Harvard University, the University of Toronto, the University of Cambridge, and the University of Oxford. In 2008, the major Internet providers Google and Yahoo combined with leading free speech advocates to formulate social responsibility standards in cyberspace via a Global Network Initiative (http://www.globalnetworkinitiative. org/)—following criticism of Yahoo provision of tracking information on political dissidents in China. While long-standing free-speech advocates like Reporters Without Borders have expanded their monitoring to track censorship and repression of electronic media, newer organizations have formed, like the Center for Democracy and Technology. Finally, movements and socially oriented firms have formed to provide technical support for digital dissidence. The most prominent is the umbrella group founded by Chinese dissidents, the Global Internet Freedom Consortium, which is comprised of two NGOs and three companies that provide downloadable software to evade censorship and repression. Their Web site states that they have "contributed significantly to the advancement of information freedom in China, Iran, Burma, and many other closed societies" (http://www.internetfreedom.org). The normative orientation of such movements is apparent in the Global Internet Consortium's statement that it is the "Underground Railroad" of digital dissidence.

Above and beyond the struggle over government control of information, this sector of global civil society struggles to control the policies and decision making processes of the hegemonic service providers, notably Yahoo and Google—which also owns YouTube and controls around two-thirds of the search engine traffic in the world. Currently, the legal and policy staff of such providers assess government requests on a case-by-case basis, balancing voluntary pledges to honor the international free speech norms which undergird their market value, contractual obligations to comply with national legislation in the countries in which they operate, and growing international "soft law" on legitimate limitations of speech and privacy rights.[1] The profit motive of commercial Internet providers works in two different directions: on the one hand, compliance with government dictates brings access to large markets but, on the other hand, maximum freedom of exchange facilitates advertising and preserves reputational market niche. In an example of choosing long-term global market niche over short-term profits, after a *New York Times* report on Microsoft's complicity with Russian authorities abusing anti-piracy laws to harass NGOs, Microsoft disabled such persecution by vastly expanding its free software licensing program to cover twelve authoritarian countries—including Russia and China—and over 500,000 advocacy groups (Levy 2010).

Internet Leviathan Google reports that its sites and applications have been directly blocked by twenty-four countries over the past few years. In many of these cases, repressive governments cite internationally recognized grounds for regulation—limiting pornography, incitement to violence, or hate speech—but apply them selectively or spuriously to political dissidents or socially stigmatized groups. In a different register, true conflicts between universal and national principles arise when countries like Thailand and Turkey demand that Google block access to sites that criticize or allegedly defame sacred founding or monarchical figures—which the provider usually honors by blocking access within the banning country while retaining access for international users. Under a system of voluntary self-regulation, Google has agreed to foster transparency and debate even when it decides to cooperate with government demands for censorship under local laws, by reporting all deleted links to chillingeffects. com, a Web site operated by the Berkman Center at Harvard (Rosen 2008). On its own, Google now provides an interactive world map and breakdown of government requests for data and removal of sites, along with Google's compliance rate in each country. Although truly closed societies like China cannot be tracked on this list, since they rely mostly on filters rather than shutdowns, the list reveals illiberal trends in curtailing free speech in democracies such as Brazil, the United States, and India (Kurczy 2010). There is some evidence of a general tilt by Google toward defending users from censorship; moving its Chinese search engine to Hong Kong, defending a dissident Georgian blogger from Russian nationalist cyber-attacks, and hosting a joint conference with Freedom House for bloggers from the Middle East in March 2010 (Morozov 2010).

Over the past decade, mobilization and solidarity in cyberspace have played a critical role in three zones of resistance to authoritarian rule, enabling new kinds of human rights claims: Iran, China, and North Africa. In each case, the power of new media can be traced to increasing the access and salience of the means of communication. Dissidents, youth, and women were able to transcend conventional channels blocked by their regimes. New media were used both for symbolism and strategy, using emotive imagery, new genres of contention such as humor, and globalized human rights rhetoric. Diffuse access and participation in cyberspace, in turn, permitted a more decentralized dialectic and helped to foster the emergence of a counter-hegemonic sector of civil society.

Iran: The Revolution will not be Televised

> The revolution will not be televised.
> —Gil Scott-Heron, *Pieces of a Man*

Iran's 1979 Islamic revolution used twentieth-century media to mobilize for fourteenth-century values. Audio and videotapes of exiled Islamic leaders inspired student protestors inside Iran, and television coverage of their protests brought the movement critical mass and international recognition. A generation later, twenty-first-century technology enables resistance to a theocracy that has failed to meet its promises to provide development, social justice, or a sustainable source of national identity. The opposition movement is defined largely by their relationship to information and globalization: students, urban professionals, the Persian diaspora, and urban, educated women.

Dissident sentiment began to emerge in Iran with the election of reformist President Khatami from 1997 to 2005, but his moderate opening proved unavailing against the power of the mullahs. They returned to dominance with the rise of President Mahmoud Ahmadinejad, who presides over a coalition of hard-liners backed by the Basij militia founded by the revolution. In 2009, dissidents united behind moderate reformer Mir-Hossein Mousavi to demand fair elections with a mandate for liberalization of the existing regime. As these limited demands were frustrated by electoral fraud and relentless repression of all forms of protest, the Green Movement began to question the fundamental legitimacy of the regime—and some even called for a secular democracy. The Green Movement label reflects the dual nature of the protests: at the same time, they sought to reclaim the mantle of Islamic revolution by adopting the Islamic color of Mousavi's campaign but also to associate themselves with the so-called "color revolutions" in other regions discussed above.

Use of new media by Iran's Green Movement was supported by several sources of transnational social capital. First, the Persian diaspora made extensive use of all of the forms of social media, and transmitted Facebook, Twitter, and Web postings onward. The fact that English was the dominant language of tweets and prominent Twitter identities such as "persiankiwi" and "oxfordgirl" testify to the transnational character of the use of these media. Second, the protests drew on and stimulated the development of a transnational network of technical support for electronic dissidence. The Toronto-based Teheran Bureau emerged as an alternative news provider and hub for electronic posting, while international electronic solidarity activists like Austin Heap and the group Haystack assisted with remote hosting of Web sites to evade government censorship. Heap stated that his servers connected around 750 Iranians at any one moment (Stone and Cohen 2009). An international Web service called "Protestor Help" even provided street-level guidance to help mobilized Iranians avoid government forces during demonstrations.

Finally, an unusual alliance developed between Chinese and Iranian dissidents for electronic collaboration to trade remote hosting sites and technology to evade state surveillance. "The Global Internet Freedom Consortium, an Internet proxy service with ties to the banned Chinese spiritual movement Falun Gong, offers downloadable software to help evade censorship. It said its traffic from Iran had tripled in the last week" (Stone and Cohen 2009). Chinese tweeters created a special hashtag, #CN4IRAN, to foster dialogue and exchange tips. In response, Iranian hackers believed linked to the government—the Iranian Cyber Army—attacked the main Chinese search engine, Baidu.cn.

International new media service providers were relatively supportive of Iran's dissidents. In Iran, Google enabled Green Revolution outreach by rushing a Persian translation service into operation and maintaining a map update of protest activities. Similarly, Facebook posted a Persian interface. Twitter postponed planned maintenance to keep protesters connected at the height of the mobilization, at the behest of sympathetic US officials (Pleming 2009).

The only media provider implicated in providing government services was cell phone company Nokia-Siemens, which helped the regime to block, trace, inspect the content, and even alter electronic communication ("deep packet inspection").

> The monitoring capability was provided, at least in part, by a joint venture of Siemens AG, the German conglomerate, and Nokia Corp., the Finnish cellphone company, in the second half of 2008, Ben Roome, a spokesman for the joint venture, confirmed. The "monitoring center," installed within the government's telecom monopoly, was part of a larger contract with Iran that included mobile-phone networking technology, Mr. Roome said. "If you sell networks, you also, intrinsically, sell the capability to intercept any communication that runs over them," said Mr. Roome. (Rhoads and Chao 2009).

Accordingly, Nokia-Siemens was subject to European boycott calls, resulting in a German government investigation in December 2009 and a European Parliament condemnation in 2010.

Several opposition media campaigns used communicative strategies of identification and framing to break silence and foster solidarity. As a chronic campaign, the opposition requested nightly rooftop chanting of prayers as a sign of support, appropriating the regime's religious imagery. Continuous and ongoing YouTube postings of chants of "Allahu Akbar" broadcast the breadth and steadfastness of opposition and encouraged others. Protesters also changed the 1979 revolution slogan from the call for an "Independent, Free, *Islamic* Republic" to an "Independent, Free, *Iranian* Republic." Moreover, one slogan specifically critiqued Ahmadinejad's accusations and censorship: "The liar is a traitor, and the traitor is fearful, and the fearful cuts off SMS!" (Gheytanchi 2010).

The bystander video of government forces' assassination of an attractive young music student caught up in the protests—Neda Agha-Soltan—widely posted on YouTube and Facebook, symbolized the viciousness and irrationality of the regime and captured the world's imagination ("Widely Seen Video" 2009). Over 64,500 videos of Neda were posted, and a group of Mourning Mothers of Iran formed at her graveside, chanting "Our Neda has not died, the Republic has died" (Gheytanchi 2010)—similar to the protest repertoire of the Mothers of the Disappeared in Argentina. Neda read to the world as a pure innocent victim, while in Iran she was symbolized as an everywoman symbol of rising youth (Afshar 2010). Meanwhile, Neda's death also played into an Iranian cultural repertoire of martyrdom.

Dissidents also used media to consciously contest the government's attempt to delegitimize the opposition as heretics and feminized traitors. An outstanding incident of digital reframing solidarity occurred when the regime tried to shame a leading opposition figure (Majid Takkavoli) by publishing his photo in a newspaper wearing a woman's veil. In response, electronic dissidents flooded their Facebook pages with photos of male supporters wearing women's veils: the I AM MAJID! Campaign.

The rebels had a cross-cutting identity as information processors. One of the key leaders of the US wing of the uprising, Mohsen Sazegara, was a disillusioned former architect of the Iranian revolution: as a speechwriter for the Ayatollah Khomeini and head of the state radio station, as well as co-creator of the Revolutionary Guard. A generation later, after fleeing Iran when reforms he advocated to reopen the political system failed, he turned to making YouTube videos instructing protestors on strategies and tactics—including evading the Revolutionary Guard he founded. Other prominent international Iranian activists were filmmakers and journalists, and the uprisings inside Iran were headed by university students (Fassihi 2009a).

Network analysis shows that Iran election tweets were bifurcated into one stream of prominent individual tags of insiders, and another of supporters (HelpIranElection) (Fisher 2010). With UC Irvine doctoral candidate and remote Web host Eric Mosinger, who had monitored the protests closely as they unfolded, we examined six months of Twitter streams from the six leading tweeters, from the contested election to the end of 2009. Opposition candidate Mousavi (*mousavi1388*) used the hashtag of the Persian date for 2009 and registered 27,594 direct followers, indicating a likely re-tweeting footprint of tens of thousands more; at the height of protests, his Facebook fan group had over 50,000 members (Stone and Cohen 2009). The single most popular Twitter, with 32,132 followers, comes from *persiankiwi*—drawing on some transnational connection with New Zealand but reporting on protests from within Iran. Similarly, one of the most prominent Twitter streams from *oxfordgirl* posts a mix of international news and appeals along with transmitting messages within Iran. *Stopahmadi*, with 12,582 followers, was the most radical and focused on strategy, while *Change_for_Iran* (25,968 followers) seemed to reflect the perspective and experiences of the student movement. Another indicator of the velocity of the new media is when *stopahmadi* posted on July 13th: "we're close to 500 followers. This account was created less than 12hrs ago. Thank you!" A smaller stream of *iran09* (6,121) posted a high level of international information into Iran and appeals outward. Finally, a stream which appeared only in August, *IranRiggedElec* quickly garnered 12,416 followers and focused heavily on strategic self-defense and bulletin board type announcements for the protest movement.

Twitters in Iran performed the full range of functions predicted for new media to expand human rights. They brought information into a closed society and monitored conditions for outside sources: announcing vote counts; worldwide protests and international reactions to the repression; listing names of the disappeared, arrested, and assassinated; posting photos and videos documenting repression (including Neda's death, which first broke on Twitter) and even identifying some repressors—to the point that within months, Basij troops began to conceal their faces during protests. When detainees were released, many posted accounts of their detention, including descriptions of torture and the growing practice of political rape (of males and females). Such accounts helped to document repression, further delegitimize the regime, and encourage international coverage. Twitters analyzed international sources of regime support, such as antiriot vehicles supplied by China, and launched the call for a boycott of Nokia-Siemens.

Several tweeters continually appealed to international media for coverage of specific events as they unfolded. But in a reverse flow, by December 2009, CNN and other international media had gone beyond monitoring Iranian Twitters to posting their own requests for local reports from tweeters on the ground. Meanwhile, Fisher's complementary network analysis shows that Twitters were a significant source of systematic cross-posting with internationally prominent bloggers, such as Andrew Sullivan and the *Huffington Post*'s Nico Pitney (Fisher 2010).

New media dialectics help to establish and evolve the frames and claims of dissidence. Several of the early Twitter streams, especially *iran09* and *stopahmadi*, blend calls for militant mobilization (such as links to recipes for Molotov cocktails) with democratic appeals. But within days, a consistent rhetoric of non-violent resistance takes hold across the cyber-community, along with frequent citations from Gandhi and international human rights documents. The culmination of this arc is the movement's adoption of the chant "Death to no one!"—subverting both religious and nationalist repertoires of "Death to America!" and previous militants' use of "Death to the dictator!" (originally used against the Shah). Electronic media originated and spread the dominant slogan of the Green Movement, which positioned it as a citizen claim for democracy: "Where is my vote?"

More broadly, digital dissidence conveys symbols that build identities and counter-legitimacy for the movement. Cyber-protest constantly evoked the global human rights frame that is more contested on the ground in Iran but also bridged to local cultural frames by labeling victims of repression as "martyrs." The apogee of this was the creation of a new hashtag (Twitter label) in the name of slain student Neda, *#neda*. Twitters disseminated calls for symbolic "greening" of public spaces, signs, and monuments with the movement's own color— so successfully that at one point the government removed repeatedly defaced pictures of the clerical leadership in Teheran, rather than risk their repeated "greening."

A number of new media rhetorical strategies seek to undermine or appropriate regime legitimacy, transforming religious or national identity. Several months into the uprising, when the government began broadcasting visibly coerced "confessions" of current or former political prisoners, the movement responded with a Web site called WatchMeConfess.org. As dissidents uploaded videos to YouTube, the site deconstructed and parodied the government-sponsored confessions with outlandish claims of fake crimes, and posted counter-confessions of dissidents avowing their "crime" of working for democracy in Iran. The movement contested the regime's nationalist mantle via Twitter rumors that the government had brought in hated foreigners—Lebanese Hezbollah militia— to assist the Basij in repression. Similarly, Qods Day holiday protest chants reported and diffused on Twitter compared the conflict in Iran to Palestine, associating the regime with the role of regional enemy Israel.

Electronic media also played a special role in strategic movement activities, helping to coordinate and shield protest, as well as evade censorship and repression. From the period just prior to the election, major Twitter streams warn Iranians to bring their own pens to polling stations, anticipating a "disappearing ink" strategy of voter fraud (in the event, it was the ballots that disappeared). In the early days, Twitter streams posted the addresses of proxy servers to evade government censorship—until other dissidents pointed out that these postings could be intercepted or hacked by the government. Later on, they called for supporters to physically distribute more USB keys to sympathizers, to enable personal downloading of proxies from authenticated sites. Twitters posted scarce self-defense information not found in the conventional media, such as first aid for teargas and guidelines for assisting rape victims. *Persiankiwi* exhorts internationals to change their Twitter location to Iran to flood regime surveillance and confound tracing. Others counsel protestors to "carry pictures of Imam Khomenei so they can't shoot at you," and if apprehended to "wash Basij markings off your doors" to ward off follow-up sweeps of larger teams of repressors in contested areas. Finally, tweeters fought to keep the lines of communication open, mobilizing Twitter, e-mail, and telephone campaigns by international followers to persuade the Twitter service provider to postpone maintenance, and YouTube to reinstate a critical video up-loader.

The Iranian government attempted to block dissident use of new media, use media to track and repress protestors, and launch counter-campaigns for legitimacy through old and new media. The government slowed the speed of Internet service on protest days and blocked access to Web sites of opposition or alternative media sources. On Election Day, text-messaging services were shut down (Stone 2009). Government agents posted photos of protestors at mosques to encourage pious loyal citizens to turn them in. In November, anticipating December protests, the government massively texted Iranians warning them: "Respected citizen, based on our information, you have been influenced by the anti-security propaganda of the foreign media. If you get involved in any illegal protest and get in touch with the foreign media..." (http://www.rferl. org). Ultimately, the government hacked opposition sites and posted challenges and threats to dissidents by the "Iranian Cyber Army." In a related vein of symbolic politics, the Iranian authorities confiscated the Nobel Peace Prize medal of dissident feminist judge Shirin Ebadi (Fathi 2009).

Iran's regime extended its campaign of Internet surveillance and repression beyond its borders, tracing and targeting physical and electronic protestors among the 4 million strong Persian diaspora. According to one *Wall Street Journal* investigation,

> Dozens of individuals in the United States and Europe who criticized Iran on Facebook or Twitter said their relatives back in Iran were questioned or temporarily detained because of their postings. About three dozen individuals interviewed said that, when traveling this summer back to Iran, they were questioned about whether they hold a foreign passport, whether they possess Facebook accounts and why they were visiting Iran. The questioning, they said, took place at passport

control upon their arrival at Tehran's Imam Khomeini International Airport. Five interviewees who traveled to Iran in recent months said they were forced by police at Tehran's airport to log in to their Facebook accounts. Several reported having their passports confiscated because of harsh criticism they had posted on-line about the way the Iranian government had handled its controversial elections earlier this year (Fassihi 2009b).

While such physical repression can delay the institutional impact of the reform movement, it cannot erase the tectonic shift in the Iranian political land-scape; digital dissidence has already given voice and membership to previously excluded students, women, and exiles. The electronic public sphere forged new solidarities, as labor and other sectors recognized their common cause, and eroded the government's symbolic legitimacy and religious mandate. The next Iranian revolution may take a year or a generation—but it will not be televised from the top down, it will be tweeted from the bottom across.

Media and Empowerment in China:
The Long March to Human Rights

China is distinguished in two ways that should have opposite consequences; it is at the same time the largest and perhaps the longest-standing dictatorship on earth and the largest community of Internet users, numbering nearly 400 million. At the same time, the post-Communist regime faces an inherent contra-diction between its twin pillars of legitimacy "the information-related needs of economic modernization and the security requirements of internal stability" (Chase and Mulvenon 2002: 46). The translation of the citizenship appeals of the 1980s Democracy Wall to the World Wide Web has been matched by the authoritarian government with the world's most vigorous strategy of censor-ship, surveillance, and prosecution—dubbed "The Great Firewall of China."

The struggle for membership, rights, and participation in China is very much a struggle for control of the means of information. In contrast to Iran, it is a chronic conflict with more limited use of electronic media and a more ambiva-lent role of transnational forces. Moreover, China's widespread Internet use is undercut by a particularly strong "digital divide" in access; by one estimate, China's cyber-citizens are 80 percent under 35, 60 percent college-educated, overwhelmingly urban, and at least 60 percent male (Chase and Mulvenon 2002: 6). Like in Iran, China's conventional broadcast media are state-domi-nated, despite recent privatization (Escarey 2006). Moreover, China has largely blocked YouTube and Facebook, especially since the 2008 Olympics. However, Guobin Yang finds that through on-line activism in the interstices of hegemony,

"Chinese people have created a world of carnival, community, and contention in and through cyberspace" (Yang 2009: 1).

Chinese citizens' grievances include the suppression of every form of free speech and political participation, repression of religion, and systematic ethnic domination of non-Han populations, especially Muslims and Tibetans. The Chinese democracy movement emerged in force with bloodily repressed student demonstrations in Tiananmen Square in 1989 and has continued among scattered groups of political exiles, academics, journalists, and alternative political organizations such as the Chinese Democracy Party. More longstanding Tibetan opposition crystallized around the government-in-exile of the Dalai Lama when he fled China in 1958 but has subsequently extended to a vigorous network of local civil society groups, transnational Buddhist solidarity, and international advocacy groups. A parallel, nonethnic form of religious resistance to Communist Party hegemony emerged through the new religious movements of the 1990s, especially the Falun Gong meditation sect centered on the charismatic leadership of Li Hongzi. This group has emphasized and deepened electronic dissidence, going beyond digital self-defense to a broader campaign and alliances for Internet freedom. While each of these sectors has mounted systematic electronic resistance to the dictatorship, there is little coordination among them and they operate mostly in tandem—in distinction from Iran's Green Movement. Beyond these parallel sectors, Yang (2009) charts the enabling potential of the Internet for newer forms of countermovement, such as disability rights, antidiscrimination, anticorruption, forced displacement, and labor rights.

In China, unlike Iran, global civil society has been a mixed influence on electronic dissidence. Although all three dissident sectors—democracy, ethnic, and religious activists—draw on a network of like-minded exiles, the broader Chinese diaspora is preponderantly apolitical. A greater proportion of electronic communication in China is strictly commercial, and China has developed alternative national service providers such as search engine Baidu.cn. And the international service providers, notably Google and Yahoo, have played an ambivalent and controversial role vis-à-vis electronic dissidence. For example, "in China in 2004, Yahoo turned over to the Chinese government important account information connected to the e-mail address of Shi Tao, a Chinese dissident who was imprisoned as a result" (Rosen 2008: 6). Yet in March 2010, after years of cooperation with government filtering requests, Google redirected its China search engine to Hong Kong rather than collaborate in the level of filtering of political Web sites required by the Chinese authorities.

Chinese dissident use of the Internet has been more informational and vertical than Iran's more mobilized electronic public sphere. Greater government technological control over Web filtering and more limited penetration of international services such as Twitter have narrowed Chinese netizens' communication options. E-mail lists have fostered the formation of political organizations such as the Chinese Democratic Party, disseminated the messages of movement leaders like the Dalai Lama, and fostered some ties between mainland groups and international supporters—especially for the Falun Gong. Web-based petitions have been important for Chinese advocacy groups like Human Rights in China and the Tiananmen Mothers' movement. Newsletters by groups such as China Watch and the International Campaign for Tibet have increased monitoring and raised consciousness internationally. Clusters of Web sites substitute virtual mobilization of resources, information, and activism for movements physically repressed on the ground. For example, Tibet Online provides fifty-six links in eighteen languages, the Tibet Fund is an entire site dedicated to fundraising, and Tibet House can mobilize demonstrations in dozens of countries (Chase and Mulvenon 2002).

While none of these modalities have mobilized the extent of horizontal real-time interaction of the Iranian tweeters (and their associated Facebook and YouTube postings), the most interactive grassroots electronic forum in China appears to be chat rooms. BBS messaging and blogging have also mushroomed in the past decade. It is here that new voices, frames, and symbols emerge—although with much less direction than dissidence elsewhere, and ample contestation and counter-agendas. Mere participation in on-line forums appears to increase political expression and foster discursive participation, social capital, and "weak ties" (Fei Shin et al. 2009). Alongside campaigns for the promotion of institutional democracy (such as Charter 08), chat rooms have served to mobilize episodic grassroots mobilization around local corruption and mishandling of natural disasters. Chat rooms have also been a site of nationalist mobilization which sometimes reinforces but occasionally exceeds government policy: in 1996 around contested islands, in 1999 when the United States bombed the Chinese Embassy in Belgrade (Chase and Mulvenon 2002), and in 2009 contesting international boycott calls for the 2010 Olympics.

And such forums have served as sites of (proto-political) satire, such as the spread of a cartoon creature—the "grass mud horse"—with a Chinese name that sounds the same as a transgressive profanity, whose heroic adventures could be read as defiance of authority. "A YouTube children's song about the beast has drawn nearly 1.4 million viewers. A grass-mud horse cartoon has logged a quarter million more views. A nature documentary on its habits attracted 180,000 more. Stores are selling grass-mud horse dolls. Chinese intellectuals are writing treatises on the grass-mud horse's social importance" (Wines 2009b).

In a more transnational version of political satire via cultural politics, dissident artist Ai Wei-wei has created critical art installations in and out of China, that often combine Chinese and global cultural repertoires. His work

is often deeply subversive through it use of irony, in a way that often resonates with Chinese publics and sometimes avoids censorship (though he has
been imprisoned). In the latest example, the Chinese dissident artist remixes the
most widely viewed international YouTube sensation of 2012, the bizarre South
Korean pop song "Gangnam Style." "The artist, who mimics the mock horse-
riding dance moves of the original while wearing handcuffs in his remix, calls
his version "Grass-Mud Horse Style," a reference to a Chinese Internet meme
that employs a pun on an obscene phrase to mock government censorship of the
Web" (Mackey 2012).

The more identity-based movements with the strongest alternative bases of
legitimacy have made the most developed uses of digital dissidence. Tibet sites
seem especially powerful at international outreach to counter domestic isolation. One of about a dozen key sites, the Tibetan Centre for Human Rights
(http://www.tchrd.org/) has a site counter and map that show almost 3,000 visits a month, concentrated around the United States and Western Europe. During
mid-2000s violence in Tibet, dissidents projected images of Chinese repression
via cell-phone cameras. The Falun Gong has significantly used the Internet for
strategic and self-defense functions on a par with the "color revolutions." For
example, the breakthrough 1999 Zhongmain demonstration by around 10,000
Falun Gong followers was organized on-line. Falun Gong Web sites have also
disseminated tactics and software to evade censorship and repression of physical mobilization.

But a new generation of urban middle-class netizens has also proliferated,
with more cultural, quotidian, yet contentious critiques of China's state and
market. Yang shows a marked increase in the prevalence, issue multiplication,
organizational base, and forms of on-line activism—often simply demanding
accountability for acknowledged rights issues that do not directly challenge
state legitimacy. Activists have appropriated and innovated highly symbolic
genres and rituals of communicative contention, from virtual sit-ins to hacking.
Like the campaigns examined above, "spontaneous online protests in response
to grave social injustices...typically involve the death of vulnerable persons
and corrupt or derelict government officials" and "convey a moral sense." For
example, one posting protesting the death of a citizen journalist beaten to death
for trying to photograph city officials beating protesting villagers lamented,
"What a world is this? If we don't push this posting, are we still human beings!
Where is Heaven's justice?" (Yang 2009: 34–36). Like in Iran, "narratives produced during protests stress the innocence of the victims and the injustices they
suffer" and are often highly emotional, using cultural forms such as visual art
and poetry (59). Some protests have bridged from virtual to physical space, as in
Iran, although not as frequently. Student activists have printed and posted bulletin board messages on campus, on-line forums have announced and coordinated

protests, and events have been broadcast on-line as they unfolded. On-line petitions have been delivered to authorities, especially on issues the regime claims
to honor, like anticorruption and discrimination.

In the process, China's cyber-citizens have helped to constitute new forms
of civil society. One of the unexpected benefits of China's uneven liberalization is that cyberspace is largely civic space. Yang's organizational research
shows that "e-government and e-commerce are both promoted by the Chinese
government, yet they have developed at a rate far slower than China's e-civil
society" (Yang 2009: 106). Above all, they have built social capital—networks
of trust and interaction—around "defining and affirming common values, the
most sacred values being those often considered damaged in contemporary
society—freedom, trust, and justice" (156). On-line communities offer experiments in self-governance of the discursive sphere and often provide solidarity
for the plight of aggrieved members.

The Chinese authorities have countered burgeoning attempts at electronic
critique with the world's most wide-ranging and systematic suppression of
access—"the Great Firewall of China." We can analyze the various aspects of
China's Firewall as a combination of regulation, filtering, surveillance, and co-
option. Regulation is the first barrier, as a 1997 Chinese law governs registration and responsibilities of Internet service providers, users (including licensing
modems), Internet cafes, bulletin boards, and even international media. All of
these entities are held liable for pornography, pirated material, anti-government
incitement, slander, and "state secrets," in a manner that civil libertarians and
Chinese advocates contend have resulted in selective prosecution of political expression and whistle-blowers. For example, in April 2010, "a Chinese
court jailed three people on Friday who posted material on the Internet to help
an illiterate woman pressure the authorities to re-investigate her daughter's
death.... The court... found the Internet activists guilty of slander" (Associated
Press, in *New York Times*, April 17, 2010). After the release of the democracy
movement's Charter 08, "by mid-February, the government effort had shut down
more than 1,900 Web sites and 250 blogs—not only overtly pornographic sites,
but also online discussion forums, instant-message groups and even cellphone
text messages in which political and other sensitive issues were broached"
(Wines 2009b). Meanwhile, a 2010 amendment to the State Secrets law further
obliges all network operators and providers to block, report, and investigate any
leaks of government-defined "information concerning state security and interests ... [that] would damage state security and interests in the areas of politics,
economy, and national defense, among others" (Ansfield 2010a: A9).

Once citizens are on-line, they are denied unfettered access by government edicts that service providers block search requests for designated sites
and terms associated with the democracy movement, Falun Gong, and Tibet,

among others. For example, the words "tank man"—evoking the iconic resistance image of the lone Tiananmen protestor defying a government tank—will return no results on China's search engines. Chinese authorities have repeatedly blocked the Web sites of major foreign news organizations such as the *New York Times* and the BBC. Similarly, the sites of foreign universities replete with educational links, including Stanford University and Cal Tech, have been blocked after hosting critical material (Chase and Mulvenon 2002).

Surveillance of what users say and do on the Web is exercised by a panoply of local and national authorities from police, Party, and Information Ministry offices. The Orwellian culmination of the institutionalization of surveillance is the 2010 establishment of a new bureau within the Information Office exclusively devoted to "police social networking sites and other user-driven forums on the Internet," as well as an Internet news coordination bureau to further manage news services (Ansfield 2010a). Such surveillance is further enabled by international service providers, with specific accusations that surveillance equipment and software have been provided by Cisco and Nokia-Siemens. As Rhoads and Chao (2009) point out, parallel to Iran, "China's vaunted 'Great Firewall,' which is widely considered the most advanced and extensive Internet censoring in the world, is believed also to involve deep packet inspection. But China appears to be developing this capability in a more decentralized manner, at the level of its Internet service providers rather than through a single hub, according to experts."

Above and beyond restricting what comes into China's cyberspace, China's authorities have begun to fill it with their own viewpoint, agenda, and information. Following summer 2009 ethnic riots in Xinjiang, Chinese officials simultaneously shut down external cell phone service and Twitter, and deluged domestic broadcast media and international news services with the government line—including invited tours of the region for foreign journalists (Wines 2009b). When an Internet campaign of thousands questioned a suspect's suspicious death in police custody, provincial officials invited a volunteer on-line committee to help investigate. The move backfired when Web users discovered that the "volunteers" were almost all state-run media employees, and the police blocked their access to evidence on the ground. The case generated over 70,000 mostly skeptical postings in one week on QQ.com, and a Web portal poll showed that 86 percent of respondents still did not believe the police version of the incident (Jacobs 2009).

However, another mode of contention in Chinese civil society is assertion of expressive autonomy through evasion of censorship. Chinese discussion forums counsel netizens on how to use proxy servers, anti-blocking software, and even rewrite programs to disable filters. Filters can be tricked through using nonliteral language, unusual spellings, homophones, and images. Activists proliferate blogs to insure the survival of some when others are shut down; Yang cites an anticorruption campaigner who used about eighty blogs, so that when thirty were intercepted, over fifty survived (Yang 2009: 61).

Finally, the diaspora of foreign students and transnational human rights advocates that gave birth to China's "e-civil society" continue to expand and defend it. Transnational on-line activism in China has three layers: the classic "boomerang" in which domestic dissidents reach out for international support against the state (Keck and Sikkink 1998), but also a significant sector of diaspora exiles and students, and finally international advocates. Transnational activist networks mount the most radical on-line campaigns, both because they are freer from state control and because they are catalyzed by experienced exiles and international human rights NGOs. Amnesty International, Human Rights Watch, Human Rights in China, and Global Voices monitor censorship, disseminate critical information via Web sites and on-line communities, and transfer capacity to local on-line activists. Even internal dissidents, often veterans of the pre-Internet 1989 struggles, campaign for Internet freedom alongside their primary grievances, and leverage transnational awareness. For example, when dissident Hu Jia was under house arrest for most of a year, "he kept a daily blog, joined a human rights debate in the European Parliament via a Webcast, went on hunger strike and made a short film of his life in detention, Prisoner in Freedom City" (*Guardian* cited in Yang 2009: 202). Finally, coalitions of diaspora individuals who are not necessarily opponents of the Chinese state have mobilized via the Internet for more transnational human rights issues, such as accountability for wartime atrocities in Japan or the rape of ethnic Chinese women following ethnic riots in Indonesia in 1998—resulting in dozens of protests in cities worldwide (Yang 2009).

Globalization has been a double-edged sword in China, enabling the modernization of a totalitarian state to "market Leninism," but at the same time catalyzing the growth of a critical class of information processors who demand fairness, accountability, and participation. Although the state still controls the means of information, through digital dissidence, wide sectors of China's citizens have gained voice, community, critical consciousness, and transnational access. The significance of what Yang labels a "communication revolution" in China can be seen by the coinage of a literal new vocabulary that allows netizens to "think different"; there are recently introduced Chinese terms for "right to know," "discourse space," and "public sphere" (Yang 2009: 217).

The Arab Spring: The Facebook Path to Freedom

After analyzing the full range of new media used in 2011 democracy movements in Tunisia and Egypt, a leading study concludes: "The Arab Spring had many causes. One of these sources was social media and its power to put a human face on political oppression" (Howard et al. 2011: 2). The report explains,

> First, social media provides new opportunities and new tools for social move-
> ments to respond to conditions in their countries. It is clear that the ability to
> produce and consume political content, independent of social elites, is impor-
> tant because the public sense of shared grievances and potential for change can
> develop rapidly. Second, social media fosters transnational links between indi-
> viduals and groups. This means that network ties form between international and
> local democratization movements, and that compelling stories, told in short text
> messages or long video documentaries, circulate around the region. (Howard
> et al. 2011: 23)

But new media did not create this effect in isolation from the full panoply of information politics—and it did not happen overnight.

The Facebook revolutions of the Arab Spring capped over a decade of increasing media access, diversification, and contestation in the Middle East. Systematic analysts of struggles for press freedom, the emergence of Al-Jazeera, and shifts in Arab public opinion contend that from the mid-1990s, these developments laid the foundation for a "new public sphere" in Arab civil society (Lynch 2006; Seib 2007). "In 1999 alone almost a dozen al-Jazeera talk shows criticized the absence of democracy in the Arab world" (Lynch 2006: 9). Another way to measure the impact of burgeoning transnational media linkages is public opinion surveys that consistently found a correlation between access to satellite television and positive attitudes toward democracy as a system of government—approval of democracy distinct from critical attitudes towards the US model and the US role in the region (Tessler 2003).

A precursor to the 2011 wave of information politics occurred in the mid-2000s. Most famously, Lebanon's 2005 Cedar Revolution was facilitated greatly by satellite TV, texting, and blogging. Also in that year, women in Kuwait helped organize protests via texts that led to voting rights for women, and then in April 2006 blogged for electoral reform—resulting in May dem-onstrations and eventually an "Orange Revolution" of new parliamentary elec-tions (Seib 2007; al-Roomi 2007). At the same time, in Bahrain, approximately sixty blogs were focused on a human rights campaign against the arrest of Abdulhadi Al Khawaja of the Bahrain Centre for Human Rights and for con-stitutional reforms. Finally, Egypt's 2004 Kefaya protest movement was led by activist bloggers who broke the story days before the mainstream media, and rose by 2005 to over 1,500 blogs in both English and Arabic. Wael Ghonim, who was tracking the region as a marketing executive before he became an activist, also points out that Internet usage in Egypt skyrocketed shortly before the protests; from 1.5 million users in 2004 to 13.6 million in 2008 (Ghonim 2012: 38).

In 2011, linked protests in Tunisia, Egypt, Libya, and Yemen in various ways brought down dictatorships, leading to the label of "the Arab Spring"— mirroring the 1968 liberalization protests of Prague Spring. The protests began in Tunisia with the December 2010 self-immolation of Mohammed Bouazizi, a Tunisian fruit vendor frustrated by his persecution and abuse by corrupt police. Nonviolent civil disobedience marches in Tunisia led to the January 2011 resignation of Tunisia's president and inspired a similar but larger campaign in Egypt, culminating in the occupation of Tahrir Square—the central public space of Cairo. Weeks of massive protest in Egypt led to the resignation of long-standing US-backed dictator Hosni Mubarak in February. More sporadic and repressed but persistent protests in Yemen throughout the year led President Ali Abdullah to broker an exit from power in November. Finally, in Libya, an initially similar democratization campaign that met with fiercer repression responded by taking up arms, leading to a civil war and international intervention—which eventually displaced Muammar Gaddafi in August. Even though some of these changes have resulted in incomplete democratization or further conflict, they all expanded political participation and broke the repression of long-standing abusive regimes. Major protest campaigns also occurred in Algeria, Jordan, and the Gulf States that had resulted in a mix of regime repression and concessions by 2012.

Throughout the region, campaigns organized through cell phones, blogs, YouTube, Facebook pages, and Twitter became instrumental to raising consciousness, mobilizing protest events, and monitoring repression, although at times virtual communication also facilitated police dispersion. A comprehensive empirical analysis concluded, "We find that conversations about liberty, democracy, and revolution on blogs and on Twitter often immediately preceded mass protests. In Tunisia, for example, 20 percent of blogs were evaluating Ben Ali's leadership on the day he resigned from office (January 14), up from just 5 percent the month before. Subsequently, the primary topic for Tunisian blogs was "revolution" until a public rally of at least 100,000 people took place and eventually forced the old regime's remaining leaders to relinquish power" (Howard et al. 2011: 3).

Old media morphed into newer modes, as Al-Jazeera posted live blogs of protest in Syria, Egypt, Yemen, and Bahrain.[2] In similar crossover from broadcast to electronic media, the Web mapping study of Egypt and Tunisia reports:

> Our evidence suggests that political organizations and individuals used Western news sites—such as the BBC and CNN—to spread credible information to their supporters through the revolutionary period. The result was that, by using digital

technologies, democracy advocates created a freedom meme that took on a life of its own and spread ideas about liberty and revolution to a surprisingly large number of people. Interestingly, not a single Egyptian political Website we mapped linked to regional news sources such as Al Jazeera and Al Arabiya before the revolution. (Howard et al. 2011: p. 3)

As in Iran and China, the new technology empowers and is most effective for youth, the rising middle class, and women. Thus, even within the region, the countries with these demographics are the most impacted. "In Tunisia, where the median age is 30 years old, approximately 23 percent of the 10 million people who live there are under the age of 14. In Egypt, where the median age is 24, 33 percent of the country's 83 million inhabitants is under 14. Cell phone use is widespread in both countries, with 93 mobile phone subscribers for every 100 people in Tunisia and 67 mobile phones for every 100 people in Egypt. What's more, in both countries the government has censured the media" (Howard et al. 2011: 5). Moreover, "30 percent of the people actively contributing to Twitter conversations inside of Tunisia were women. Women made up 33 percent of the people actively tweeting inside Egypt during the revolution" (6).

In Tunisia, viral videos of the protest suicide and the virtual public sphere of blogging catalyzed the revolution. "By the third week of January, 18 percent of all Tunisian blog posts talked about revolution; 10 percent discussed liberty. That week marked the climax of protester turnout with estimates ranging from 40,000 to 100,000 people in the streets. The primary topic of political conversation in Tunisian blogs then became "revolution" until a public rally of at least 100,000 people on February 27, after which Ghannouchi was forced to resign. In Tunisia, the blogosphere anticipated what happened on the ground by days" (Howard et al. 2011: 13). Government blocking of social media sites and arrests of bloggers were unavailing, as activists found technological evasions of censorship, including remote hosting and transnational support. "Outside the country, the hacker communities of Anonymous and Telecomix helped cripple government operations with their 'Operation Tunisia' denial-of-service attacks, and by building software activists used to get around state firewalls" (8). Hence, the events in Tunisia rapidly diffused electronically throughout the region: "This figure reveals that at the peak of events in Tunisia, there were 2,200 tweets outside Tunisia but in the region about Ben Ali's resignation" (15).

Egypt's revolution, like Tunisia's, was sparked by images of the violent death of a single individual who came to symbolize the corruption and repression of a dictatorship. The beating of Khaled Said went viral and led a young dissident Google executive, Wael Ghonim, to create a Facebook page, "We are all Khaled Said"—like Neda in Iran. Images of Khaled Said were also circulated directly via cell phones. Ironically, Said was a fellow blogger, who had been assassinated by the police for exposing corruption and malfeasance on-line. Ghonim reports that 36,000 members joined the Facebook page in the first day, that comments showed tremendous identification with an ordinary middle-class victim compared to previous martyred activists, and that he posted powerful visual documentation of Said's death and subsequently related incidents of torture that garnered huge public response (Ghonim 2012: 62). As Ghonim points out, "The page developed its own culture, and its members began to feel that they belonged to a community." Solidarity sites for Khaled Said were also established in Tunisia and Yemen (84–85). Organizer Ghonim himself was arrested when his Facebook page reached 300,000 members, but the protests continued unabated ("The Facebook Freedom Fighter" 2011).

Although police were investigated for the death of Said, their light sentence led to the January 25th protests that launched the eighteen-day civil society siege of Tahrir Square. As in Tunisia, virtual traffic precedes, accompanies, and diffuses the protest; "Over the course of a week before Mubarak's resignation, the total rate of tweets from Egypt—and around the world—about political change in that country ballooned from 2,300 a day to 230,000 a day" (Howard et al. 2011: 4). Although the Mubarak regime shut down Internet service for five days by banning local ISPs, international groups evaded the censored Egyptian service providers with dial-ups, and Google and Twitter provided a "speak-to-tweet" service that posted voicemails.

Electronic media carried content aligned with other elements of symbolic politics. The path-breaking appearance of women in public space, and the violation of women's dignity was also a powerful cultural appeal that legitimized dissidence in Egypt. Images of the beating and sexual assault of women protesters—and even a foreign female journalist—inflamed public and international opinion. Inside Egypt, a YouTube video called "Blue Bra Girl" that depicted the beating and exposure of a vulnerable young woman, identifiable only by her blue bra, became a rallying point for a broad spectrum of activists, from conservatives to feminists (Higgens 2011).

Protestors drew on a variety of languages and modes for their appeals, from slogans to posters to rhyming couplets to jokes. Protest placards mixed local Arabic, international English, and even ancient hieroglyphics—placing Mubarak as the Pharaoh. But the new wave of protestors also added the new transnational vocabulary of technology. The youth protests featured signs that said, "Mubarak is offline," "Mubarak Fail," and "Delete Mubarak." (Zimmer 2011). A key turning point in the diffusion of protests across the region came in mid-January 2011, when Ghonim changed the Facebook page "We Are All Khaled Said" photo to an Egyptian flag—with a Tunisian symbol embedded in the center (Ghonim 2012: 136).

In his memoir, *Revolution 2.0* (2012), "Facebook revolutionary" Wael Ghonim himself assesses how new media reshaped democratic activism in Egypt. Ghonim states that "the Internet has been instrumental in shaping my experience as well as my character.... [creating a] virtual network with hundreds of youth worldwide" (24) Although Ghonim is a pious Muslim somewhat critical of the West, he speaks of the democratizing influence of "Google culture," which is information-based, nonhierarchical, experimental, and favors employee autonomy (26). After living abroad and completing his studies, Ghonim had repeatedly applied and campaigned for a job with Google throughout his twenties. When he finally secured a post in 2008, before becoming a cyber-activist, Ghonim stated his social purpose to his new employer, "Why Google?: I want to be actively engaged in changing our region. I believe the Internet is going to help make that happen" (26).

Kony 2012: When Buzz is not Enough

But media mobilization is not sufficient for the success of a human rights campaign, and media is a more significant force multiplier under the conditions outlined above, when media access is breaking a bottleneck in information politics and there is clear leverage to displace the source of abuse. The "Kony 2012" campaign bears analysis as a communication politics crash. In the spring of 2012, the California advocacy group Invisible Children brought the full force of social media to bear on the very real problem of war crimes and the abuse of child soldiers in Eastern Africa—and ultimately failed to elicit solidarity. In retrospect, the campaign was ill-conceived, overly reliant on narrow leadership, and attempted to substitute rhetorical sizzle for political substance.

The single-issue, regional solidarity group Invisible Children was founded in 2004, when three young Southern California activists traveled to northern Uganda and made a documentary about the widespread abduction and internal displacement of schoolchildren in that country's civil war. Although government forces were implicated in some abuses, the preponderance of the kidnappings of child soldiers, murders and mutilations of civilians, and sexual enslavement of girls was committed by a bloody and cultish paramilitary force called the Lord's Resistance Army (LRA), under the direction of Joseph Kony. After the release of the film, *Invisible Children,* the organization launched a mission to raise broader awareness of these atrocities, particularly among youth. The Invisible Children organization became very popular on high school and college campuses, in church groups and humanitarian organizations, sponsoring free film screenings, classroom speakers, and frequent fund-raising drives. The issue of vulnerable children cruelly abused by a maniacal warlord in Africa resonated strongly with American youth; dozens of my students participated in campus and national awareness and protest events, and hundreds of student members of the organization were inspired to pursue further study and activism in wider human rights, peace, and development classes and campaigns.

Invisible Children went on to sponsor several massive protest performance events, such as outdoor "sleep-ins" replicating the conditions of displaced Ugandan children, who fled their villages and slept outdoors to avoid capture by LRA guerrillas. In the 2006 Global Night Commute, over 80,000 activists went to city centers in seven countries and slept out with signs to raise awareness of the Ugandan "night commuters." In April 2007, the group organized an event called "Displace Me," in which 67,000 activists throughout the United States slept in the streets to raise awareness about the displaced—including schoolchildren sleeping in the bush, and refugees in abusive conditions in Ugandan government camps. The same year, the American band Fall-Out Boy recorded a hit song about Ugandan children that was featured on MTV and circulated widely on YouTube, drawing further attention. As a result of these events and other celebrity endorsements, over 150,000 Americans contacted their local representatives requesting political action, and the United States appointed a US diplomatic representative to attend peace talks in Uganda (http://invisiblechildren.com/playlist/about-invisible-children/).

Meanwhile, pursuit of the abusers continued on the ground. In 2005, the International Criminal Court had indicted Joseph Kony for war crimes. After failed peace negotiations with the Ugandan government in 2006, the LRA left Uganda and retreated to southern Sudan, the Democratic Republic of Congo, and the Central African Republic, where they continue to inflict massive violations on civilians, pillage villages, and kidnap children. The nature of the issue shifted into postwar mode in Uganda, and the Invisible Children organization correspondingly shifted out of communication politics and into more conventional movement activities.

Invisible Children changed its focus to reconstruction and resettlement in the war torn areas of Uganda. They began the *Schools for Schools* program, to raise funds for rebuilding schools and providing supplies to Ugandan students. They also launched the *Bracelet Campaign*, a micro economic initiative to provide jobs and training for displaced persons, funded by bracelets made in displacement camps and sold through Invisible Children. Invisible Children also lobbied for 2010 US legislation, the Lord's Resistance Army and Northern Uganda Recovery Act, that sent US military advisors and aid to militaries in the region to assist with the defeat of the LRA.

But in 2012, Invisible Children returned to information politics and launched a new, wildly popular social media initiative: the Kony 2012 video, again decrying the warlord's crimes and calling for his capture. The half-hour video went viral, reaching an estimated 100 million views in six days, over 3 million "likes" on Facebook, and hundreds of thousands of followers on Twitter (http://www.guardian.co.uk/news/datablog/2012/apr/20/kony-2012-facts-numbers). It was tweeted by Oprah, Justin Bieber, and Ryan Seacrest. "Kony 2012" represents the epitome of information politics, in that it calls upon a diverse group of twenty "culture makers" distinguished mainly by name recognition for help disseminating the message—from Colbert to Lady Gaga to Rush Limbaugh to Mark Zuckerberg to Rick Warren ("Kony 2012: Which Celebrities are Targeted to Help?" 2012). As media analysts commented:

> But the real pipeline to big numbers was the Kony 2012 website, which features "The Culturemakers," a slick, visual chart of twenty celebrities, including Oprah, Justin Bieber, Jay-Z, Angelina Jolie, Bill Gates, Bono, and more. 'When they speak, the world listens,' the website says. And to encourage them to speak, clicking on any of the celebs' photos automatically crafts a tweet directed at the Culturemaker, complete with the Kony 2012 web address and two related hashtags.[3] The interface is easy, it's quick—messaging all twenty celebs would take less than two minutes—and most importantly, it allows anyone to feel like they're making a difference." (Coscarelli 2012)

Secondarily, "Kony 2012" appealed to a similarly diffuse group of twelve "policy makers" for unspecified action to capture Kony: including George W. Bush, Condoleezza Rice, John Kerry, Bill Clinton, Harry Reid, John Boehner, Mitt Romney, Stephen Harper, Ban Ki Moon, and Patrick Leahy.

In more conventional mode, the film encouraged viewers to "Take the pledge" to help stop Kony and donate a few dollars through the Invisible Children's preexisting program. The film explained that the campaign would culminate in a day of action called *Cover the Night*, during which they would encourage supporters to "cover" their neighborhoods in Kony 2012 propaganda: posters, stickers, and yard signs—acquired by buying the $30 Kony Action Kit. It was the translation of the on-line campaign back into these classic modes of mobilization that ultimately fizzled, following criticism of both the media and the messenger.

The "Kony 2012" campaign was criticized for the film's own claims and strategy, and this spilled over into broader questioning of the Invisible Children organization—which was hoisted by its own petard in the blogosphere. Knowledgeable journalists and area experts from international and human rights organizations claimed the campaign was oversimplified, misleading, pointless, and even potentially dangerous. Perhaps the most thorough and widely circulated critique came from freelance journalist Michael Wilkerson via the Foreign Policy blog, in a piece titled "Joseph Kony is not in Uganda (and

Other Complicated Things)" (Wilkerson 2012). As one critic put it, "Why now? What does it profit to market the infamy of a man already famous for his crimes and whose capture was already on the agenda?" (Orden and Bariyo 2012). The contention that "Kony 2012" could actually be dangerous is because Invisible Children calls for aid to the abusive Sudanese and Ugandan militaries in their pursuit of Kony—the campaign has lobbied for Western intervention in support of these controversial forces that are arguably worsening war crimes in the region. The Invisible Children organization released a follow-up video and media campaign responding to these charges regarding the film, with mixed results (Invisible Children's Response to critiques: "Q & A with Invisible Children" from their Web site, http://invisiblechildren.com/critiques/#BBB; Ben Keesey, CEO, Responds to Criticism on Vimeo.com, http://vimeo.com/38344284).

Invisible Children's organizational finances, personal leadership, and non-profit philosophy were also subjected to scrutiny. Within two days of the film's release, Grant Oyston, a 19-year old student from Nova Scotia, created a blog called "Visible Children" on tumblr.com (Goodman and Preston 2012). The blog received millions of hits in just a few days and sparked many questions regarding Invisible Children's financial accountability and direction of resources to advocacy over direct relief. Oyston quotes Jedidiah Jenkins, Invisible Children's Director of Ideology, breaking down the organization's finances:

> Thirty-seven percent of our budget goes directly to central African-related programs, about 20 percent goes to salaries and overhead, and the remaining 43 percent goes to our awareness programs....But aside from that, the truth about Invisible Children is that we are not an aid organization, and we don't intend to be. I think people think we're over there delivering shoes or food. But we are an advocacy and awareness organization. (Oyston 2012)

This raised debate over the efficacy and necessity of "awareness programs." Katie Cronin-Furman and Amanda Taub (2012) of the *Atlantic* wrote at length about the failed philosophy of awareness campaigns, including those of Invisible Children.

More tellingly, Invisible Children's youthful, charismatic leaders were criticized for personalizing the story of Uganda as their own, and their unaccountable, visionary leadership style. The Kony 2012 video had highlighted the personal journey of Invisible Children co-founder Jason Russell, including footage depicting his young son, in an attempt to replicate the relatable quality of the original Invisible Children film. But an exhausted, emotionally fragile Russell consequently received very personal attacks in the blogosphere's criticism of the campaign and organization. On March 16th, Russell suffered a public and embarrassing breakdown during which the organizer was filmed running naked on the street in San Diego, slapping the ground and ranting about the devil ("Kony 2012-Jason Russell's Naked Meltdown" on YouTube). The video was picked up by TMZ, posted on YouTube, and made headlines in tabloids around the country. In an article in *The Atlantic*, Megan Garber wrote about the connection between personal narrative, social media, and social movements noting that "Russell's breakdown and subsequent arrest complicated an already complicated story line by injecting his personal troubles into the public conception of the campaign itself" (Garber 2012). She analyzes the Twitter discussion revolving around Kony 2012, observing that "the conversation faded on its own, then surged back to a smaller spike with, around March 16, the news of Russell's breakdown. And then: flatline.... Suddenly, a Facebook Like of Kony 2012 or a Twitter mention of Invisible Children wasn't just a vote against Kony's atrocities... it was also a de facto endorsement of that crazy guy who lost it on that street in San Diego" (Garber 2012).

Media can be a powerful tool to deliver a political message, but the media is not the message—and media mobilization focuses attention on the movement's analysis, rights claims, organizational soundness, and policy prescriptions, for better or worse. Invisible Children's campaign focused on real suffering, but promoted a false or outmoded understanding of the causes, rights relevance, and policy solutions for that suffering. In this case, there were also flaws in almost every other aspect of the movement's communication politics beyond the mobilization of social media buzz: inappropriate personification, murky representation claims, speakers' loss of credibility, obsolete frame, and poorly scripted plot. Buzz is not enough—and bad rhetoric can undermine a good cause.

Conclusion

Is there an app for mobilizing media in information politics? The current generation of media does build social capital across borders, new repertoires of political action, and a cross-cutting issue network of advocates for an open society. The most horizontal, interactive media appear to have the most profound political impact, although the impact of media is highly contingent on social context. Like the printing press, newspapers, or radio, new media are a resource—not an ideology—that can be used for a variety of purposes. But like these previous waves of media, electronic media do eventually democratize control of the means of information. This means that when access to information politics is a major barrier to human rights struggles, this app reaches critical mass.

Table 6.1 Human Rights Campaigns: Media

Case	Voice	Frame	Performance	Media
Tibet	Dalai Lama	Self-Determination	Protest	Web sites
Dreyfus	Cause célèbre	Democracy, citizenship		J'accuse
Spanish Civil War	Writers	Democracy		Arts
Holocaust	Anne Frank, Elie Wiesel	Genocide	Testimonial	Photo, film
Arab Spring	Khaled Said	Democracy, citizenship	Protest, parody	Facebook
South Africa	Nelson Mandela	Discrimination	Protest, testimonial	Newspapers, film
Burma	Aung San Suu Kyi	Democracy	Protest	All
Argentina	Mothers of the Disappeared	Torture, disappearances	Protest, testimonial	Newspapers, photos
AIDS	Doctors, Victims Movement	Health rights	Protest	Health campaigns
Violence vs. women	Amartya Sen	Violence	Testimonial, protest	Film, television
US death penalty	Weak celebrities		Protest	
Trafficking	Child victims	Sex slavery	Testimonial	Movies, Kristof
Female genital mutilation	Child victims, doctors	Violence, health rights		Academic, films
Colombia		Crime		
Darfur	Celebrities	Genocide	Testimonial	All
Congo	Weak celebrities	Barbarism		
US civil liberties	Stephen Colbert	Democracy, discrimination, detention	Testimonial, parody	Television, print
India	Anna Hazare	Citizenship	Protest	All
Russia	Pussy Riot	Democracy, citizenship	Protest, parody	All
Iran Green	Neda	Democracy, torture	Protest	Twitter, Facebook
China	Cause célèbre	Democracy, civil rights	Parody, testimonial	Chat rooms, other cyber
Kony 2012	Invisible Children	Child soldiers		YouTube
Academic freedom	Limited cause célèbre	Civil rights	Limited testimonial	
Armenia		Genocide	Limited Protest	
Israel/Palestine		Genocide, refugees	Protest	Web sites
Liberia	Mothers	War crimes	Protest	Print, radio

Table 6.1 charts the forms of media used by the human rights campaigns throughout the book, alongside the previously profiled elements of voice, frame, and performance.

Once human rights claims are voiced, framed, and projected, they must be received by an attentive audience. Communication power is dialectical, so we will now turn to the receivers who turn rhetoric into recognition, solidarity, and action.

7

AUDIENCES

Constructing Cosmopolitans

The whole world is watching.
—Todd Gitlin

The final phase of communicative contention is reaching a receptive audience. While some struggles quickly become so widely diffused and resonant that "the whole world is watching," often an attentive audience must be targeted, cultivated, and constructed by the politics of persuasion. Like nations, audiences are "imagined communities" (Anderson 1991)—like the ironic "Colbert Nation"—so a sense of common cause and identity both precedes and follows the reception of human rights rhetoric. Construction of an audience involves raising awareness, focusing attention, creating cognitive receptivity, and establishing channels of communication with some subset of the global public. In the process of targeting an audience, the identities of victims and supporters focus awareness of grievances, community networks and organizations provide selective channels of communication, while bridging narratives articulated by both advocates and audiences translate local suffering into global norms and shared history.

If audiences are made, not born, receptive attention should follow the same pattern of the concentric circles of cosmopolitan solidarity: radiating outward from the core of kindred identities, then traversing the inner penumbra of distinctive groups linked by common norms and values, then finally reaching the thin outer layer of global citizens (Appiah 2006). We tune in first to the suffering of kin, then fellow travelers, and finally generic humanity—if we have been schooled to do so by some universalizing ideology and directed by communication politics. The rhetorical process of diffusion of a human rights campaign must then consist of multiple layers of audience construction—first forging new circuits of direct transnational identification with victims of persecution, then evoking supportive attention among diverse communities by linking cognate narratives, and finally raising critical consciousness among the widest swathe of global bystanders with an evolving social imaginary.

The first layer of audience building, the transnational construction of new attentive constituencies, can be modeled in networks of professional solidarity—modernity's form of fictive kinship. Such networks often begin as functional information exchanges that establish transnational channels of communication. Transnational professional roles with normative dimensions may then go on to develop as attentive audiences for collective self-defense when the professional function is threatened, or reach out as role-based advocacy groups for professions in more secure circumstances, as discussed above for Doctors Without Borders. Thus, we see writers, journalists, scholars, and other information processors mobilize as a community of fate across borders, to monitor and defend their exercise of freedom of thought and expression. Like transnational religious groups or ethnic diasporas, human rights networks organized around professional identity are a naturally receptive audience for appeals for solidarity from kindred communities persecuted on the basis of that identity. Professional role-based groups like the writers' organization PEN, The Committee to Protect Journalists, and Scholars at Risk illustrate the construction of specific identities around functional requisites of modernity and globalization (Meyer et al. 1997), and consequently give preferential collective attention to the persecution of the republic of letters.

The next layer of audience construction connects two or more distinctive identities through some common normative understanding, epitomized in the unusual but persistent test case of interethnic solidarity. Disparate groups can become an ongoing attentive constituency for the claims of others who have experienced a similar genre of suffering or defend a common principle, and such allied audiences may even become a transmission belt for publicizing these claims to wider audiences. Previously persecuted groups become attentive and receptive to current victims through the projection of a bridging narrative.

The most powerful bridging narratives are those that project an analogous shared trauma central to the group's identity. The construction of such narratives depends on the elements of memory, analogy, and social learning (Edkins 2003). In order to identify with another struggle, the victimized group must be able to articulate an established history of its own persecution that is available for analogy with another experience (Khong 1992; Lakoff 1990); it must not be perceived as wholly unique. The analogy must be a good fit with the form of persecution suffered by the older victim community. Finally, the coalition partners must have compatible "lessons of history" (May 1973).

Moving outward to the widest audience of bystanders, the most ubiquitous and generic problem is how to focus audience attention and cognitive receptivity when the whole world is watching—but not seeing. The most interesting test case of consciousness-raising of bystander audiences is the mobilization of male awareness of women's human rights, crossing the most universal and definitive identity barrier. Men and women are not a community of fate, many men are latent potential beneficiaries of structures of oppression of women—regardless of individual intentions—and inattention to suffering is intertwined with the construction of modern masculinities. However, significant numbers of male individuals, mixed-gender social movements, and male-dominated institutions have become much more habitually attentive to gender inequity and violence against women. Women's human rights appeals have reached a bystander audience of sympathetic attention among modern males through a combination of relational appeals, micro-channels of communication, the leading role of public intellectuals and charismatic figures, and a global shift in expectations of appropriate masculine roles toward an ethos of care.

Finally, the construction of cosmopolitan audiences is intertwined with the construction of cosmopolitan institutions.[1] Cosmopolitan institutions serve informational functions as arenas for voice and performance, sources of framing and branding, channels of attention, and fora for audience agglutination. The whole world is watching international organizations—but what, how much, and how they are watching varies. UN conferences and treaty monitoring bodies are strong sources of issue identification, the creation of networks of attention, and testimonial performance for issues of discrimination, health, and vulnerable populations (Thakur, Cooper, and English 2006). The more diverse combinations of election monitoring organizations, incorporating international, foreign policy, and NGO entities construct attentive constituencies for civil and political rights (Legler, Lean, and Boniface 2007). Purpose-driven interstate bodies like the OSCE and the Community of Democracies also establish focused circuits of awareness and reporting on political and minority rights conditions in diverse and often obscure settings (Brysk 2009). Regional organizations with human rights bodies, such as the EU and OAS, add a layer of "neighborhood watch" consciousness to regionally relevant human rights concerns like indigenous rights in the Americas. Finally, issue-specific monitoring groups—usually nongovernmental but sometimes intergovernmental—build ongoing niche audiences through reports, conferences, social media dissemination, and certification regimes. Groups like CorporateWatch, Global Witness, Amazon Watch, and Transparency International begin to build communication channels for the cosmopolitan community; dedicated frequencies for tuning in to naming and shaming on a particular genre of concern.

Protecting the Power of the Pen

In the era of globalization, professional organizations that began as local or national guilds have become transnational networks of information exchange. In some sectors of the international public sphere, information professionals have become a community of fate, subject to similar forms of persecution for "speaking truth to power." Authors, journalists, and scholars now collaborate across borders both to improve the flow of information that sustains their role—and to protect their threatened colleagues. A critical element of this new attentive constituency is identification with the professional role beyond national, religious, or personal ties. This imagined kinship is situated in commitment to a common set of "family values" shared by the members of the profession: international human rights, and specifically freedoms of expression and information. Such groups are at the same time forming an audience for the welfare of colleagues, protecting their professions' role as a global audience for repression worldwide, and informing wider publics about the suffering of individuals in socially valued roles.

The international writer's organization PEN calls itself "a global literary community, promoting free expression and celebrating literature." PEN was founded in 1921 in response to the ethnic divisions of interwar Europe and now has 144 centers in 101 countries. Alongside its primary mission of promoting writers' professional development and exchange, the organization quickly developed a self-defense and advocacy role for authors persecuted by their governments. The organization's "Freedom to Write" division advocates for human rights and freedom of expression policies worldwide, as well as campaigning for writers who are abused, arrested, or exiled. The Rapid Action Network, similar to Amnesty International Urgent Action campaigns, was established in 1991. Recently, PEN has launched a special campaign for China, letter-writing campaigns for a dozen writers in peril from Uzbekistan to Iran, and helped to resettle Iraqi journalists and translators displaced by that conflict. They actively critique US policies such as the Patriot Act that affect rights to expression, privacy, and due process (http://www.pen.org).

Hundreds of journalists are killed worldwide for their reporting each year, and this has inspired the formation of several self-defense groups. Since many are foreign journalists reporting on dictatorships or war zones, their plight is inherently transnational but has extended to a universalist defense of the rights of local reporters vis-à-vis their home governments. The Committee to Protect Journalists, Reporters Without Borders, and the International Commission of Journalists are the main self-sponsored professional organizations. But they operate in tandem with a broader network of over seventy organizations that defend their freedoms, coalescing in the International Freedom of Expression Exchange. The Committee to Protect Journalists was established by American overseas correspondents in 1981. Its annual incident report *Attacks on the Press* and press freedom awards have been influential in mobilizing the diplomatic efforts of sympathetic democratic governments to press authoritarian or warring regimes for protection of the press (http://www.cpj.org). Reporters Without Borders, consciously echoing the name of Doctors Without Borders, was started in France in 1985. In addition to a different form of country-by-country monitoring of press freedom (the Worldwide Press Freedom Index), this organization publishes handbooks for journalists—and specifically for bloggers—operating in dangerous environments on self-protection and evading censorship. Reporters Without Borders gives both conventional press awards and honors cyber-dissidence and "Netizen of the Year"—and provides small grants to sustain imprisoned journalists for legal expenses or family support (http://www.rsf.org).

The academic sector has also mobilized for freedoms of expression and inquiry, and protection of its members worldwide. The American Association for the Advancement of Science has monitored the freedom of natural and social scientists since the Cold War era and established an umbrella research and advocacy Science and Human Rights Coalition in 2009 (http://shr.aaas.org/aaashran/csfrlets.php). In similar fashion, several US-based international academic associations whose overseas members face high risks of persecution established academic freedom protection mechanisms during the 1990s. The Middle East Studies Association and Latin American Studies Association, comprising thousands of members each, have regularly campaigned for imprisoned colleagues and even conducted fact-finding overseas missions (http://www.mesa.arizona.edu/). Other academic associations have more sporadic but influential activities; in 2010 the American Political Science Association helped secure the release of a Saudi Arabian political scientist imprisoned there for reporting on prison conditions, including letters of concern from professional colleagues who had served in US administrations (http://www.apsa.org). In 2006, I participated in the establishment of an Academic Freedom Committee in the Human Rights Section of the International Studies Association, which was adopted by the wider body in 2009.

One new organization was founded exclusively to advocate for and assist persecuted academics: Scholars at Risk (SAR). The Council for Assisting Refugee Academics, a precursor organization that has now joined forces with SAR in the United Kingdom, was established in 1933 by a group including John Maynard Keynes, in response to the persecution of academics by fascist governments. Scholars at Risk was founded by Robert Quinn at the University of Chicago in 1999 to facilitate academic freedom and prevent violence against academics throughout the world, by bringing scholars facing human rights abuses to positions at institutions in safe countries. The network was launched with a major international conference at the University of Chicago in 2000. According to the organization's mission statement:

> Scholars at Risk seeks to protect and empower threatened academics, while simultaneously honoring the memory of threatened scholars from prior generations,

who had no such support network. Drawing upon remembrance of the exile of scholars from Constantinople in 1453, the exodus and purging of Russian scholars in Soviet Russia, and the widespread attacks on academics in the WWII era, Scholars at Risk seeks to prevent such events from reoccurring. (http://www.scholarsatrisk.nyu.edu)

In 2001, SAR joined over twenty other human rights organizations and academic institutions to launch NEAR (Network for Education and Academic Rights), an organization whose function is to facilitate international collaboration between organizations active on issues of academic freedom. That same year, SAR began accepting applications from academics abroad. In 2002, SAR joined with the Institute of International Education to help establish the Scholar Rescue Fund. In May 2008, SAR partnered with nine Spanish universities. In October that year, SAR helped create the African Academic Freedom Network, whose membership consists of Ghana, Ethiopia, Rwanda, Kenya, Senegal, Somalia, Tanzania, and Uganda. In 2009, Iranian scholar in exile and Nobel Laureate Dr. Shirin Ebadi founded the Irish section of SAR. Currently, SAR works with 220 universities in twenty-nine countries (http://www.scholarsatrisk.nyu.edu). Since its creation, SAR and its affiliates have rescued over 400 scholars from thirty different countries.

In the twenty-first century, writers, reporters, and scholars form an attentive constituency for common threats to kindred spirits. Through communication networks, those who live by the pen try to protect each other from those who live by the sword. But even when the sword falls on strangers, attention must be paid when they tell a tale of kindred suffering.

"My Brother's Keeper": Memories across Borders

The Universal Declaration of Human Rights exhorts us to act "in the spirit of brotherhood," but distinctive ethnic groups struggle to identify with the suffering of strangers bonded to each other and bounded from outsiders by race, religion, language, or history. In many languages, the word for human being is the term for members of the group—suggesting that recognition across ethnic lines constitutes a key challenge for cosmopolitan solidarity. Therefore, it is important to map how interethnic coalitions can occasionally build bridges of attention, through projecting memories into common narratives. In a model of cosmopolitanism based on Appiah's idea of concentric circles reaching outward from solidarity within one's own community toward true universalism, it is a critical intermediate step to move from collective self-defense to become "my brother's keeper"—a supporter of a distinct yet related community.

Why and how do communities that have been victims of human rights abuse themselves come to recognize new, unrelated victims of ethnic persecution? Interethnic solidarity begins with breaking the recognition barrier and reaching an audience with an appeal to shared suffering and an implied wider community of fate. The solidarity appeal of Holocaust survivor Pastor Martin Niemoller demonstrates this projection of interdependence: "When the Nazis came for the communists, I remained silent; I was not a communist.... When they came for the Jews, I remained silent; I wasn't a Jew. When they came for me, there was no one left to speak out." (http://isurvived.org/home.html#Prologue). The key communication politics for linkage is the projection of a bridging narrative of rights claims and frames, based on common memories central to the group's identity. Bridging narratives must be structured communications that promote diffuse Other-identification between community leaders or organizations with social capital and charismatic status.

Interethnic solidarity challenges materialist views of ethnic communities as interest groups and shows the exception to the general pattern of in-group self-defense and withdrawal from the suffering of strangers (Horowitz 1985; Esman 1994). Indeed, a study comparing support for affirmative action policies that explicitly redistribute social resources shows that individuals' political principles are the most important determinant of their support for privileging disadvantaged Others, with the self-interest of their own ethnic group the least significant variable (Lien and Conway 2000; Sonnenshein 2001). But material constraints do mark the parameters of the space for speaking rights and target audiences; solidarity among oppressed ethnic groups is uncommon because the groups most likely to recognize another's suffering must combine a history of suffering with current security. Groups that have not suffered are less attentive to abuse, but groups that are still suffering are usually not positioned to form a coalition with peers. As former victim groups become more secure and attain higher status, they also tend to have superior communicative resources such as education and media access, which enable them to interpret and memorialize their own experience, gain awareness of the experience of distant neighbors, and project appeals within their own society and the international arena.

Interethnic human rights solidarity is uncommon, but persistent and meaningful. For example, during the emergence of the Latin American indigenous rights movement from the 1970s through the 1990s, Indians of the Americas received disproportionate support and critical infusions of resources from European ethnic minority groups who identified with their quest for autonomy—from Basques to Irish (Brysk 2000). American Jews played a disproportionate role in raising awareness for Darfur; African Americans overcame domestic disempowerment to lead the antiapartheid movement; and Northern Irish Catholics have mobilized information campaigns for Palestinian self-determination (Brysk and Wehrenfennig 2010). Japanese Americans stood among the sparse advocates for Arab Americans during the post-9/11 detentions. In similar fashion, Armenian Americans have recently broadened the struggle for recognition of their own genocide to global awareness of contemporary crimes against humanity. These groups have formed an attentive coalition and receptive audience on the basis of matching memories to rubrics of suffering, from wartime detention to genocide, from racism to self-determination. Kindred fellow sufferers can form a limited but powerful target audience for human rights claims.

African Americans and Antiapartheid Solidarity

Although African Americans have been consumed with their own struggle for survival during most of their beleaguered tenure in the United States, defensive pan-Africanism did extend to true interethnic advocacy by the 1970s—a mere decade after American blacks secured full formal legal equality under the 1964 Civil Rights Act. America's 40 million citizens of African descent remain the largest most persistently and broadly disadvantaged ethnic group in most categories of social resources: 27 percent of blacks live in poverty, diminishing the group's political capital (National Poverty Center, University of Michigan 2010). Even the basic indicators of biological survival—infant mortality and life expectancy—show significant gaps, with black infant mortality around twice the national average and a life expectancy gap of almost ten years between black and white males (US Department of Health and Human Services 2012).

For the century following the end of slavery, a combination of violent prejudice, poverty, and continuing civic disenfranchisement under Jim Crow legislation isolated and demobilized the majority of the African American community, blocking significant foreign policy advocacy well into the 1960s (DeConde 1992:108, 145). The destructive power of the legacies of slavery beyond simple racial bias in impeding group mobilization by African Americans is highlighted by the relatively higher social mobility and civic participation of Caribbean black migrants to the United States, who were voluntary migrants with ongoing transnational ties to intact and literate societies (Alex-Assensoh and Hanks 2000). While there are numerous African American national organizations, the major civic bodies such as the National Association for the Advancement of Colored People (NAACP) historically had only a sporadic foreign policy focus; the latent social capital of black churches eventually focused on civil rights at home, but they did not generally engage in international activity. Until the antiapartheid campaign, African American consciousness and criticism of US foreign policy was remarkably high and consistently anti-imperialist, but specific coalitions and impact were low (Krenn 1999).

From the 1950s onward, some African American churches and community advancement organizations did organize relief efforts and early petitions to the United Nations for the minority-ruled African settler states of Southern Africa, in association with anticolonialist and nonaligned movements. Since most African Americans' roots were in Western or Central rather than Southern Africa, black Americans were not identifying with ancestral homelands, nor did they widely critique postcolonial African leaders' oppression of their own people. Rather, US blacks criticized white settler regimes' slavery-like and Jim Crow-like abuses toward unrelated "fellow Africans."

Black American antiapartheid activism took off during the 1970s, following a decade of educational and electoral reforms that brought significant numbers of African Americans into policy-making circles; African Americans had now passed the threshold of empowerment to advocate for other groups. Catalytic figures like Carter's UN Ambassador Andrew Young and grassroots organizer Randall Robinson linked normative appeals against apartheid to civil rights movement networks and values, and founded the new organization Transafrica in 1976. By 1978, the organization had 10,000 members (DeConde 1992: 177). The bridging narrative involved frequent parallels between the US civil rights movement and the struggles of South African blacks for legal equality. Key South African communicators Nelson Mandela and Bishop Desmond Tutu framed their conflict in parallel terms for a US audience, and frequently stated that the South African struggle was inspired by the American civil rights movement.

Meanwhile, newly empowered black legislators established the Congressional Black Caucus, which quickly took up apartheid as its main international issue. Congressman Ron Dellums drafted an early sanctions bill at the request of South African black unions, which formed the basis of eventual US restrictions, after over a decade of struggle.

> The Black Caucus was also the source of the Comprehensive Antiapartheid Act of 1986 that transformed U.S. policy toward South Africa. This collaboration between congressional leaders and human rights activists was reflected in the Free South Africa Movement, which organized the arrests of thousands of demonstrators outside the South African Embassy in Washington D.C. in the early 1980s. During the demonstrations numerous African American Congressmen were arrested along with ordinary citizens and celebrities in the sit-ins outside the South African Embassy. (Nesbitt 2004: 4–5)

Robinson, the Pan-African Liberation Committee, and the Harvard divestment movement also organized 1970s boycotts of Gulf Oil over Portuguese colonialism and later lobbied for more humanitarian action on Haiti (Robinson 1998), but without receiving the grassroots black support or US policy response of the antiapartheid campaign.

The identification of African Americans with South African blacks and their projection of this identity into American political discourse in the post–civil rights era were clearly key to the success of antiapartheid mobilization in securing US and global sanctions that contributed to the transition to majority rule in South Africa.

American Jews: "Never Again"?

Contrasting with African Americans, American Jews are perhaps the leading case of a massively and chronically persecuted minority achieving security and success within one generation of immigration. One sociological study summarizes the combination of economic, educational, and civic insertion of American Jews with the statistic that Jewish individuals comprise roughly 40 percent of a list of the wealthiest Americans, 40 percent of American winners of Nobel prizes, and 40 percent of the partners of the leading law firms in Washington and New York (Lipset and Raab 1995: 26–27). Seeking to transcend racist genetic or conspiracy theories of this phenomenon, a careful sociological analysis traces the success of American Jews to a strong fit between the compensatory skills Jews gained in a history of forced Diaspora and the needs of America as a globalizing pluralist superpower: an economic "middleman minority" and a diffusely literate religious tradition (Hollinger 2006: 135–165). Moreover, American Jews quickly transformed a legacy of strong communal religious organizations into dozens of civic and promotional bodies (Mittleman, Sarna, and Licht 2002), gaining a high level of network "social capital."

Thus, Jewish community organizations quickly assumed a foreign policy orientation, in part due to ongoing uncertainties within the Diaspora. By 1905, in response to a horrific pogrom in Odessa, 50,000 American Jews marched through the streets of New York—and the following year established the flagship American Jewish Committee, which by 1912 had secured the abrogation of an anti-Semitic US treaty with Russia (DeConde 1992: 70–71). However, unavailing appeals by well-situated and well-organized American Jews to rescue their brethren during the Holocaust planted a strong sense of the limits of assimilation and American civic universalism, evoking a back-up strategy of communal self-defense culminating in Zionism (Spiegel 2001). Jewish American intra-ethnic advocacy for Soviet Jews during the Cold War appears to have served as a critical intermediate phase between inward-looking Zionism and cosmopolitan outreach to unrelated groups (Galchinsky 2008). When Jews reached out across ethnic lines, leading Jewish figures in international human rights and Jewish organizations clearly adopted the message that Kantian cosmopolitanism was the ultimate guarantee of "never again." American Jewish NGOs lobbied for forty years for the Genocide Treaty despite US isolationism, under the aegis of the Ad Hoc Committee on Human Rights and Genocide Treaties, and helped to draft the United Nation's Declaration on the Elimination of All Forms of Religious Intolerance (Galchinsky 2008: 36).

Yet the organized American Jewish community has varied tremendously in its relationship to the persecution of similarly situated groups, depending in part on the presence and strength of bridging narratives. During the 1960s and 1970s, US Jewish organizations strongly supported the African American civil rights movement, often adopting biblical metaphors of Jewish enslavement in Egypt. African American public intellectual Cornel West explains the narrative match, following Thomas's observations, that both African Americans and US Jews share a "nagging moral conscience owing to an undeniable history of underdog status and unusual slavery-to-freedom narratives in authoritative texts" (Lerner and West 1995: 2; Thomas 1999). Regarding Jewish Americans' disproportionate participation in the US civil rights movement advocating for African Americans, pluralistic rabbi and political activist Michael Lerner explains, "It was for the underdogs, the Jews of that situation" (Lerner and West 1995: 42).

But American Jews had a mixed record opposing apartheid in South Africa, which resonated more with American than Jewish history—with American Jewish institutions lagging behind the global Jewish community and even South African Jewish peers in lower levels of antiapartheid activism. Confronting genocidal persecutions in distant lands during the following decades, American Jews spoke out against refugee quotas for persecuted Cambodians and urged US intervention in Bosnia, but were relatively silent on Rwanda (Galchinsky 2008:100–102). And the American Jewish community has been notoriously reluctant to criticize human rights abuses in Israel, only slightly mitigated by the recent emergence of a few dissident American Jewish organizations focused on Mideast peace.[2]

However, by the twenty-first century, interethnic solidarity with unrelated groups linked to Holocaust recognition came to play a central role in constituting Jewish identity, especially among non-religious and younger generation Jews. This is exemplified in an interview with Edgar Bronfman, a nonobservant Jewish "billionaire philanthropist who has spent much of his fortune battling anti-Semitism worldwide," in which he responds to the question:

Q: Why is it important to you that Judaism continues?
A: There are things we have to do. For instance, Darfur, Cambodia, Rwanda. There have been holocausts since our Holocaust. We should be the first people to

stand up and say this is unacceptable, but we don't. We say, "Never again," just for us. We have to say, No, it's for everyone, this "Never again." (Solomon 2008)

The internationalist projection of "never again" reached its apogee in an unlikely identification with distant victims of a barely comprehensible genocide in Sudan—as in Bosnia, claiming mostly Muslim victims. After years of retreat from internationalism over quandaries related to global condemnations of Israel's human rights record, the American Jewish community rallied around the cause of Darfur. Information was available: the 2004 attacks in Darfur followed increasing publicity of the thirty-year North–South Sudanese civil war by American humanitarian groups, as well as increased media attention to African regimes linked to global terror following 9/11. Moreover, key community leaders articulated a bridging narrative; the Holocaust Museum sponsored the founding conference for concern about Darfur, and Nobel Laureate Elie Wiesel explicitly labeled the conflict as a genocide. By 2004, the American Jewish World Service had established a coalition of 170 NGOs, the Save Darfur Coalition. The coalition lobbied President Bush for multinational intervention, raised over $4 million, and led rallies throughout the United States. In parallel fashion, the Jewish press and numerous synagogues publicized and raised funds for Darfur relief. Activists sported buttons that read "Never Again—Darfur" and drew explicit comparisons to the Holocaust. A Jewish college student, the grandchild of four Holocaust survivors, raised $250,000 from fellow students to fund African Union peacekeepers and established a new social action organization, the Genocide Intervention Network (Galchinsky 2008: 84, 103). In a primal ritual of identification, the US national Jewish students' organization Hillel sponsored weekly baking and sale of the highly symbolic Sabbath bread for Darfur relief at dozens of American universities.

On the other hand, the limits of interethnic solidarity by American Jews are dramatically illustrated by the organized Jewish community's equivocation over recognition of the World War I era Armenian genocide, when a bridging narrative was trumped by a regression to perceived communal self-protection. It is deeply ironic, in that one of the lessons of the Armenian experience was the consequence of international passivity toward genocide for the next victims—in this case, the Jewish Holocaust. In planning the Final Solution, Hitler overcame his own generals' concern over international reaction stating, "Who today still speaks of the massacre of the Armenians?" (Power 2002: 23).

The foundation for American Jewish passivity was set by Israeli policy:

Israeli officials sometimes engaged in realpolitik that prevented them from taking a universalist stance on genocide. During the 1980s, for example, Israel was attempting to build an alliance with Turkey....So valuable was this alliance that in 1982, the Israeli government refused to condemn the Turkish genocide of Armenians, despite the existence of a sizable Israeli Armenian minority, and it acted to prevent an international genocide conference in Tel Aviv from going forward because the conference contained a panel on the Armenian genocide. (Galchinsky 2008: 87)

Recurrent attempts by Armenian American activists to appeal for Jewish support produced individual sympathy but organizational torpor, frustrating the Armenian community that sought to draw on the Jewish precedent to galvanize wider acknowledgement in the United States. The Holocaust Museum and Reform religious movement explicitly recognized the genocide, but key gatekeeper organizations such as B'nai Brith and the American Jewish Committee demurred. This chronic tension resurfaced in 2007, as a US Congressional Resolution to recognize the Armenian genocide wound its way through the legislature—and some Jewish organizations actually worked to oppose the measure, on the grounds that it would threaten the US and Israeli strategic alliance with Turkey.

In arguing for a more principled position by the American Jewish community, widely respected French Jewish philosopher Bernard Henri-Levy explicitly contrasted interethnic identity to interest group alliance. Contesting some Jewish groups' concerns that some Armenians had failed to ally with Jewish concerns or even denied the Holocaust, the philosopher argued, "I don't care what the Armenians expect. What I expect from myself is faithfulness to the Jewish message, which is a message of universality, and my neighbor's lack of faithfulness in the idea of universality does not give me the right not to be faithful myself....I feel a kinship with the sons and grandsons of the survivors of the Armenian genocide....we must break the competition of victimhoods....Compassion is not a cake, from which nothing is left for others if you take too big a piece" (Sanders 2008).

On August 21, 2007, the Anti-Defamation League finally issued the following statement:

We have never negated but have always described the painful events of 1915–1918 perpetrated by the Ottoman Empire against the Armenians as massacres and atrocities. On reflection, we have come to share the view of Henry Morgenthau, Sr. that the consequences of those actions were indeed tantamount to genocide. If the word genocide had existed then, they would have called it genocide....Having said that, we continue to firmly believe that a Congressional resolution on such matters is a counterproductive diversion and will not foster reconciliation between Turks and Armenians and may put at risk the Turkish Jewish community and the important multilateral relationship between Turkey, Israel and the United States. (Harris 2007)

The episodic interethnic altruism of American Jews can be modeled by the variance in communicative fit. Overall, US Jews easily surpass the threshold of community security, organizational capacity, and communication density. The Jewish community can draw from several widely disseminated bridging narratives—from slavery to religious discrimination to genocide—that often pull American Jewish organizations up to a higher level of interethnic attentiveness than similarly situated Americans of other ethnic groups.

However, the Armenian dilemma shows how the massivity of the Holocaust trauma makes American Jews vulnerable to regress to a defensive mode of chronically incomplete assimilation that revives geopolitical insecurities, along with a related nationalist narrative of exceptionalism that "burns the bridge" of the bridging narrative. Much debate in the Jewish community on the Armenian genocide revolved around the perceived uniqueness of the Shoah, disabling purely symbolic recognition of an objectively parallel experience (Rosenbaum 2001). Meanwhile, Israel--the homeland of Diaspora defensiveness--itself is in flux. In December 2011, the Israeli Knesset opened debate on recognition of the Armenian genocide, and some Israeli lawmakers finally took up the universalist appeal. At the same time, almost a century after their own trauma, some Armenians have begun to reach outward to other afflicted groups.

Memory and Analogy: "Who Remembers the Armenians?"

Armenians themselves have struggled for recognition of the genocide of over one and a half million people for almost a century. The first genocide of the twentieth century was committed by the Ottoman Turks in 1915–23, with systematic execution, torture, forced marches, and starvation of the Christian Armenians. The Armenian Diaspora numbers 5–6 million individuals; the descendants of survivors make up the majority of the Armenian community worldwide. Decimated, dispersed, and unacknowledged, Armenians were not available for attention or coalition until several generations had been established in secure receptive societies such as the United States. As Armenians campaigned for recognition of their own suffering, they gradually became socialized to the rubric of genocide and circulated in international settings. The Armenian Church provided charismatic voice and some organizational linkages. Moreover, Armenian organizations that had formed for self-defense developed outreach to similarly situated communities.

A Southern California Armenian cleric is representative of Armenian Church interethnic outreach at the grassroots level. Father Vazken Movsesian started the organization "In His Shoes." Its mission statement reads in part: "In His Shoes was created in response to acts of Genocide perpetrated against the Armenian nation in 1915. Those who have suffered evil have a responsibility to take action against injustice to others. In His Shoes provides aid through rallies, information programs and fund raisers" (In His Shoes 2011). As a typical activity, the organization held a fast April 22, 2011 (right before Armenian Remembrance Day on April 24) at Glendale Community College to bring attention and awareness to Darfur and raise funds for refugee camps. In His Shoes has donated hundreds of thousands of dollars to populations affected by genocide. Father Vazken visited Rwanda in 2006 and uses his experiences there to make connections between the Armenian and Rwandan genocides for American audiences—and to show the importance of action against the genocide in Darfur. In a clear use of bridging narrative, he tells Armenian Americans that the images he sees at the Genocide Museum in Rwanda remind him of his grandparents. The Rwandans, in turn, have dedicated two rooms to the Armenians at their Genocide Museum (In His Shoes 2011).

The Armenian Assembly of America is the largest non-partisan Washington-based lobbying organization for Armenian issues (Armenian Assembly of America 2011). They have also engaged in advocacy for the Bosnian, Rwandan, and Darfur genocides. In 2007, they lobbied for the passage of the Genocide Accountability Act, which provides jurisdiction under US law to prosecute US residents accused of perpetrating genocide overseas. "This legislation would hold accountable those people who commit crimes of genocide outside of the United States also accountable under U.S. law" ("Representatives Berman and Pence Introduce Genocide Accountability Act" 2007). The head of the Armenian Assembly, Bryan Ardouny, testified before the Senate for the Accountability Act, while the Armenian Assembly also offered testimony advocating the more specific Darfur Accountability and Divestment Act. This act "prohibits U.S. government contracts with companies that conduct business operations in Sudan, with the purpose of exerting economic pressure against the government of the Republic of Sudan for its role in, and responsibility for, the continuing grave abuses of human rights on the territory of its Darfur province, including the crime of genocide, and with a goal to stop the atrocities" ("On the Darfur Accountability and Divestment Act" 2007).

The Armenian National Committee of America (ANCA) is the second of the two main Armenian lobbying organizations in Washington and state capitals. In 2007, the organization protested when the Turkish government blocked an exhibit on the Rwanda genocide. The reason given by the Turks was an indirect reference to the genocide of the Armenians through a quote by Jewish Holocaust memorialist Raphael Lemkin—the bridging narrative appeal ("ANCA Criticizes Turkey for Blocking U.N. Exhibit on the Rwanda Genocide" 2007). The ANCA has also worked to foster greater awareness through grassroots workshops such as "New Jersey Voices against Genocide," which had panels discussing Rwanda and Darfur ("Momentum Builds in North Jersey" 2009). Another regional attentive coalition is the Florida Armenian National Committee, which organized a similar panel on Darfur along with the Jewish Community Relations Council ("ANC of Florida Joins Launch of Genocide" 2009).

Finally, the Armenian Youth Federation has formed a United Human Rights Council. This group sponsored a five-day fast in front of the Los Angeles Turkish Consulate to draw attention to both recognition of the Armenian genocide and Darfur. The fast was held with representatives of the California Assembly offering words of encouragement and featured images of the genocides perpetrated in Rwanda and Bosnia—to show that the cycle of genocide does not end without recognition ("Fast for Justice Press Conference Draws Attention to Global Cycle of Genocide" 2011).

"So It Won't Happen Again:"
Japanese Americans and Post-9/11 Detentions

One of the earliest defenses of Arab Americans from post-9/11 detentions in the United States came from the unlikely quarter of Japanese Americans. This unusual coalition between completely unrelated US ethnic groups suffering similar persecution fifty years apart illustrates the power of the projection of memories to overcome the politics of fear. The Japanese American Citizens' League (JACL), established in 1929 to combat legal discrimination against Japanese migrants, suffered the World War II-era massive internments of over 120,000 members of its community with little capacity to resist. Decades later, in the 1980s, the JACL secured retroactive remedies for the abuses through litigation but subsequently assumed a much lower profile—monitoring civil liberties in the relatively secure Asian American community. Throughout the 1990s, the JACL did occasionally participate in broader civil rights initiatives—especially protesting hate crimes against other Asian Americans.

Yet after the 2001 attacks, the JACL surprisingly increased and broadened its activities, as an active legal challenger to the illicit detentions of Arab Americans undertaken in the name of the "war on terror." The two groups had little prior contact and no common interests—in fact, Arab Americans were widely stigmatized and unlikely allies who had to be located by Asian American sympathizers. In a press release issued by the JACL the day after the September 11th attacks, National President Floyd Mori immediately invoked a bridging narrative, stating: "While we deplore yesterday's acts, we must also protect the rights of citizens. *Let us not make the same mistakes as a nation that were made in the hysteria of WWII following the attack at Pearl Harbor*" (Japanese American Citizens League 2001, emphasis added).

In the wake of the September 11, 2001, terrorist attacks, over 1,200 Arab and North African noncitizens were swept into detention without trial. Thousands more male noncitizens of Middle Eastern or Islamic origin were profiled, monitored, and interrogated by the FBI, INS, and police. Military tribunals were established to try "enemy combatants," who were not accorded the status or protection of prisoners of war under the Geneva Conventions nor common criminal suspects under the U.S. Constitution. While the USA Patriot Act curtailed habeas corpus, free speech, and privacy rights for all citizens, many migrants from Islamic countries were subjected to extraordinary scrutiny, denials of asylum, unprecedented detention for status offenses, and even summary deportation. In offshore detention facilities like Guantanamo, CIA "black sites," and foreign jails to which Middle Eastern origin suspects were "rendered," torture and inhumane conditions were prevalent, and redress was absent (Forsythe 2007). While a few civil libertarians spoke out early against these abuses, most of American civil society was silent or even supportive. In one Gallup poll, one-third of Americans believed that we should intern wide swathes of Arab Americans (Volpp 2002).

Japanese Americans, a generally secure, middle-class, and law-abiding "model minority," were one of the few groups that spoke out early and often. The 24,000-member JACL participated in a steady and wide-ranging campaign of monitoring, advocacy, and legal defense for Arab Americans. In 2002, they lobbied President Bush against a Department of Justice proposal to establish detention camps for "enemy combatants." In 2003, they joined the ACLU lawsuit challenging the USA Patriot Act and protested the Homeland Security special registration of Muslim men. The following year, the JACL joined an amicus brief in *Rumsfeld v. Padilla* (542 U.S. 426 (2004) and campaigned for a Civil Liberties Restoration Act to contest the limitations of the Patriot Act. The JACL lauded Senator John McCain's 2005 anti-torture legislation and urged congressional leaders to reject the use of military tribunals to try terrorism suspects. As recently as 2009, the JACL joined the Supreme Court case of *al-Marri v. Spagnone*, (555 U.S. 1220 (2009) contesting the constitutionality of holding a US legal resident in indefinite military detention. For over a decade, the organization issued regular press releases highlighting each abuse, lobbied congressional representatives it had come to know through the redress campaign for its own historic vindication, and provided legal assistance to the growing civil libertarian coalition contesting the abuses (http://www.jacl.org; Japanese American Citizens League 2007).

The JACL's legal and policy advocacy was matched by cultural programming and outreach. As early as March 2002, the New England chapter held a forum on civil liberties "After Pearl Harbor and 9/11" at MIT. During the following years, they paired with the Arab-American Anti-Discrimination Committee to sponsor talks, theatrical performances, and roundtables. Later, the national organization hosted teacher training workshops comparing 1941 and 2001, as well as special sessions on contemporary persecution of Arab Americans at its JACL annual conferences. Local chapters on the West Coast were particularly active in providing speakers to schools and media defending their Muslim neighbors.

Meanwhile, a smaller, newer, more radical Japanese American organization also explored new identities and forged new alliances in the aftermath of 9/11. The Nosei group of young descendants of survivors held a Bay Area event titled "So It Won't Happen Again" that included strong critiques of US racial and foreign policies. As one of these newer activists explains, "If there is one thing we can learn from 9-11, it's that we need to critique the master narrative of our history. World War II was not just about internment. It was about non-citizens and what they went through: being restricted, picked up, and being victims of human rights violations before internment. That is a direct parallel to what's happening now and we shouldn't forget it" (Naber 2002: 227).

A key factor in forging the revived consciousness was articulation of the bridging narrative by Japanese American community leaders and survivors with charismatic credibility. JACL Director Floyd Mori speaks of his consciousness-raising as he returned to the United States from a peace conference in Japan on September 10, 2001, and watched events unfold with horror—"my first thought after 9/11 was: will they try to blame Muslim-Americans like they did to us?" (Mori 2008). Similarly, a Japanese former detainee who resumed activism in 2003, at the age of 81, told an interviewer, "I see a lot of parallels between what happened to Japanese Americans and people who are Arab or look Arab." That year, the elderly Japanese American woman attended three demonstrations against the Arab American detentions, and she spoke at numerous schools about the historic parallels to her father's incommunicado detention by the FBI in 1942 and her own experience of receiving her bachelor's degree from UC Berkeley while being detained in a horse stall at a California racetrack used as a detention center (Chung 2003). One catalyzing event was Representative Howard Coble's (NC) 2003 statements justifying both Arab American detentions and the prior Japanese American internments as national security policies—a statement protested by both Asian and Arab organizations. Accordingly, one of the last acts of the plaintiff in the famous Korematsu redress case for Japanese American internments, before his death in 2005, was to file a brief in support of Guantanamo detainees.

Just as younger and less religious American Jews found a renewed sense of purpose in principled interethnic advocacy, Japanese American organizations bolstered their own identity through recognition of analogous trauma. Former Director Floyd Mori discussed the shifting mandate and role of the JACL. In the initial postwar years, as both discrimination and Japanese immigration waned, the organization slowed. Japanese American identity and activism were reanimated by the redress struggles of the 1980s, but at the price of a controversial intergenerational succession. Then the agenda shifted again: "After 1988, we had to ask ourselves: now that we have redress, and a declining Japanese population due to immigration and inter-marriage, why are we relevant as an organization? We realized we had to reach out to a broader Asian population, and to broader immigration and civil liberties issues" (Mori 2008).

After 9/11, Mori knew that the redress campaign had socialized the Japanese community to the lessons of their own experience, but they lacked linkages with the current wave of victims—so he and National Executive Director John Tateishi prioritized outreach, consciously constructing an attentive constituency (Mori 2008). As early as September 21, 2001, Tateishi sent a memo warning of hate crimes and scapegoating of Arab Americans, stating that "what Japanese Americans went through following the attack at Pearl Harbor is being relived today in the reactions against Arab Americans." Chapter Presidents were urged to go through local phone books to locate Arab community organizations and mosques, and contact them to offer support. The JACL instructs its Regional Offices to "reach out to Arab, Muslim, Sikh, and Islamic communities," "offer to do joint press conferences with Arab organizations in your area," "select a chapter spokesperson to be interviewed about the JA experience during WWII," and "notify your local police departments to investigate cases involving Arab Americans as hate crimes"—among other measures. He reminds local Japanese American leaders, "As a national civil rights organization representing the only community that has experienced the consequences of the type of backlash that is occurring today, the JACL has a responsibility to stand firm to protect the rights and welfare of those who are being victimized in the aftermath of the September 11th attacks" (JACL Action Memorandum, September 21, 2001).

The Council on American-Islamic Relations, a leading voice of the victim community, stated that US Muslims "have found steady allies in the Japanese American community, both groups all too familiar with being the target of 'anti-terror' xenophobia and discrimination during war time." In one response of social learning, more than 100 Muslim American community leaders and students joined the Japanese annual pilgrimage to Manzanar, the California desert detention center where tens of thousands of Japanese Americans were interned ("CAIR-CA: U.S. Muslims Find 'Steady Allies' in Japanese American Community" 2008). National Director Floyd Mori was presented with the

Voices of Courage Award by the Islamic Cultural Center of Fresno for speaking out against racial profiling ("JACL Director Honored by Islamic Cultural Center" 2008).

Although many ongoing violations of human rights remain in US counter-terror policy, there has been some positive change on some of the aspects highlighted by the JACL: anti-immigrant profiling and biased detention policies. By the end of 2003, the Department of Homeland Security suspended the special registration of Muslim visitors and the pre-Iraq War detention of asylum seekers from Middle Eastern countries. National origin profiling allegations continue but have been met with reforms by the FBI, TSA, and local police. The series of legal cases in which the JACL participated have also generated some policy change; a series of Supreme Court decisions invalidated "enemy combatant" status, granted military detainees a right to trial, and limited the conditions for military detention of civilians. Broader civil liberties concerns of the JACL, such as the Patriot Act and legislation against the use of torture by US authorities, have been only slightly reformed and remain vigorously contested.

Dueling Denials:
Burning Bridges and the Tragedy of Israel–Palestine Conflict

The importance of audience construction is highlighted in a negative way when the same rhetorical strategies that build interethnic solidarity are used to burn the bridging narrative, refusing empathy. Although there are many material and geopolitical influences on Israel's systematic denial of Palestinian rights, and Palestinian war crimes in attacks on Israeli civilians, failures of communication play a surprisingly large role in undermining attention, solidarity, and response—even compared to objectively similar conflict in Northern Ireland (Wehrenfennig 2009). A 2004–2008 research survey of 4,000 Palestinians and Israelis ranging from Hamas supporters to Israeli settlers shows that even absolutists who reject any possible two-state or land-for-peace material trade-off would accept equivalent peace proposals that incorporated significant symbolic acknowledgements, like Israel's right to exist on one side or an apology for Palestinian displacement on the other (Atran 2010). Meanwhile, international actors have offered numerous practical peace plans from Camp David to Oslo that fail to address symbolic issues and break down. But even worse, the transnational allies of both parties have deepened the symbolic dimensions of the conflict further by engaging in negative framing of the Other's central trauma that arouses fear and impedes empathy. In order to address this costly and tragic human rights deadlock, alongside analysis of the roots, rights, and wrongs of the conflict on the ground, we must explore the negative features of symbolic representation and strategic communication of rights claims.

On one side, supporters of Palestinian rights have received increasing international support as many have turned away from armed struggle to appeal to universal norms of self-determination, principled nonviolence, human rights standards, and international humanitarian law to contest Israeli policies in the Occupied Territories. The Gaza aid flotilla of 2010 embodying this approach was widely supported by many Europeans and the Jewish left. Although tremendously controversial and only partially accurate, the apartheid analogy critiquing Israel's Occupation of Palestinian areas has won some additional support in media and public opinion in the global South and generated principled though contested divestment campaigns in international labor and progressive religious organizations, and even on contested college campuses like UC Irvine (Armony 2011). (http://www.jewishjournal.com/community/article/israeli_apartheid_week_at_uc_irvine_brings_conflict_to_fore_20100511).

Yet all of this rhetorical progress in building audience receptivity for Palestinian rights has at times been undermined by the questionable deployment of the genocide frame, and in some locations derailed by Holocaust denial by a small minority of Palestinian activists and advocates. This rhetorical misstep came to the fore at Iran's 2006 Holocaust denial conference, which included several Palestinian advocates whose international credibility for their own rights claims was undermined by their attendance, signaling a failure of recognition of the Other (Karon 2006) (http://www.time.com/time/world/article/0,8599,1570116,00.html). More broadly, the genocide frame for Palestinian rights is a bad narrative fit, blocks the intended shaming effect with rage, and blinds its target audience. Even the well-documented, egregious, and massive violations of Palestinian civilians' rights to life, liberty, and health do not yet fit the rubric of the Genocide Convention, which requires intent, racial profiling, and elements such as policies intended to prevent reproduction of the targeted group. Accusations that Israel is committing genocide against Palestinians are intended to shame with the trump card that legitimates the Jewish state. But instead they create a nefarious competitive dynamic that diminishes real Palestinian suffering by comparing it to the distinct Jewish horror. Moreover, they attack the central narrative of contemporary Jewish identity and global guilt that legitimates Israeli nationalism, thereby unwittingly uniting in opposition religious and nonreligious Jews—including many critics of Israel—as well as reviving international Palestinian rights sympathizers' counter-concerns with anti-Semitism. It is a marker of the failure of this frame that the West Bank Palestinian Authority, whose leader Mahmoud Abbas had published a book diminishing the Holocaust in 1983, now sends envoys to Holocaust memorials—and that the rival Hamas movement that arguably benefits from conflict continues to condemn Holocaust recognition (Ghosh 2012). (http://www.ibtimes.com/articles/369675/20120802/palestinian-gaza-hamas-bandak-auschwitz-jews-holocaust.htm).

Conversely, on the other side of the symbolic divide, Jewish denial of the central Palestinian narrative of the Naqba—expulsion—and refugee status equally impedes the recognition that is a foundation for a rights-based resolution. Following the practice of the Israeli government, the AIPAC lobby (American Israel Political Action Committee), and major American Jewish organizations such as the Anti-Defamation League put the terms *rights, refugees*, and especially *right of return* in quotations throughout their public statements when referring to Palestinians. This is especially striking for the Anti-Defamation League (ADL), as a civil rights organization that claims its mandate has expanded from defense against anti-Semitism to cover all groups. Moreover, AIPAC uses the term "deportation" on its Web site only to refer to the proposed dismantling of illegal Jewish settlements in the Occupied Territories—and never to Palestinians. The ADL and AIPAC both pair a very partial account of the 1948 Palestinian displacement with the contemporaneous movement of Jews from Arab countries into the new state of Israel, claiming a numerical and moral equivalence that does not accord with international standards. For example, Palestinians displaced by war clearly fall under the Refugee Convention but some of the post-1948 North African Jewish migrants who were not formally expelled may not—but the Jewish organizations do not acknowledge this difference. The ADL further attempts to distinguish the status of Palestinian refugees from the 1967 war from "real" refugees (with internationally recognized rights under both the Refugee and Geneva Conventions), assigning them instead the label of "displaced persons." Moreover, the Jewish organization does not accord any status at all to a third group: "expired permit Palestinians" who emigrated at some point and have not been allowed by Israel to return to the West Bank and Gaza—even if their migration was forced, or induced by Israeli expansion of occupation due to settlement and unilateral redrawing of boundaries (http://www.adl.org).

It is instructive to compare the collisions of these dueling denial frames across American college campuses, which have become a microcosm of debate and mobilization on this issue. At UC Irvine, one of the most contentious campuses, Palestinian advocates were channeled mainly through the religious and radicalized Muslim Student Union (rather than a more secular or pluralistic group)—and regularly protested by both Jewish religious organizations like Hillel and Zionist advocacy groups like "Anteaters for Israel." The framing organizations were based on identity rather than rights claims. Muslim students at UCI sponsored an annual "Israel Awareness Week" (sometimes called "Israel Apartheid Week" and other years "Israel Genocide Week") that featured displays such as a mock concentration camp labeled "Gaza," exhibits of paired Holocaust and Gaza photos, and wall paintings of a Star of David, an equal sign, and a swastika. The 2009 event was called "Israel: The Politics of Genocide" and featured a photo of Anne Frank wearing a Palestinian headdress. To demonstrate the negative impact of these representations on the interethnic audience, they were among the complaints brought by Jewish students to the US Office of Civil Rights in 2007 alleging hate speech (the complaint was ruled to fall outside the mandate of the Office).

While the Palestinian genocide analogy displays were presented alongside accurate documentation of Israeli abuses of international standards and rights-based political advocates for Palestinians, the factual and universalist materials were crowded out in campus consciousness and media coverage by the offensive appeals. Beyond the opposing Jewish organizations, the Anti-Defamation League, the UC administration, and a petition by dozens of Irvine faculty expressed concern about the inflammatory and frankly anti-Semitic speeches of MSU guest Amir Abdul Malik Ali. Ali's 2010 speech, titled "Death to Apartheid," compares Jews to Nazis, decries alleged Jewish control of the media, and calls for the destruction of the state of Israel ("Anti-Semitism at UC Irvine" 2012) (http://www.adl.org/main_Anti_Israel/Anti-Semitism+at+UC+Irvine.htm). Although the Jewish student organizations did not engage in this level of rhetorical provocation, their sponsored events did reiterate the mainstream American Jewish organizations' Palestinian refugee denial frame. And there were scattered incidents of hate speech by a few Jewish student and community participants in campus protests, such as occasional signs or chants labeling Arab or Muslim students as "terrorists."

Throughout the late 2000s, Irvine was the site of physical, as well as verbal, confrontations between Muslim and Jewish students, intermittent police presence at Mideast themed events, the administration's controversial arrest of militant Muslim protesters of an Israeli official—and a campus climate of fear and alienation. When I was the faculty advisor to the student Amnesty International campus group, in order to hold a debate on human rights violations in the Israel–Palestine conflict we were required by the Dean of Students to hire the Irvine police, who were posted around the inside of the conference hall as the event unfolded—a rather harsh contrast to Habermas's "ideal speech situation."

By contrast, at neighboring UC Santa Barbara, the conflict is real, but communication is possible (most of the time). Palestinian advocates are not identity-based and their more pluralistic organization is called "Students for Justice in Palestine." Protest events have a more informational character, use more human rights language, and receive greater recognition by the broader campus community, despite some ongoing controversies with Jewish student organizations and speakers. The Palestinian solidarity season is called, "Palestine Awareness Week," focusing on the victims and raising consciousness, and widely attended by both faculty and students. The only major contentious incident in this campus's recent history was when a faculty member invoked a Holocaust analogy against Israeli policy, comparing the Gaza Strip to the Warsaw Ghetto. This professor's remarks sparked outrage by Jewish organizations and an attempt to censure him but also a campus-wide defense of his academic freedom and free speech rights—as frames collided, on this campus rights trumped.

One pathway out of the tragedy of dueling denials is simply to open up the audience and rebuild an attentive constituency for potential solidarity. In response to the microcosm of conflict at UC Irvine, a group of local students and community activists (the Center for Citizen Peace-Building) created a new kind of dialogue group, the Olive Tree Initiative. The Olive Tree, informed by research in communications and conflict resolution, seeks to push beyond the various interfaith and youth exchange programs in and about the region with a more concerted communicative action strategy. The Olive Tree is a campus-based education, dialogue, travel, and publication program with a universal human rights ethos. It is comprised of Jewish, Muslim, and unaffiliated students who study together for a term and then travel to Israel/Palestine for several weeks. The students meet with a wide variety of participants to understand the conflict in its own terms, participate in structured dialogues with each other throughout the trip, and communicate with the wider campus community on their return. There is no attempt at conflict resolution—rather, the goal is simply to achieve a principled understanding of the conflict and create respectful public space at a grassroots level for exchange of views. Although initially controversial, the program was considered so successful at Irvine that it has now spread to over a dozen US campuses—and has been adopted as an official program of the university (http://www.olivetreeinitiative.org).

Such programs can never hope to overcome the many material obstacles to peace in the Middle East, but greater consciousness of communication politics can help to build a more constructive transnational audience among dueling diasporas. In the journal the Olive Tree students published on their return, a Jewish campus activist whose account of the journey is titled, "Transformation," writes that the director of the Wi'am Palestinian Conflict Resolution Center in Bethlehem told him, "Peace will come when Israelis understand the Palestinian narrative, and Palestinians understand the Israeli narrative." The Jewish student leader states: "I think every Israeli and supporter of Israel needs to understand that Palestinians have a reason to be desperate and angry about living under occupation—you would be, too" (Yerushalmi 2010).

In parallel fashion, after her stay in Israel/Palestine, a Persian student who joined the trip after taking a Human Rights course with me, and researching this section of the project, concluded: "While I easily identify with the suffering of Palestinians, I consider myself above all an advocate for human rights....both peoples deserve the inalienable rights to human dignity and self-determination.... This is the story of Israelis and Palestinians: two peoples who are separated by physical and mental barriers, but recognized as equal under God and international law. In that sense, they are separate but equal. I hope that one day they will just be equal and treated accordingly" (Aghapour 2010).

We can learn to act "in the spirit of brotherhood" that the Universal Declaration of Human Rights prescribes when disparate and far-flung communities articulate a language of kinship, based in common vulnerability and bridging universal principles. Through common consciousness of common suffering, we become our brother's keeper. The final frontier in constructing cosmopolitans is to widen the audience to the outer circle of true universality: bringing in the sisters.

Across the Great Divide: Men Who Care about Violence Against Women

In my lifetime, violence against women has shifted from a silent or marginal issue discussed only by crusading feminists to a routine concern of scholars, journalists, and mass publics of both sexes. In 1992, I recall a young, liberal male colleague at a leading university who was mystified by my inclusion of a lecture on rape as a war crime in an International Relations course. "But rape has always been a part of war," he protested; I responded, "Yes, that's the problem." Twenty years later, audience attention to wartime sexual abuse is so well-established that it has formed the plot of several episodes of "Law and Order."

Modern male consciousness of women's suffering has been constructed through many forms of voice, including relational appeals to care, grassroots dialectics, the call to conscience of public intellectuals and charismatic figures, and the diffusion of global messages regarding appropriate gender roles. We can trace some of these dynamics in the emergence of male norm entrepreneurs, diffuse intergenerational shifts in male attitudes worldwide, and bystander state attention to women's rights in patriarchal societies.

"Looking for a Few Good Men": Male Feminist Norm Entrepreneurs

An increasing number of male public intellectuals and community leaders speak out on issues of violence against women, linking female suffering to universal moral frameworks, personal compassion, and global problems. Public intellectuals like Amartya Sen, campus and community groups like Men Against Violence and Men Against Rape, and groups with overlapping norms such as physicians and male gay rights activists have all brought sympathetic attention to women's human rights, and the prevalence and impact of abuse worldwide.

The identity basis of such norm promoters can be seen in the mission statement of the organization National Organization for Men Against Sexism (NOMAS)—in Spanish, their acronym means "no more." In the statement "Why Are Anti-Sexist Men Confronting Violence Against Women?" they reject explanations based on either guilt or self-interest. Instead, these activists cite:

—a genuine belief in *justice;*
—plain, old-fashioned *idealism;*
—a desire to make the world a better place;
—admiration for the courage and integrity of women we have known and cared about;
—and, frequently, by genuine indignation and anger at what sexism and male violence have done to our own sisters, mothers, wives, daughters, and friends.

After comparing their movement to white supporters of African American civil rights struggles and citing the Hillel quote that opens this text, they conclude: "Men in NOMAS do not take pride in simply being *men* (like half of the human race), but in being *men who are trying to make a difference*" (http://www.nomas.org/node/165).

As an individual, *New York Times* columnist Nicholas Kristof has made a signal contribution to emotionally connecting American readers to reproductive rights issues, sexual violence, and the dark side of globalization in distant locales. In dozens of influential columns, Kristof documents and personalizes stories of maternal mortality, human trafficking and sexual slavery, sexual violence during war, and gendered violence such as acid attacks and honor killings. His pieces on women's issues highlight individual stories, which he has discussed as a deliberate journalistic strategy. But Kristof presents his subjects as more than victims, as he highlights cases of courage and resistance, including the efforts of local organizations and campaigns. He emphasizes simple technological, development, and policy solutions, and actively encourages individual readers to contribute financial resources and lobby US policy makers to combat specific local wrongs. Kristof has written several books with his wife, the journalist Sheryl Wu Dunn, including *Half the Sky: Turning Oppression into Opportunity for Women Worldwide* (2009). His reporting has begun to influence US foreign policy, as evidenced by an exchange between Barbara Boxer and Hillary Clinton during Clinton's confirmation hearing as Secretary of State, when both women referenced Kristof's work on acid attacks and sexual slavery and the need for US action through policy (Kristof 2009a). Kristof's articles were also specifically mentioned in the announcement for a subcommittee on global women's issues led by Boxer (Kristof 2009c).

Kristof builds audience attention through an appeal to care and the global commons in the "21st century manifesto" he penned with his wife Sheryl Wu Dunn:

> The oppression of women worldwide is the human rights cause of our time. And their liberation could help solve many of the world's problems, from poverty to child mortality to terrorism. In the 19th century, the paramount moral challenge was slavery. In the 20th century, it was totalitarianism. In this century, it is the brutality inflicted on so many women and girls around the globe: sex trafficking, acid attacks, bride burnings and mass rape. (Kristof and WuDunn 2009a: 28-29)

Leadership by male experts and advocacy movements has a unique capacity to reshape the moral agenda to increase male attention to female suffering. Moving from advocacy to empowerment, direct personal voice by women, as well as increased dialogue with men, has improved their consciousness and even behavior.

Changing Roles: "Use Your Words"

One of the most powerful sources of change in consciousness of gender relations and reproductive rights is "small talk"—engaged micro-level communication in households and small group settings in civil society. Research in Africa has found that the greatest determinant of optimal family planning and female freedom to use contraceptives is free communication between men and women in the household. Even joining evangelical churches that ostensibly defend patriarchal family values but give women a voice and social role that translates into greater domestic equity results in a tremendous increase in discussion and use of contraceptives, as well as a decrease in domestic violence (Epstein 2011). Similar effects have been observed in indigenous areas of Latin America, where evangelical churches empower women's voice and campaign against domestic violence—and associated alcohol abuse—even though they reassert biblical models of imagined traditional gender roles (Brysk 2000). Universalist vocabularies and the practice of personhood may be more important than the manifest content of religious teachings.

The story is similar at a society-wide level. In a 2010 report, UN General Secretary Ban Ki Moon identified a number of effective programs around the world to help prevent violence against women. Alongside the standard government programs, law enforcement, and support services, these "best practices" include several key communicative strategies. The report highlights awareness projects involving the media, community and religious leaders, young men, and high-level government officials; using educational curricula to address women's issues; training journalists to report on violence against women in a gender sensitive manner; and workshops and national campaigns targeting young men to help them develop skills for nonviolent issue resolution (Moon 2010).

Along these lines, the UN Population Fund identified several communicative strategies that were successful in four different programs to address reproductive health and domestic violence in Armenia, Turkey, Romania, and Ukraine. Targeting family members and community leaders helped to overcome male apathy to discussing gender issues. In the case of Romania, the subject of women's rights was discussed by police authority figures, which helped reduce resistance. In Armenia, male resistance was overcome by focusing on the effects on family health. In Turkey and Romania, police assertively responded to resistance and hostility, but also created an empathic bridge by linking women's issues to female family members. Finally, both male and female trainers simultaneously spoke to individuals to share experiences and give alternative perspectives. This method conveyed a respectful relationship between genders and led to a shift in attitude among the men in the audience (United Nations Population Fund 2010). Effective use of media also helped by provoking interest, raising awareness, and shifting attitudes through repetition.

In a similar program in another region, a study of young men in Mumbai found that more equitable gender attitudes among young men could be fostered by small group discussion sessions led by peer educators and gender specialists. Traditional attitudes toward masculinity favored dominance and sexual prowess, while condom use was often stigmatized. The study found that the young men were eager to participate in the groups because of the opportunity to discuss relationship and gender issues with other men. At the end of the workshop, the researchers found that gender attitudes had positively shifted to be more equitable (Verma et al. 2006).

Reinforcing these dialectics, listening to the opposite gender pays off in personal well-being for modernizing men. The positive social reinforcement for men from shifting attitudes and domestic decision-making is greater relationship and sexual satisfaction, which is demonstrated in a range of studies, and eventually permeates broader cultural awareness. A wide-ranging study in the United States shows that perceived housework equity led to higher marital happiness and lower likelihood of divorce (Frisco and Williams 2003); while a broader parallel study showed that other dimensions of domestic equity also have a significant positive effect on marriage quality, across a wider variety of American ethnic groups (Perry 2004). Feminist attitudes among men in couples produced a significant improvement in relationship satisfaction by both partners (Rudman and Phelan 2007). At the global level, a 2004 study of 13,882 women and 13,618 men from twenty-nine countries found that individuals from male-centered pairs experienced lower sexual satisfaction, while those from the most equal couples reported the highest sexual satisfaction (Laumann et al. 2004). This is reinforced by a similar study from the culturally distinct milieu of rural China, which focused specifically on decision-making power over sexual relations—and again demonstrated that shared power brings the greatest happiness (Lau et al. 2006).

This global cultural shift in relationship models is reflected and may be deepened by the emergence of numerous streams of dramatic broadcast media that give female characters voice to male audiences and depict modern participatory responses to domestic and gender inequities. Even in Afghanistan, where the Taliban's regressive patriarchy specifically banned women's voice, popular female vocalists now perform in reality TV competitions, domestic abuse is decried in widely viewed soap operas, and advice shows deliver a model of consultative family management (Rubin 2010). There are commercially broadcast soap operas popular with both sexes in Iran, Turkey, and India that highlight sympathetic female characters suffering from patriarchal family patterns—like India's drama, *The Mother-In-Law was Once the Daughter-In-Law*. Even the dozens of Islamic Afghan male students I taught at a provincial Indian university aspired to modern families with educated wives, resented older generation pressures for patriarchal marriage that they felt restricted their own freedom, and empathized with women's suffering. One of them told me, "You know, we watch movies. We know how love can be happy."

Voice matters: men can and do become more attentive to women's rights and needs when women are simply empowered to speak up—and men become increasingly aware of incentives to listen. Moving from the individual to the social to the global level, gender rights also improve when entire countries become attentive to the plight of women worldwide.

Bystander States, Cosmopolitan Institutions, and Violence against Women

State support for women's human rights overseas must reflect some conversion of male public sympathy, along with the growing influence and solidarity of women in developed democracies, since men are equally present and usually still dominant in foreign policy decision making. A litmus test for state-level principled support for women's rights is the introduction of gender-based asylum, starting with Canada in 1993 and subsequently diffusing to a dozen other countries. Gender-based asylum means that women who have been persecuted on the basis of dissidence from sex roles are treated like political dissidents, that women subjected to sexual violence as a form of state political persecution receive equal refugee recognition as men violated in other ways, and that women denied protection from private violence—by states that defer to patriarchal families and religious authorities—have the right to seek refuge in a state that ensures equal protection to all of its citizens.

Following a communication campaign by asylum seekers and advocacy groups, Canada drafted new refugee admission standards and processes to encompass gender-based persecution, defined to include: state-negligent and severe domestic violence, FGM, and prosecution for resistance to discriminatory restrictions on dress and social behavior. These new refugee policies resulted in a measurable increase in refugee admissions on the basis of gender, that brought acceptance rates for gender-based claims on a par with other forms of persecution (roughly 58 percent), affecting thousands of women (Alfredson 2009). The content of the Canadian model reflects progressive socialization on the nature and causes of sex discrimination, encompassing four gendered categories of persecution: gendered forms of harm (such as sexual violence) for persecution on some other basis, persecution of women on the basis of kinship, state collusion or negligence in protecting female citizens from severe discrimination or violence by private actors, and persecution for "transgressing, certain gender-discriminating religious or customary laws and practices" (Alfredson 2009: 5–6). Such recognition of a new and complicated basis for refugee admissions clearly contradicted the default state interest in controlling migration and the bureaucratic politics of immigration officials, who stated their resistance the previous year on precisely these grounds. But the Canadian state reversed course and even became a model for other bystander states, after a concerted campaign that appealed to core Canadian values and universal women's rights.

The core of the communication campaign was a set of media statements and interviews by half a dozen representative asylum seekers who told their stories, as well as group statements by women refugees from eighteen different countries, capturing the public imagination. One level of impact was simply to put a human face on the suffering of these women refugees—several were mothers who spoke of their fears for their children. Another effect was to educate the Canadian public about the scope of gender persecution in the home countries, and the inadequate response of their governments. These speakers were supported by highly legitimate refugee, women's, and religious organizations in a country with a relatively influential and internationalist civil society (Brysk 2009). Favorable media coverage successfully linked the women's struggle for recognition to human rights frames well-established in Canada; one story was titled "Is Sexual Equality a Universal Value?" while an editorial in the *Montreal Gazette* contended "Indivisible: Until Women's Rights Are Human Rights, We Have Far to Go" (Alfredson 2009:197–199).

When the Canadian flagship human rights organization ICHRDD (International Centre for Human Rights and Democratic Development) joined the campaign, they appealed to transnational socialization and cosmopolitan institutions: "If [Nada] is forced to return to her country, Canada will be sending out a signal that it will not act to oppose the systematic violation of women's human rights....This would be most unfortunate, given the important initiatives that Canada has taken on behalf of gender equality and human rights in the Francophonie, the Commonwealth, and the Organization of American States" (Alfredson 2009: 195). The domestic mobilization of shame deepened when the president of the ICHRDD, former MP Ed Broadbent, wrote an editorial for the country's two leading newspapers (the *Globe and Mail* and *La Presse*) that a colleague explained "embarrassed the hell out of the government." When the government defended itself with an argument of cultural relativism and refusal to "impose its values on the rest of the world," it unwittingly radicalized the public debate as Canadian civil society groups asserted that women's rights were not the property of any culture. As a result, the Minister ended up retracting his statement, promising new refugee policy guidelines, and announced representations to the United Nations (Alfredson 2009: 202–204).

Why did Canada come to protect, and later globally promote, the rights of powerless non-citizens suffering from private wrongs? First, the "innocent victims" became charismatic speakers who communicated directly with a receptive public. Their claims were reinforced by a coalition of highly legitimate insider advocates. The message that "private" violence against women was a public problem resonated strongly with well-established domestic values, as a 1991 federal report on violence against women in Canada had stated: "These assaults on the person, dignity and rights of women as equal citizens undermine the values Canadians revere and upon which they are trying to build a tolerant, just and strong nation" (Alfredson 2009: 258). Providing refuge to abused women reinforced Canada's self-image as a humanitarian internationalist, at a time of growing migration tensions, inaction in Bosnia, and debacle in Somalia. Thus, the Canadian courts became a life-saving audience for abused women worldwide, and provided a role model for the establishment of refuge from sexual violence in over a dozen democratic countries.

A measure of the success of socialization on this issue was its rapid diffusion to a set of diverse but "like-minded" humanitarian states, such as Ireland, South Africa, Australia, and Sweden, at a time when most were grappling to restrict migration on other grounds. The culmination of this modeling was the 2002 adoption of UN High Commission on Refugees Guidelines on International Protection: Gender-Related Persecution (HCR/GIP/02/01). The United Nations explicitly cited the influence of pilot standards in Canada, the United States, and Australia, and the European Union generated a corresponding directive in 2004.

Table 7.1 Human Rights Campaigns: Audience

Case	Voice	Frame	Performance	Media	AUDIENCE
Tibet	Dalai Lama	Self-Determination	Protest		Cosmopolitan public
Dreyfus	Cause célèbre	Democracy, citizenship		J'accuse	Cosmopolitan public
Spanish Civil War	Writers	Democracy		Arts	Cosmopolitan public, International Left
Holocaust	Anne Frank, Elie Wiesel	Genocide	Testimonial	Photo, film	Cosmopolitan public, Diaspora
Arab Spring	Khaled Said	Democracy, citizenship	Protest, parody	Facebook	Cosmopolitan public, youth
South Africa	Nelson Mandela	Discrimination	Protest, testimonial	Newspapers, film	Cosmopolitan institutions/ public, ethnic
Burma	Aung San Suu Kyi	Democracy	Protest	All	Cosmopolitan public
Argentina	Mothers of the Disappeared	Torture, disappearances	Protest, testimonial	Newspapers, photos	Human rights movement, exiles, women
AIDS	Doctors, Victims Movement	Health rights	Protest	Health campaigns	Gays, humanitarians
Violence vs. women	Amartya Sen	Violence	Testimonial, protest	Film, television	Human rights movement, women, men, cosmopolitan states
US death penalty	Weak celebrities		Protest		
Trafficking	Child victims	Sex slavery	Testimonial	Movies, Kristof	Human rights movement, religious, women

Female Genital Mutilation	Child victims, doctors	Violence, health rights		Academic, films	Cosmopolitan institutions, women, humanitarians
Colombia		Crime			International Left
Darfur	Celebrities	Genocide	Testimonial	All	Cosmopolitan public, ethnic
Congo	Weak celebrities	Barbarism			
US civil liberties	Stephen Colbert	Democracy, discrimination, detention	Testimonial, parody	Television, print	Ethnic, "Colbert Nation"
India	Anna Hazare	Citizenship	Protest	All	Diaspora
Russia	Pussy Riot	Democracy, citizenship	Protest, parody	All	Cosmopolitan public, youth
Iran Green	Neda	Democracy, torture	Protest	Twitter, Facebook	Cosmopolitan public, Diaspora, youth
China	Cause célèbre	Democracy, civil rights	Parody, testimonial	Chat rooms, other cyber	Human rights movement, exiles
Kony 2012	Invisible Children	Child soldiers	Limited testimonial	YouTube	Youth
Academic freedom	Limited cause célèbre	Civil rights	Limited Protest		Professional networks
Armenia		Genocide			Ethnic
Israel/Palestine		Genocide, refugees	Protest	Web sites	Diaspora
Liberia	Mothers	War crimes	Protest	Print, radio	Religious, women

Cosmopolitan institutions like the United Nations and the European Union provided attention and diffusion for gender-based asylum, tapping into but also expanding the global audiences.

Conclusion

Communicative appeals for human rights can reach—and construct—a sympathetic audience, but the process is not automatic. Targeting and building an audience is one more rhetorical task that must be consciously strategized, but fortunately it overlaps with some of the mechanisms of voice, framing, plot, and media. Human rights campaigns can forge transnational identities, project bridging narratives, and foster cosmopolitan consciousness across many kinds of boundaries. We can learn to pay attention to the suffering of distant victims if we identify with their role, understand the form of their persecution, or glimpse a common human vulnerability and a common investment in improving the imperiled human condition. Table 7.1 completes our map of the rhetorical elements of human rights campaigns, adding the audiences constructed by each campaign to its use of voice, frame, performance, and media.

Thus, we have traveled the full circle of communication, from attention to voice to message to interpretation to consciousness. Now, we can analyze what we have learned about using rhetoric for rights.

8

CONSTRUCTING POLITICAL WILL

Another World is Possible

> Pessimism of the intellect, optimism of the will.
> —Antonio Gramsci

Above all, this book has tried to show that another world is possible: a world in which we care for strangers. Again and again, in a world of pain, fear, and oppression, someone has summoned the will to resist—and someone has managed to send a message that gains attention and support for their struggles. Appeals to identity, principle, and interdependence are how we recognize ourselves, our fellow humans, and their suffering. And when such appeals resonate widely, over time they may transform the parameters of political possibility.

We have examined dozens of cases of strangely successful symbolic struggles for human rights, along with a few instructively unsuccessful efforts. What have we learned about how to construct political will for solidarity? How can the politics of persuasion promote a global social imagination of human rights? And which rhetorical strategies deliver the message of care, connection, and responsibility? These questions have implications for the academic study of social movements, human rights, communications, and global governance.

First, we will summarize the lessons learned. Then we will examine a portrait of contemporary communication power, a very "hard case" that shows how the right kind of appeals transformed the brutality of the Liberian civil war. Finally, the book will outline best practices for human rights rhetoric.

Constructing Political Will

The power of persuasion depends on engaging hearts and minds with a narrative of compassion, justice, and cosmopolitan commonweal. Such a narrative directs the specific claims, venues, and forms of evidence needed to support a human rights campaign. Successful human rights rhetoric provides both a story of suffering, and a dialectical emotive response to the counter-narratives of dominance; pitting pity against terror, agency against despair, and bonding against boundaries.

Communication begins with sending a recognizable message about bad things happening to good people in a way amenable to our intervention. We cannot support what we cannot see. Thus, the book traced the difference in global response to Darfur and the objectively worse carnage of Congo largely to the difference in the availability of information structured in a comprehensible narrative that fit contemporary understandings of human rights abuse. Darfur was seen as a state-sponsored genocide, while Congo was less reported and framed as a miasma of tribal violence—even though there were nonethnic and nonstate elements of the abuses in Darfur, and state-sponsored war crimes including ethnic atrocities in Congo.

The distinguishing elements of a comprehensible narrative are voice, plot, argument, performance genre, media, and audience. These elements are interconnected, but may vary in strength and number, as long as several are present in a form appropriate to the social context. It is also critical that none of these elements strongly contradict the zeitgeist, as we saw in Colombia. A persuasive narrative may expand its reach over time, as when a charismatic speaker articulates a new plot, or an existing symbolic campaign reaches a new audience through new media. Successful rhetorical campaigns also adapt dialectically in response to the reception of their claims, as when Latin American Indian rights movements expanded from cultural preservation to environmental protection appeals (Brysk 2000).

We saw how the repertoire of response was established in the European heartland of the international human rights regime. The Dreyfus Affair set the grammar of the cause célèbre through symbolic identification with an individual, framing his struggle against prejudice as a claim for justice and citizenship, and pitting communicative appeals against the weight of military and Church power and reactionary nationalist honor. Decades later, the Spanish Civil War tested principled solidarity across borders. Even the massive and pervasive horror of the Holocaust was not recognized fully until it was memorialized in symbolic and narrative form, with compelling characters, testimonials, and the new frame of genocide.

We have analyzed each element of the narrative arc to learn what works. First, struggles gain greater attention and response if narratives are voiced by credible and charismatic speakers. Direct victims are usually most credible, but the charisma of outsider advocates and witnesses such as celebrities and experts may reach broader global audiences. It is important to recognize that speakers can be cause célèbre, leaders who represent a broader class of victims, or advocates who inhabit a collective charismatic role. Poster children—Sikkink's "innocent victims who suffer physical harm"—have had tremendous influence in the campaign against human trafficking. We saw how cause célèbre Nelson Mandela consciously used his repertoire of identities to embody suffering to a global audience, and at the same time to deliver a message of principled appeal to global norms. Aung San Suu Kyi similarly combined representation of hidden victims, principled appeals, and a stronger ethos of martyrdom, in a very different cultural register and gender role. Argentina's Mothers of the Disappeared echo these roles in collective form, in yet another location. Public intellectuals like Amartya Sen have a singular power to discover patterns in suffering, frame and position new issues on the global agenda, and provide credible evidence of structural causality of hidden abuse. Collectively, Doctors Without Borders combines these functions with humanitarian service.

Framing and argument determine the power of plot. Appropriate framing draws on an existing and widely supported claim, and fits well with the priorities and culture of the international human rights regime, as we have seen with genocide in Darfur and transnational sex trafficking. The claims carried by strong frames are universal and inalienable, and stand up against countervailing appeals for sovereignty, security, or cultural difference. Good frames offer a compelling causal narrative of government repression of innocent dissidents, as Colombia and Congo failed to do. Powerful frames also imply a response and offer a leverage point; this was initially problematic for FGM as a "private wrong," but was resolved when the struggle to end female circumcision was reframed as a health right, appropriate for international collaboration and public–private partnership.

Format and genre based in performance can deliver more effective human rights messages. Testimonials provide humanizing identification with victims and structure suffering as a narrative amenable to intervention, as we have seen in the Voices of Witness project, the Vagina Monologues, and political theater worldwide. Allegory links diffuse social problems into powerful preexisting frames that resonate with national and/or global culture, and historic modes of mobilization. This genre was profiled in the tale of India's Anna Hazare but is also visible in protest performances of Argentina's Mothers of the Disappeared, many mobilizations in Iran and Egypt, and some global campaigns against violence against women. As we have seen in the diverse contexts of Putin's Russia, the Arab Spring, Chinese cyber-protest, and twenty-first-century America, political satire can reshape agendas, challenge authority, and break through fear and apathy.

Transnational communication campaigns have been invigorated by new electronic media, just as previous waves of citizenship and civil liberties struggles benefited from the new media of their eras: from newspapers to radio, from faxes to CNN. New media in Iran, China, and the Arab Spring has been most helpful to human rights where it has granted access to new voices excluded from the traditional public sphere, such as women and youth. Cyberspace also facilitates the performance-based genres such as testimonial and parody, emotive imagery, and decentralized dialectic. However, electronic media still suffer from a digital divide in access in many regions and sectors, and some forms are more easily repressed by certain regimes than traditional media or physical grassroots contact. Appropriate use of conventional media such as newspapers, radio, television, and film has also notably enhanced communication power in all of our historic cases (Dreyfus, the Spanish Civil War, the Holocaust, Argentina, South Africa), Nicholas Kristof's columns on violence against women, India, and the Liberian civil war (below). The media is not the message, as we saw in the failure of the Kony 2012 campaign, but more accessible and salient forms of media—digital or broadcast—can often boost human rights appeals.

Finally, we saw that audiences for human rights appeals are made, not found. The public sphere is constructed and layered from an attentive core of kin outward toward a true global constituency. Human rights campaigns can learn to construct channels of reception that enable solidarity by projecting bridging narratives of identity and principle. The inner core consists of crafting new forms of identity based on functional roles, such as transnational professional solidarity networks, that also serve as transmitters outward to global audiences—writers, scholars, and journalists. The next layer are distinctive ethnic or religious communities with analogous experiences of suffering, illustrated in the multifarious bridges of interethnic attention and solidarity by African Americans, Japanese Americans, American Jews, and Armenians to current victim communities from South Africa to Arab Americans to Darfur. Even the largest social divide of gender can be crossed to constitute a sympathetic audience, as male norm entrepreneurs, male members of local civil societies, masculine global publics and foreign policy elites become sensitized to violence against women through compelling narratives of relationship and interdependence.

The academic implications of this project speak to our broader analysis of social movement campaigns, international relations, and the study of human rights. This study provides strong support to the cultural and identity-based approach to social movements and develops further avenues of investigation for the dynamics of the mobilization and impact of human rights campaigns. For the study of social movements, our findings suggest greater attention to charismatic forms of movement leadership and projection—and the social salience of mobilization by occupants of charismatic roles. It affirms the importance of social movement framing of claims, but highlights frame evolution and the power of frame shift. *Speaking Rights to Power* reinforces recent attention to social movement protest as performance and analyzes the impact of specific performance genres. This book shows the importance of social movement alliances and coalitions as attentive constituencies and information transmission belts—not just material supporters—while providing a rubric for such relation-ships via concentric circles of other-identification.

At the global level, this book fills in the constructivist perspective on inter-national relations, showing how the power of ideas works through building new transnational interests and identities. It shows how agents work from above and below to craft new social imaginaries like human rights that open new pos-sibilities for counter-hegemony. This study demonstrates how communication helps to constitute global governance—and the capacity for its transformation. It adds to constructivist approaches an emphasis on how global civil society helps to condition inter-state "international society." These cases also comple-ment the constructivist emphasis on cognitive rationalist norm change, by high-lighting the normative and affective dimensions of persuasive argumentation in the global public sphere.

Finally, *Speaking Rights to Power* attempts to contribute to a dynamic under-standing of the power of persuasion in the politics of human rights. The book documents how rights are constructed by political practice, not just transmitted as a preconstituted body of law. It shows the differential power of different kinds of rights claims, going beyond the study of power vs. principle—our cases show that it matters which principle speaks rights to power. This study deepens my own prior work and related research that demonstrate how rights are claimed dialectically, by counterpoising the legitimacy base of rights strug-gles to competing norms of identity and security. In this process of constructing rights norms, human rights become not just ideas, but identities, and the process of socialization and affective appeals to these identities is a critical component of the politics of human rights. Finally, this book suggests that the rights we care about are grounded in a global ethic of care, and that such an ethos is the most sustainable and dynamic basis for the development of human rights as global social imagination.

To bring together all of these arguments and findings, let us visit one last case of surprising social change. I began my journey through the power of speaking rights in 1980s Argentina, when fourteen mothers mourning their murdered kin donned white headscarves and brought down a brutal dictatorship. Thirty years later, the mothers of Liberia garbed themselves in white robes and stopped a vicious civil war.

Symbolic Politics in Hard Times:
The Liberian Women's Peace Movement

On January 16, 2006, Ellen Johnson Sirleaf became the first female African head of state. She was elected the president of Liberia, a country that for decades had been torn by civil war. Fourteen years of war that had killed an estimated 250,000 citizens—around one-quarter children—was ended by symbolic protests by women peace activists, who touched the conscience of the world, and even the brutal troops and warlords responsible for the violence. Their surprising success against all odds was traceable to a strong and systematic use of narrative: charismatic voice, compelling frames, performance of resonant plots, construction of audience, and diversified use of media. The appeal to hearts and minds was no accident; as protest leader Leymah Gbowee relates in her account, "It was prompted by emotion—by women's exhaustion and desperation—but there was nothing spontaneous about it....I was the strategist and coordinator of our actions; I talked to the media and got everyone fired up about continuing to fight" (2011a: 138).

The Liberian conflict occurred in two waves, and began in 1989, when the much-loathed government of Samuel Doe was overthrown, leading to eight years of civil war. During these eight years, it is estimated that 1.2 million Liberians were displaced, 168,000 women were victims of rape, and there were 200,000 casualties (Cain 1999). The First Liberian Civil War came to an end with the 1996 ceasefire and subsequent election of Charles Taylor. Taylor, a US-educated Liberian government worker–turned rebel fighter–turned warlord, was elected largely on the understanding that his rule would end violence and bring stability. But Taylor's government was characterized by extortion, embezzlement, violence, and illegal resource exploitation. Taylor's predatory government was challenged in 1999, when various Liberian dissident groups coalesced into Liberians United for Reconciliation and Democracy (LURD). LURD forces attacked from Guinea and Sierra Leone, and as the insurgency dragged on, both sides engaged in even more widespread and profound violence against civilians. In this second wave of conflict, an estimated one-third of the population was displaced and 75 percent of the country's physical infrastructure was destroyed (Gbowee 2011b).

In 2002, at the height of the conflict, a social worker named Leymah Gbowee helped begin a women's peace movement, originally based in the Christian churches. Gbowee (2011b), a survivor of atrocities, forced displacement, and domestic violence, stated that the situation was so bad that "women had nothing left to lose." Gbowee was also highly influenced by the Christian liberation texts of her childhood, readings of Gandhi and Martin Luther King, Jr. during her belated education between wars, work with international organizations, and even a biography of Hillary Clinton she was reading during the 2003 protests—including an epochal quotation from Harriet Tubman.[1] Her regional co-organizer Thelma Ekiyor, a Stanford-trained lawyer from Nigeria, was inspired to establish a regional women's peace-building network by the global norms of UN Resolution 1325, and selected Gbowee as its leader in Liberia (Gbowee 2011a, b).

The foundation of the women's movement was a series of prior organizational efforts that imparted the importance of storytelling, consciousness-raising, and identity appeals. Chief organizer Gbowee had worked as a social worker for a UNICEF program for Sierra Leone refugees in Liberia in 1991, and noted how rape victims' political framings helped them to survive horrific personal violations. Later, after a stint exiled in Ghana with an abusive husband, she returned to Liberia in 1996 and worked with the Lutheran World Federation Trauma Healing and Reconciliation Program—and by 1999, had initiated separate women's storytelling sessions for recovery and humanization. After narrating her own tale and the story of how her movement grew to stop a war in 2004, Gbowee summarized her outreach philosophy: "Every conflict has a face, many faces. Every problem touches your heart" (2011a: 207).

Leymah Gbowee recounts a biblically inspired dream which told her to "Gather the women to pray for peace," leading her to form the Christian Women's Peace Initiative in the spring of 2002. The peace movement began in a Christian church, but soon reached out to the minority Muslim community and established a presence in public space. Asatu Ben Keneth was a pioneering Muslim woman police official, inspired by professional norms to work for conflict resolution and gender equity, and the President of Liberia's National Law Enforcement Association. Together, they created the Liberian Women's Mass Action for Peace. For six months in 2002, the women reached out systematically to the key spheres of civil society; Gbowee directed the activists to visit mosques on Friday, markets on Saturday, and churches on Sunday. The activists connected to other women in these locations by telling their own stories of violence—Gbowee recalls "using shared personal revelation to organize was completely new" (2011a: 128).

Meanwhile, a novel form of outreach for male support which secured widespread attention—especially among rural Christians—was a sex strike by the peace activists. The sex strike, in a negative echo of the link between consciousness-raising and relationship interdependence cited above, was based in a biblical model of fostering women's chastity to increase their spiritual power to secure peace through prayer. Husbands were invited to supplement their chaste wives' prayers with more material efforts to resolve the conflict, so that peace would hasten reunion with their wives.

After initial marches on symbolic sites such as City Hall and later Parliament, the women's peace movement established a permanent sit-in on the roadside of the main boulevard to the capital. They sat dressed in white and bearing peace signs, greeting the president's daily convoy and passersby. In spring 2003, a new wave of fighting targeted NGOs, displaced 360,000 refugees and internally displaced persons (IDPs), and fighting approached the capital. In response, the Women's Peace Network launched a "media peace blitz," marched for a ceasefire, and in early April, established a permanent encampment. Three days later, they blockaded Parliament. On April 23rd, these tactics secured a meeting with President Taylor. The women appealed to him as mothers, and eventually he agreed to participate in peace negotiations under international auspices in Sierra Leone (2011a).

The leaders of the LURD rebel groups were pressured to attend the meeting by appealing to their personal and communal relationships with the women. The power of the women's identity appeal was seen when they sent pickets and mobilized local displaced women in Sierra Leone to push the exiled rebel leaders to the peace table. "Our mothers came all the way from Liberia to talk to us," the men told [movement leaders] Asatu, Grace, and Sugar. "Well, mothers, because of you, we will go" (Gbowee 2011a: 143).

After the conflict was not resolved in 2003, a new round of peace talks were set for June 2004 in Ghana, again with international supervision and again with Liberian women's mobilization of hundreds of pickets. But this time, when the meetings in Ghana stalled and fighting in Liberia intensified, the women invaded the negotiation hall and blocked the doors to prevent any of the negotiators from leaving the building. When security guards came to arrest the women, the female peace activists threatened to remove their clothes, invoking an African cultural taboo on seeing a mother's nakedness that amounts to a curse. Following this confrontation, the negotiations reached an agreement: Charles Taylor would be exiled to Nigeria and a transitional government would give way to elections (*Pray the Devil Back to Hell* 2008).

After Charles Taylor stepped down, there was a drive to disarm fighters to facilitate the transition. When one of the disarmament drives became violent despite UN presence, the women stepped in again to keep the peace. Some of the fighters would only give up their arms to the women. When asked why they trusted them, one of the fighters remarked, "They are our mothers" (*Pray the Devil Back to Hell* 2008). To further guarantee the return of democracy, in the first election in 2005, the women's movement embarked on a voter registration campaign—and increased female registration from 15 percent to 51 percent. During the elections, the women campaigned vigorously for a female candidate with a peace platform, building a strong support network for Ellen Johnson Sirleaf (Gbowee 2011a).

The following year, the movement was profiled in a powerful documentary by influential filmmaker Abby Disney, *Pray the Devil Back to Hell*. In 2008, the film was screened in over twenty countries, including many conflict regions such as Cambodia and Bosnia, and hundreds of US cities. In 2010, the movement led the first "women's peer review" of the new president, resulting in the introduction of a new rape law and free primary education—in the face of an estimated 50 percent illiteracy rate among girls (Gbowee 2011a). The Liberian movement has reached out to regional peers in Sierra Leone and the Ivory Coast, sending a "Liberian Peace Train" to lobby for peace negotiations and an end to sexual violence in those troubled neighboring countries. Finally, in December 2011, the Nobel Peace Prize was presented to three women's rights activists, two from Liberia—Leymah Gbowee and President Ellen Johnson Sirleaf.

The Liberian Women's Mass Action for Peace's methods built and projected voice through identity as innocent women vulnerable to sexual violence, maternal roles, and apolitical spiritual leaders. This identity allowed them to transcend ethnic, religious, and class differences to reach out to all Liberian women. The women were trusted mediators, who gained the confidence of rebels and international workers. The degree of trust was indicated by the UN's eventual submission to the women's suggestions regarding the disarmament process. Additionally, because the conflict was attributed to the failures of men, women were perceived as less threatening. Leymah Gbowee was designated as the sole, charismatic spokesperson for the movement. She was an attractive, articulate, and skilled community organizer, a Christian social worker and mother of four, and a woman whose life experience represented many of the forms of suffering of her peers, who modeled agency in overcoming trauma.

The movement framed the issue in terms of a non-partisan desire for peace and condemnation of war crimes, both well-established claims. By avoiding taking sides, they were able to gain a degree of legitimacy that led to popular and international support, which Taylor could not ignore. The violence against women frame also had a shaming effect on some leaders and international publics, including some of the UN and ECOWAS (Economic Community of West African States) negotiation brokers. At the critical juncture in the 2004 peace negotiations, the women changed their placards from "Women Want Peace" to the more accusatory "Butchers and murderers of the Liberian people—STOP" (Gbowee 2011a: 161).

These claims were performed in public space and drew on testimonials, allegories from religious traditions, and culturally situated rituals. The white T-shirts and head-ties worn by the members of the Liberian Women's Mass Action for Peace were an effective symbol of unity and increased their visibility. White is a global symbol of peace and purity. The "women in white" created a new repertoire that is now well recognized throughout West Africa.

The Women of Liberia Mass Action for Peace initially communicated their message through participation in religious rituals and peaceful marches but also campaigned through locally relevant media of radio, television, and newspapers. Additionally, the recent rise of cell phones contributed to their effective coordination. As their struggle reached critical mass and secured the breakthrough in peace negotiations, the subsequent documentary *Pray the Devil Back to Hell* disseminated their message and repertoire. This brought increased

Table 8.1 Constructing Political Will

Case	Voice	Frame	Performance	Media	Audience	Outcome
Tibet	Dalai Lama	Self-Determination	Protest		Cosmopolitan public	Solidarity
Dreyfus	Cause célèbre	Democracy, citizenship		J'accuse	Cosmopolitan public	Policy change
Spanish Civil War	Writers	Democracy		Arts	Cosmopolitan public, International Left	Solidarity
Holocaust	Anne Frank, Elie Wiesel	Genocide	Testimonial	Photo, film	Cosmopolitan public, Diaspora	Recognition
Arab Spring	Khaled Said	Democracy, citizenship	Protest, parody	Facebook	Cosmopolitan public, youth	Policy change
South Africa	Nelson Mandela	Discrimination	Protest, testimonial	Newspapers, film	Cosmopolitan instituitional/ public, ethnic	Policy change+
Burma	Aung San Suu Kyi	Democracy	Protest	All	Cosmopolitan public	Policy change
Argentina	Mothers of the Disappeared	Torture, disappearances	Protest, testimonial	Newspapers, photos	Human rights movement, exiles, women	Policy change+
AIDS	Doctors, Victims Movement	Health rights	Protest	Health campaigns	Gays, humanitarians	Policy change
Violence vs. women	Amartya Sen	Violence	Testimonial, protest	Film, television	Human rights movement, women, men, cosmopolitan states	Policy change-
US death penalty	Weak celebrities		Protest			X

Trafficking	Child victims	Sex slavery	Testimonial	Movies, Kristof	Human rights movement, religious, women	Policy change
Female genital mutilation	Child victims, doctors	Violence, health rights		Academic, films	Cosmopolitan institutions, women, humanitarians	Policy change-
Colombia		Crime			International Left	X
Darfur	Celebrities	Genocide	Testimonial	All	Cosmopolitan public, ethnic	Policy change
Congo	Weak celebrities	Barbarism				X
US civil liberties	Stephen Colbert	Democracy, discrimination, detention	Testimonial, parody	Television, print	Ethnic, "Colbert Nation"	Recognition
India	Anna Hazare	Citizenship	Protest	All	Diaspora	Policy change-
Russia	Pussy Riot	Democracy, citizenship	Protest, parody	All	Cosmopolitan public, youth	Solidarity
Iran Green	Neda	Democracy, torture	Protest	Twitter, Facebook	Cosmopolitan public, Diaspora, youth	Solidarity
China	Cause célèbre	Democracy, civil rights	Parody, testimonial	Chat rooms, other cyber	Human rights movement, exiles	Solidarity
Kony 2012	Invisible Children	Child soldiers		YouTube	Youth	X
Academic freedom	Limited cause célèbre	Civil rights	Limited testimonial		Professional networks	Solidarity
Armenia		Genocide	Limited Protest		Ethnic	
Israel/Palestine		Genocide, refugees	Protest	Web sites	Diaspora	X
Liberia	Mothers	War crimes	Protest	Print, radio	Religious, women	Policy change+

international support and funding for their post-conflict disarmament, electoral, and women's rights activities in Liberia, and enhanced regional networking and cross-regional influence of women's peace groups in West Africa.

The Liberian Women's Mass Action for Peace maintained its solidarity and built a core attentive constituency by emphasizing a common identity based on womanhood. Religious, class, or social differences were marginalized in favor of a common identity that had gained salience because of the high frequency of sexual violence. Historically, Liberia has had a very socially stratified society, with "American" Liberians having a higher social position than "African" Liberians. To bridge this socioeconomic gap, the groups emphasized wearing plain white garments without jewelry and discouraged the use of "big English" at meetings (Ellis 2009). The white clothing came to represent unity among the movement. The peace movement gained a broader popular audience by appealing to religious leaders and across ethnic divides. One of their bridging frames was an appeal to common vulnerability, with the slogan: "Does the bullet know Christian from Muslim?" (Gbowee 2011a: 128). Finally, they sought an international and pan-African audience with rhetorical linkages and social ties the women had learned in refugee camps, periods of exile, study abroad, and work for international organizations. They mastered the international lexicon of conflict resolution and peace-building, took journalists and NGOs on tours of the conflict region to gather testimonials, and lobbied visiting international officials for the participation of civil society.

Leymah Gbowee (2011b) summarized the lesson of her movement, "No matter how bad a situation, the people possess some power." Her successful campaign, and the other cases profiled in this study, show what a difference communication strategies can make in finding that power.

Table 8.1 shows the conclusions of this study: how human rights rhetoric constructs political will for social change. For each campaign, the elements and absences of information politics are labeled: voice, frame, performance, media, and audience. Then a rough estimate of the campaign's results are indicated: from lack of impact to recognition to solidarity to policy change. Policy change is differentiated as weak (-), moderate, or strong (+). This is a map of the pathways for speaking rights to power.

Acting Globally

As we struggle for care in a world of woe, what do the patterns of the politics of persuasion teach us about how to craft rhetorical appeals for human rights? Victims, advocates, and policy makers in the international human rights regime already know that information politics is important. But we can learn to assess this channel of influence more systematically and use it more effectively, and even activists who are skilled at some dimensions of communication strategy may be less aware of others. Students, journalists, and concerned international publics observing communication campaigns can also benefit from analyzing the rhetorical strategies that may inflate, distort, or underplay the suffering a human rights campaign seeks to address.

These are the communication tasks and associated best practices suggested by this study:

(1) *Focus attention.* First, open the eyes to suffering and the mind to understanding by mapping the prevalence and patterns of violations. Imagery, analogy, and charismatic speakers are the gateways to focus attention, but if they are not followed with credible information, principled claims, and direction toward response, information campaigns will quickly yield to attention fatigue. While it is important to begin with people at risk, we must push past preconceptions about the vulnerability of particular cultures, regime types, and roles—for example, not abandoning a country once it becomes an electoral democracy, since the preconditions and consequences of dictatorship are likely to persist and may easily manifest in new violations. Monitoring must be a continuous and roving process, and newly emerging types of victims and genres of abuse must be actively positioned in public consciousness.

(2) *Diagnose and communicate the political pathology causing violations.* Simple humanitarian depictions of suffering without interpretation may seem to carry more universal appeal, but unstructured empathy without connection is more likely to result in compassion overload or distorted response. Scattered, hidden, or personalized abuse must be revealed as a public and political problem. Poster children must be framed as victims of an abuse of power. What is this a case *of*? An accurate causal account will also help to secure a good fit for venues of appeal, and direct advocates more precisely to seek transferable lessons from cognate experiences. At the same time, it is important that the public projection of the pathology be labeled in the most widely acceptable terms— that is, an abuse of military control by an occupying power will prosper further as "war crimes" rather than "imperialism."

(3) *Identify when and how a problem is "ripe for rhetoric."* Information politics are powerful but not omnipotent, and are more effective at some stages of a problem and world history than others. Communication is less likely to avail at the two extremes of a truly closed society where information is simply unavailable and, conversely, when problems have already been publicized and received significant reform response. In the first case, speaking rights to communication precedes a right to power, and in the latter, more institutional lobbying and leverage of existing channels are more important. Moreover, in a world

of widespread suffering where we must sometimes triage our efforts, rhetorical efforts will be most effective for problems that match or can be pitched to match some aspect of the *zeitgeist*, such as a global wave of democratization, world-wide development crisis, or international cultural awakening like indigenous rights.

(4)   *Inventory your rhetorical resources and opportunities.* Different populations, pathologies, rights claims, and cultures offer different communicative strengths and weaknesses. Does the affected population possess charismatic speakers? If not, which transnational charismatic roles are linked to the situation? Does the pathology of abuse fit well with a locally or globally resonant allegory? Can testimonials be gathered to put a face on structural or hidden abuse? Is there a clear fit with a universal norm—and if not, how can the claim be reframed; for example, violence against women rather than an abusive cultural practice? Where is the physical or virtual public space where appeals can be performed? Do victims, advocates, or policy makers have access to appropriate media, or can new forms of media be utilized? Are there trade-offs between media self-generation and dissemination, and how can media be managed to reach multiple audiences? What are the existing attentive constituencies for this issue, and how can they be expanded? Does the violation potentially affect members of a shared transnational community, echo the historic form of suffering of an unrelated group, or possess emotional resonance with universal primary relationships?

(5)   *The message matters.* Human rights rhetoric must do more than communicate suffering or claim principled protection, though it must begin there. Successful appeals must carry the key elements of humanization, connection, agency, and alternatives. The emotional tone of the message is also critical, as it must promote both pity and hope over fear. Clearly, often a campaign will need to coordinate a series of messages or modalities to cover these distinct facets of the message.

(6)   *Harness communication consciously to the stages and tasks of the campaign.* We have already seen some distinct dynamics of drawing initial attention to an unrecognized problem. Information campaigns must also traverse the following range of tasks, often but not always in sequence, and the communicative elements like voice and framing may work differently for each. First, all movements must shift the social agenda to gain recognition of a public political problem that affects morally worthy members of the community. At this stage, humanization and voice are critical. The problem must then be linked to a causal story, which often invokes a frame. Next, communication must establish a connection between the suffering and the audience, which involves either a community of fate or a relation of responsibility. Imagery and performance tend to be the forefront of this phase or facet. Now, the campaign must make

a principled claim for protection and entitlement. This rights claim is quickly engaged in a dialectic with competing logics such as nationalism and security. Responding to counter-claims is the task most often missed or mishandled by movements. This critical middle stage requires a renewal or shift of charismatic voice, frame matching, and performance of bridging narratives—not simply broader use of media or more evidence for the initial appeal.

(7) *Coordinate the dynamics of each communicative element as the dialogue unfolds.* The communicative arc generally emerges as a unified whole, with designated speakers, frames, performances, media, and audiences. But over time, diverse streams of communication may develop within a campaign, some communicative elements may grow or deteriorate, or the elements may become disconnected. Diversification of streams safeguards against the vagaries of charisma and has the potential to reach multiple audiences, but may sacrifice coherence or introduce contradictory frames. The development of consistent core narratives is probably the most sustainable strategy, which can be voiced by different speakers, performances, and media. It is also helpful if ongoing social movement, scholarly, or journalistic institutions command a "brand" of authenticity that can cue, commend, or curtail the proliferation of speakers, messages, and formats.

(8) *Offer an empowering and appropriate solution.* Human rights campaigns must identify leverage points for response and present an appropriate solution. This means directing information politics beyond general consciousness-raising and forestalling alienation, overload, and psychic numbing by emphasizing the resistance, agency, and incremental accomplishments of both victims and publics. But it also counsels caution in hasty campaigns for controversial responses that may involve unacceptable trade-offs, inappropriate transfer from previous issues, or unpalatable frames. Communication campaigns must avoid confounding debates on controversial means to the end—blunt instruments like boycotts, sanctions, or intervention should only be proposed if they can be painstakingly justified and carefully tailored. Instead, many campaigns will do better to propose starter consensus measures to engage mass publics and policy makers: constructive, incremental, well-framed responses that resonate with audiences—even if they are partial and less satisfying to activists.

(9) *Start from where you are, but keep moving.* Every struggle has a history and location that set parameters for international human rights appeals. Some unfold far from the gaze of global publics or in obscure languages; others involve victims who are former oppressors, or forms of abuse deeply contested as cultural expressions. There are vocabularies of care and justice somewhere in every culture that can be used to frame abuse, and channels of global communication that can be turned to convey suffering in far-flung locations. In

these situations, the role of advocates and transnational allies may shift from transmitters to architects and engineers of information politics. As engineers, global citizens from inside and outside a historical and cultural tradition can build bridges among different cultural dialects of universal human rights, and promote participation in multi-level appeals that socialize both speakers and audiences. As architects, we can build spaces for intercultural dialogue and historical learning in the international human rights regime. One of the most important lessons is to expand the legal roots of human rights accountability to take account of more complex causal patterns and the intergenerational and inter-group repetition of trauma. Start from the history of your struggle, but foster learning and adaptation.

(10) *Construct cosmopolitans.* All of the specific campaigns profiled in this study draw upon a global human rights consciousness, repertoire, and response that have been constructed over generations and must be continually nurtured and renewed. Globalization makes increasing numbers available for global citizenship, but global communication and ideology must construct the political will to act as such in the face of ongoing deprivation, insecurity, and dehumanization. In every generation, advocates for universal human rights must seek allies and audiences in widening circles of identity, from kin to colleague to co-religionist. We must foster bridging ideologies of community that articulate moral universalism, agency, and compassion within the grammars of particular cultures, religions, and political philosophies. Above all, we must continually make the case for human rights as global social imagination under changing conditions; in the words of the Vienna Conference, universal, interdependent, and indivisible. This book has been a part of that project.

Conclusion

Another world is possible, by speaking rights to power. Human rights campaigns pit the power of love against the love of power. And sometimes, words save lives. To become fully human, we must raise our voice.

NOTES

INTRODUCTION

1. The strategic use of communication, distinct from material leverage, to secure social change is variously labeled by different traditions as rhetoric (Aristotle), information politics (Sikkink), communication politics (Castells), symbolic politics (Edelman), political theater (various), and communicative action (Habermas). This book will use the broader label "the politics of persuasion" to encompass the overlapping process addressed by all of these labels. In most situations, "rhetoric," "communication politics," "information politics," and "symbolic politics" may be used interchangeably to describe speaking rights. But "political theater" and "communicative action" point to narrower processes that assume different conditions and dynamics, so their use in this text will be restricted to the subset of situations that meet their criteria.

CHAPTER 3

1. Pioneers operate in informal systems yet relying on networks, taking risks to establish new patterns. Dissidents work within more formal systems but function as individuals outside networks, breaking rules to tame anxiety about social problems. Heroes and champions are found in situations of greater uncertainty; heroes counterpoise charismatic inspiration to formal systems, while champions seek to rationalize their challenge to more informal authority and often serve as advocates.

CHAPTER 4

1. There are three types of FGM. Type 1: clitoridectomy, where part or all of the clitoris is removed. Type 2: excision, which involves complete clitoridectomy and removal of part or all of the labia minora. Type 3: infibulation, the most severe form of FGM where the clitoris and labia minora are removed, and the labia majora are cut and sewn together.

CHAPTER 5

1. The eight books include:
   • Surviving Justice: America's Wrongfully Convicted and Exonerated

- Voices from the Storm: The People of New Orleans on Hurricane Katrina and Its Aftermath
- Underground America: Narratives of Undocumented Lives
- Out of Exile: The Abducted and Displaced People of Sudan
- Hope Deferred: Narratives of Zimbabwean Lives
- Nowhere to be Home: Narratives from Survivors of Burma's Military Regime
- Patriot Acts: Narratives of Post-9/11 Injustice
- Inside This Place, Not of It: Narratives from Women's Prisons

2. Post-Independence India has seen influential protest movements at the local or sectoral level protesting development displacement, labor rights, caste and religious oppression, among others. Political parties have also mobilized massive numbers nationwide. The anticorruption protests were distinctive as the first nationwide, multiclass, non-partisan, systematic challenge to the post-liberalization political model. Although left intellectuals criticized Hazare's movement for lack of structural analysis and grassroots ties, he was ultimately supported by the National Alliance for People's Movements, rooted in environmental and indigenous resisters to the Narmada Dam project.

3. As Sengupta 2012 reports, Indian trade unions of the traditional left, Muslim and Dalit leaders, and left intellectuals were deeply suspicious of Hazare due to his alliance with the Hindu nationalist Chief Minister of Gujarat, Narendra Modi, a leader of the Hindu Nationalist Bharatiya Janata Party (BJP) implicated in 2002 anti-Muslim riots. Hazare had also criticized government affirmative action policies and decried corruption in caste preferences, which many Dalit organizations saw as their sole recourse—although some Dalit individuals supported him, and the Hazare movement was popular with impoverished members of lower-caste groups who did not qualify for government "reservations."

4. Although most of Colbert's civil liberties claims coincide with the Democratic Party platform, he is ostensibly nonpartisan, strongly supports the US military, regularly critiques the Obama Administration's contradictions on rights issues, has approvingly hosted conservative civil libertarians, co-hosted the Rally to Restore Sanity with Jon Stewart that protested both parties, and continues to indict manipulations of media by both Democrats and Republicans (to the point that Democratic leader Nancy Pelosi ordered House Representatives not to appear on his embarrassing "Better Know a District" segment).

CHAPTER 6

1. Interestingly, some governments push Google for greater privacy rights for their citizens rather than seeking surveillance. In April 2010, Canada's privacy commissioner joined with nine OECD counterparts to express concern over Google applications that provide universal personal and residential information about users—in this case, Google Buzz social networking and Google Street View.

2. *Syria*

Hourly live blog of marches, protests, counting deaths, diplomatic statements (http://blogs.aljazeera.net/liveblog/Syria)

Egypt

"Egypt as a new political landscape,"

Mubarak trials, protests, update on the march toward Tahir Square (organized for January 25)

(http://blogs.aljazeera.net/liveblog/Egypt)

Yemen

Unrest in Yemen—antigovernment rallies, refugee crisis, security

(http://blogs.aljazeera.net/liveblog/Yemen)

Bahrain

Shia-led protests for political rights,

antigovernment protests

(http://blogs.aljazeera.net/liveblog/Bahrain)

3. A hashtag is a word or phrase prefaced with the # symbol that allows Twitter and its users to categorize topics that people are "tweeting" about. A tweet with a hashtag will show up on a page with every other tweet that included that hashtag. If a hashtag becomes popular enough it is said to be "trending" on Twitter. Twitter also directs tweets at people by using the @ symbol followed by a username.

CHAPTER 7

1. I am indebted to an Oxford University Press reviewer for directing me to this point.

2. These include the Jewish Voice for Peace, the transnational Brit Tzedek, and the new "J Street."

CHAPTER 8

1. The quote Clinton attributes to Tubman speaks of persistence in struggles for rights by women: "If you are tired, keep going. If you are scared, keep going. If you are hungry, keep going. If you want to taste freedom, keep going."

REFERENCES

ABA (American Bar Association). 2007. "ABA Study: State Death Penalty Systems Deeply Flawed." ABA Press Release. October 29. http://apps.americanbar.org/abanet/media/release/news_release.cfm?releaseid=209.

Academy of Achievement. 2008. "Giving Voice to the World's Voiceless." http://www.achievement.org/autodoc/page/kri0int-1.

Ackerman, Peter, and Jack Duvall. 2000. *A Force More Powerful: A Century of Non Violent Conflict.* New York: Palgrave.

ACLU (American Civil Liberties Union). 2001. "The Case Against the Death Penalty." September 1. http://www.aclu.org/capital-punishment/case-against-death-penalty.

Acuff, Jonathan. 2010. "Social Networking Media and the Revolution That Wasn't: A Realistic Assessment of the Revolutionary Situation in Iran." In *Media, Power, and Politics in the Digital Age: The 2009 Presidential Election Uprising in Iran,* ed. Yahya Kamalipour. Lanham, MD: Rowman & Littlefield Publishers.

ADB (Asian Development Bank). 2003. *Annual ADB Report.* http://www.adb.org/documents/adb-annual-report-2003.

Afshar, Sareh. 2010. "Are We Neda?: The Iranian Women, the Election, and International Media." In *Media, Power, and Politics in the Digital Age: The 2009 Presidential Election Uprising in Iran,* ed. Yahya Kamalipour. Lanham, MD: Rowman & Littlefield Publishers.

Aghapour, Aran. 2010. "Separate But Equal." *Expressions/Impressions.* Spring. Irvine, CA: University of California, Irvine.

Agustin, Laura Maria. 2007. *Sex at the Margins: Migration, Labour Markets and the Rescue Industry.* New York: Zed Books.

Akerlof, George, and Richard Schiller. 2009. *Animal Spirits: How Human Psychology Drives the Economy, and Why It Matters for Global Capitalism.* Princeton, NJ: Princeton University Press.

Alex-Assensoh, Yvette M., and Lawrence J. Hanks, eds. 2000. *Black and Multiracial Politics in America.* New York: New York University Press.

Alfredson, Lisa S. 2009. *Creating Human Rights: How Noncitizens Made Sex Persecution Matter to the World.* Philadelphia: Pennsylvania University Press.

Alinsky, Saul David. 1969. *Reveille for Radicals.* New York: Vintage Books.

Al-Marri v. Spagone. 555 U.S. 1220 (2009).

Al-Roomi, Samar. 2007. "Women, Blogs, and Political Power". In *New Media and the New Middle East,* ed. Phillip Seib. New York: Palgrave Macmillan

Alyokhina, Maria, Nadezhda Tolokonnikova, and Yekaterina Samutsevich. 2012. "Pussy Riot Closing Statements." *N+1 Magazine.* http://nplusonemag.com/pussy-riot-closing-statements.

American Program Bureau. n.d. "Nicholas Kristof." http://www.apbspeakers.com/speaker/nicholas-kristof.

Amnesty International. 2007. *Annual Report.* http://report2007.amnesty.org/.

Amnesty International 2011a, *Annual Report.* http://www.amnesty.org/en/annual-report/2011

Amnesty International USA. 2011b. "Masses Converge in Atlanta to March for Troy Davis as Call for Clemency Strengthens." http://www.amnestyusa.org/news/press-releases/masses-converge-in-atlanta-to-march-for-troy-davis-as-call-for-clemency-strengthens.

Amnesty International. n.d. "Abolish the Death Penalty." http://www.amnestyusa.org/our-work/campaigns/abolish-the-death-penalty.

"Amnesty International: Many Rights, Some Wrong." 2007. *The Economist*, March 24.

Anaya Munoz, Alejandro. 2011. "Explaining High Levels of Transnational Pressure over Mexico: The Case of the Disappearances and Killings of Women in Ciudad Juárez." *International Journal of Human Rights* 15(3): 339–358.

"ANCA Criticizes Turkey for Blocking U.N. Exhibit on the Rwanda Genocide." 2007. *Armenian National Committee of America.* http://www.anca.org/press_releases/press_releases_print.php?prid=1127.

"ANC of Florida Joins Launch of Genocide." 2009. *Armenian National Committee of America | Home.* March 25. http://www.anca.org/press_releases/press_releases.php?prid=1680.

Anderson, Benedict. 1991. *Imagined Communities: Reflections on the Origin and Spread of Nationalism.* London: Verso.

Anderson, John. 2009. "Monks, Tanks and Videotape." *New York Times*, May 17.

An-Naim, Abdullahi Ahmed, ed. 1992. *Human Rights in Cross-Cultural Perspectives: A Quest for Consensus.* Philadelphia: University of Pennsylvania Press.

Ansfield, Jonathan. 2010a. "Amendment Tightens Law on State Secrets in China." *New York Times*, April 30.

Ansfield, Jonathan. 2010b. "China Starts New Bureau to Curb Web." *New York Times*, April 17.

"Anti-Semitism at UC Irvine." 2012. http://www.adl.org/israel-international/anti-israel-activity/c/anti-semitism-at-uc-irvine.html#.UT_RctHwKah

Anti-Slavery International. http://www.antislavery.org.

Appiah, Kwame Anthony. 2005. *The Ethics of Identity.* Princeton, NJ: Princeton University Press.

Appiah, Kwame Anthony. 2006. *Cosmopolitanism: Ethics in a World of Strangers.* New York: W. W. Norton.

Appiah, Kwame Anthony. 2010. *The Honor Code: How Moral Revolutions Happen.* New York: W. W. Norton.

Arendt, Hannah. 1958. *The Human Condition.* Chicago: University of Chicago Press.

Arendt, Hannah. 1963. *Eichmann in Jerusalem: A Repot on the Banality of Evil.* New York: Viking Press.

Arendt, Hannah. 1972. *Crises of the Republic: Lying in Politics, Civil Disobedience on Violence, Thoughts on Politics, and Revolution.* New York: Harcourt Brace Jovanovich.

Armenian Assembly of America. 2011. April 18. http://www.aaainc.org/index.php?id=2.

Armony, Lisa. 2010. "Israeli Apartheid Week at UC Irvine Brings Conflict to Fore." http://www.jewishjournal.com/community/article/israeli_apartheid_week_at_uc_irvine_brings_conflict_to_fore_20100511

Arthur, Paul. 2008. Interview by Daniel Wehrenfennig. November 16. Irvine, CA.

Ashley, David. 1982. "Jürgen Habermas and the Rationalization of Communicative Interaction." *Symbolic Interaction* 5(1): 79–96.

Associated Press. 2010. "3 Jailed for Online Posts." In New York Times. April 17. http://query.nytimes.com/gst/fullpage.html?res=9F06EFDC133AF934A25757C0A9669D8B63

Astrasheuskaya, Nastassia. 2012. "Russian Election Satire Takes Putin's Manhood Away." *Reuters.* March 2.

The Atlantic Online. 1999. "Humane Development: An Interview with Amartya Sen." December 15. http://www.theatlantic.com/past/docs/unbound/interviews/ba991215.htm.

Atran, Scott. 2010. *Talking to the Enemy: Faith, Brotherhood, and The (un)making of Terrorists.* New York: Harper Collins.

Attorney General. 2006. "Attorney General's Annual Report to Congress on US Government Activities to Combat Trafficking in Persons, Fiscal Year 2005." http://www.usdoj.gov/ag/annualreports/tr2005/agreporthumantrafficing2005.pdf.

Attorney General. 2008. "Attorney General's Annual Report to Congress and Assessment of the U.S. Government Activities to Combat Trafficking in Persons, Fiscal Year 2007." http://www.usdoj.gov/ag/annualreports/tr2007/agreporthuman-trafficing2007.pdf.

Aung San Suu Kyi. 1991. *Freedom from Fear and Other Writings.* Edited with an introduction by Michael Aris. Foreword by Vaclav Havel. New York: Penguin.

Axelrod, R. 1984. *The Evolution of Cooperation.* New York: Basic Books.

Baer, M., and A. Brysk. 2009. "New Rights for Private Wrongs: Female Genital Mutilation and Global Framing Dialogues." In *The International Struggle for New Human Rights,* ed. C. Bob. Philadelphia: University of Pennsylvania Press.

Bales, Kevin. 2004. *Disposable People: New Slavery in the Global Economy.* Berkeley: University of California Press.

Barry, Ellen. 2011. "On TV, Putin is Dismissive of Critics Far and Near." *New York Times.* December 15.

Bauman, Richard. 1992. *Folklore, Cultural Performances, and Popular Entertainments.* New York: Oxford University Press.

Baxell, Richard. 2004. *British Volunteers in the Spanish Civil War: The British Battalion in the International Brigades, 1936–1939.* London: Routledge.

BBC. 2001. "DR Congo's Troubled History." *BBC News—Home.* January 16. http://news.bbc.co.uk/2/hi/africa/1120825.stm.

BBC. 2003. "DR Congo Pygmies Appeal to U.N." *BBC News- Home.* May 23. http://news.bbc.co.uk/2/hi/africa/2933524.stm

Beevor, Anthony. 2006. *The Battle for Spain*. Boston: Penguin.

Beitz, Charles. 2009. *The Idea of Human Rights*. New York: Oxford University Press.

Bell, Daniel A., and Jean-Marc Coicaud. 2007. *Ethics in Action: The Ethical Challenges of International Human Rights Non-Governmental Organizations.* New York: Cambridge University Press.

Benhabib, Seyla. 1996. *The Reluctant Modernism of Hannah Arendt.* Thousand Oaks, CA: Sage.

Benkler, Y. 2006. *The Wealth of Networks: How Social Production Transforms Markets and Freedom.* New Haven, CT: Yale University Press.

Bennetts, Michael. 2012. "In Putin's Russia, Little Separation between Church and State." *Washington Times.* Aug 13. http://www.washingtontimes.com/news/2012/ aug/13/putin-russia-little-separation-church-state/?page=all.

Bergner, Daniel. 2010. "Attention-Grabber for Sudan's Cause." *New York Times.* December 2. http://www.nytimes.com/2010/12/05/magazine/05sudan-t. html?pagewanted=all.

Beverly, John, and Marc Zimmerman. 1990. *Literature and Politics in the Central American Revolutions.* Austin: University of Texas Press.

Bob, Clifford. 2001. "Globalization and the Social Construction of Human Rights Campaigns." In *Globalization and Human Rights*, ed. Alison Brysk. Berkeley: University of California Press.

Bobbio, Norberto. 1996. *The Age of Rights/Norberto Bobbio.* Translated by Allan Cameron. Cambridge, UK: Polity Press; Blackwell Publishers.

Boehmer, Elleke. 2010. *Nelson Mandela: A Brief Insight.* New York: Sterling.

Boli, J., and G. M. Thomas. 1999. *Constructing World Culture: International Non-Governmental Organizations since 1875.* Stanford, CA: Stanford University Press.

Boltanski, L. 1999. *Distant Suffering: Morality, Media, and Politics.* New York: Cambridge University Press.

Booker, Salih, and Ann-Louise Colgan. 2011. "Genocide in Darfur." *The Nation.* January 18. http://www.thenation.com/article/genocide-darfur.

Boulware-Miller, Kay. 1985. "Female Circumcision: Challenges to the Practice as a Human. Rights Violation." *Harvard Women's Law Journal* 8: 155–177.

Bouckaert, Peter. Remarks at UC Santa Barbara, November 5, 2011; April 27, 2012.

Bourdieu, Pierre. 1989. "Social Space and Symbolic Power." *Sociological Theory* 7(1): 14–25.

Boyle, Elizabeth Heger. 2002. *Female Genital Cutting: Cultural Conflict in the Global Community.* Baltimore: Johns Hopkins University Press.

Brinkley, Joel. 2006. "Modern-Day Abolitionist Battles Slavery Worldwide." *New York Times*, February 4.

Brittain, James. 2006. "Censorship, Hegemony and the Media in Colombia." *Colombia Journal,* November 27.

Brome, Vincent. 1966. *The International Brigades: Spain, 1936–1939.* New York: Morrow.

Brookings Institute. 2006. "The Gender Perspective: What Difference Does It Make?" http://www.brookings.edu/events/2006/1011poverty.aspx.

Brysk, Alison. 1994a. *The Politics of Human Rights in Argentina: Protest, Change, and Democratization.* Stanford, CA: Stanford University Press.

Brysk, Alison. 1994b. "The Politics of Measurement: Counting the Disappeared in Argentina." *Human Rights Quarterly* 16(4): 676–692.

Brysk, Alison. 1995. "Hearts and Minds: Bringing Symbolic Politics Back in." *Polity*, 27(4): 559–585.

Brysk, Alison. 2000. *From Tribal Village to Global Village: Indian Rights and International Relations in Latin America.* Stanford, CA: Stanford University Press.

Brysk, Alison, ed. 2001. *Globalization and Human Rights.* Berkeley: University of California Press.

Brysk, Alison. 2005. *Human Rights and Private Wrongs: Constructing Global Civil Society.* New York: Routledge.

Brysk, Alison. 2007. "Making Values Make Sense: The Social Construction of Human Rights Foreign Policy." *Journal for Human Rights* [Zeitschrift für Menschenrechte], Volume 2 69–80.

Brysk, Alison. 2008. "Democratic Reform and Injustice in Latin America." *Whitehead Journal of Diplomacy.* Winter/Spring. 55–70.

Brysk, Alison. 2009. *Global Good Samaritans: Human Rights as Foreign Policy.* Oxford: Oxford University Press.

Brysk, Alison, and Austin Choi-Fitzpatrick, eds. 2012. *From Human Trafficking to Human Rights: Reframing Contemporary Slavery.* Philadelphia: University of Pennsylvania Press.

Brysk, Alison, and Claude Denis. 2010. "Norm Entrepreneurs and Human Rights Promotion." *International Studies Association*, New Orleans, February 17.

Brysk, Alison, and Aditee Maskey. 2012. "Reframing Trafficking: Power, Profit, and Prostitution in India." *Global Dialogues 14* (2):

Brysk, Alison, and Gershon Shafir, eds. 2004. *People Out of Place: Globalization and the Citizenship Gap.* New York: Routledge Press.

Brysk, Alison, and Gershon Shafir, eds. 2007. *Human Rights and National Insecurity: Democracies Debate Counter-Terrorism.* Berkeley, CA: University of California Press.

Brysk, Alison, and Daniel Wehrenfennig. 2010. "My Brother's Keeper? Inter-Ethnic Solidarity and Human Rights." *Studies in Ethnicity and Nationalism*, Spring. 1-18.

Budabin, Alexandra. 2012. *Citizen's Army for Darfur.* Dissertation. New York: New School for Social Research.

Bunch, Charlotte. 1995. "Transforming Human Rights from a Feminist Perspective." In *Women's Rights Human Rights: International Feminist Perspectives*, ed. Julie Peters and Andrea Wolper. New York: Routledge.

Burgerman, Susan. 2001. *Moral Victories: How Activists Provoke Multilateral Action.* Ithaca: Cornell University Press.

Burnett, Victoria. 2009. "Families Search for the Truth of Spain's 'Lost Children'". *New York Times.* February 28. http://www.nytimes.com/2009/03/01/world/europe/01franco.html?_r=0

Burns, Michael. 1999. *France and the Dreyfus Affair: A Documentary History.* Boston: Bedford/St. Martin's.

Burwell, Catherine, and Megan Boler. 2008. "Calling on the Colbert Nation: Fandom, Politics and Parody in an Age of Media Convergence." *Electronic Journal of Communication* 18: 2. http://www.cios.org/www/ejc/EJCPUBLIC/018/2/01845. html

Cain, Kenneth L. 1999. "The Rape of Dinah: Human Rights, Civil War in Liberia, and Evil Triumphant." *Human Rights Quarterly* 21(2): 265–307.

"CAIR-CA: U.S. Muslims Find 'Steady Allies' in Japanese American Community." 2008. http://sun.cair.com/ArticleDetails.aspx?ArticleID=24772&currPage=1.

Cardenas, Sonia. 2007. *Conflict and Compliance: State Responses to International Human Rights Pressure*. Philadelphia: University of Pennsylvania Press.

Carpenter, R. Charli. 2006. *Innocent Women and Children: Gender, Norms and the Protection of Civilians*. Burlington, VT: Ashgate.

Carroll, William K., and R. S. Ratner. 1994. "Between Leninism and Radical Pluralism: Gramscian Reflections on Counter-Hegemony and the New Social Movements." *Critical Sociology* 20: 3–26.

"The Case of Juan Garza." n.d. http://www.capitalpunishmentincontext.org/cases/garza/ posttrial.

Castells, Manuel. 2000. *The Rise of the Network Society*. Malden, MA: Blackwell Publishers.

Castells, Manuel. 2009. *Communication Power*. New York: Oxford University Press.

"Celebrities Promote Humanitarian Causes | Congo Planet." 2009. *Congo Planet— News, Music, Videos, Pictures from the Congo*. April 20. http://www.congoplanet. com/article.jsp?id=45261418.

"Celebrities Raise Hope for Congo." 2009. *Celebrity Charity News, Events, Organizations & Causes*. July 10. http://www.looktothestars.org/ news/2789-celebrities-raise-hope-for-congo.

Charlesworth, Hillary. 1994. "What are Women's International Human Rights?" In *Human Rights of Women: National and International Perspectives*, ed. Rebecca J. Cook. Philadelphia: University of Pennsylvania Press.

Chase, Michael, and James Mulvenon. 2002. "You've Got Dissent! Chinese Dissident Use of the Internet and Beijing's Counter-Strategies." RAND.

Chung, L. A. 2003. "Speaking Out on Liberties since 9/11/01." *San Jose Mercury News*, February 21.

Coalition Against Trafficking in Women. http://www.catwinternational.org/.

Cohen, Noam. 2009. "Twitter on the Barricades: Six Lessons Learned." *New York Times*, June 21.

Collins, R. 2001. "Social Movements and the Focus of Emotional Attention." In *Passionate Politics: Emotions and Social Movements*, ed. J. Goodwin, J. Jasper, and F. Polletta. Chicago: Chicago University Press.

Columnist Biography: Nicholas D. Kristof. n.d. *New York Times*. http://www.nytimes. com/ref/opinion/KRISTOF-BIO.html.

"Congo-Kinshasa: FDLR Threat Continues in Kivus." 2009. *ReliefWeb*. July 23. http:// www.reliefweb.int/rw/rwb.nsf/db900SID/VDUX-7U8JPB?OpenDocument.

Cook, Judith. 1979. *Apprentices of Freedom*. London: Quartet.

Cooper, Andrew F. 2008. *Celebrity Diplomacy*. Boulder, CO: Paradigm Publishers.

Cooper, Stephen D. 2006. *Watching the Watchdog: Bloggers as the Fifth Estate*. Spokane, WA: Marquette Books.

Corradi, Juan E. 1987 "The Culture of Fear in Civil Society." In *From Military Rule to Liberal Democracy in Argentina*, ed. M. Peralta-Ramos and Carlos H. Waisman. Boulder, CO: Westview Press.

Coscarelli, Joe. 2012. "Why Kony 2012 Went Viral." *New York Magazine*. March. http://nymag.com/daily/intelligencer/2012/03/why-kony-2012-went-viral.html

Criminal Justice Project. 2012. *Death Row USA*. NAACP Legal Defense and Educational Fund, Inc. http://www.deathpenaltyinfo.org/death-row-usa.

Cronin-Furman, Kate and Amanda Taub. 2012. "The Exclusive Club of Moral Authority: From Nick Kristof to Kony 2012." http://www.theatlantic.com/international/archive/2012/04/the-exclusive-club-of-moral-authority-from-nick-kristof-to-kony-2012/256287/

Curtin, Michael. 2003. "Media Capital: Towards the Study of Spatial Flows." *International Journal of Cultural Studies* 6(2): 202–226.

DeConde, Alexander. 1992. *Ethnicity, Race, and American Foreign Policy: A History*. Boston: Northeast University Press.

"Democracy Tax is Rising." 2008. *The Economist*. December 11. http://www.economist.com/node/12749771.

"Democratic Republic of the Congo—Children and Armed Conflict." 2012. *UN— Children and Armed Conflict*. January 23. http://childrenandarmedconflict.un.org/countries/democratic-republic-of-the-congo/

Denbar, Rachel. 2012. "We Were There: Pussy Riot Verdict." *Human Rights Watch*. http://www.hrw.org/node/109629.

Derflier, Leslie. 2002. *The Dreyfus Affair*. Westport, CT: Greenwood Press.

DeVoe, D. n.d. "Saying 'No' to 'The Cut' in Kenya." http://crs.org/kenya/alternative-rite-of-passage/.

Donnelly, J. 1998. "Human Rights: A New Standard of Civilization?" *International Affairs* 74(1): 1–24.

Donnelly, Jack. 2006. "Human Rights." In *Oxford Handbook of Political Theory*, eds. Dryzek, John S., Bonnie Honig, and Anne Phillips. New York: Oxford University Press.

Donnelly, Jack. 2007. *International Human Rights*. Boulder, CO: Westview.

Dorkenoo, Efua. 1995. *Cutting the Rose: Female Genital Mutilation: The Practice and Its Prevention*. London: Minority Rights Publications.

Doyle, Mark. 2009. "DR Congo Outsources Its Military." *BBC News—Home*. February 27. http://news.bbc.co.uk/2/hi/africa/7910081.stm.

"DRC: MONUC Sticks to Its Guns—Analysis." 2009. *IRIN • Humanitarian News and Analysis from Africa, Asia and the Middle East—Updated Daily*. June 22. http://www.irinnews.org/Report.aspx?ReportId=84943.

"DR Congo: Conflict History." 2011. *AfricaFiles*. January 23. http://www.africafiles.org/article.asp?ID=23163.

"DR Congo Launches 'Amani Leo' Military Operation | Congo Planet." 2010. *Congo Planet—News, Music, Videos, Pictures from the Congo*. January 2. http://www.

congoplanet.com/news/1577/dr-congo-launches-amani-leo-military-operation-monuc-kimia-fdlr-fardc.jsp.

"DR Congo: Top UN Humanitarian Official Condemns New 'Terror and Upheaval.'" 2009. *Welcome to the United Nations: It's Your World.* April 30. http://www.un.org/apps/news/story.asp?NewsID=30649&Cr=monuc&Cr1=.

Dunne, Tim, and Marianne Hanson. 2009. "Human Rights in International Relations" In *Human Rights: Politics and Practice*, ed. Mark Goodhart. New York: Oxford University Press.

Dutton, William H. 2009. "The Fifth Estate Emerging through the Network of Networks." *Prometheus 27/1* (March): 1–15.

Edelman, M. 1977. *Political Language: Words That Succeed and Policies That Fail.* New York: Academic Press.

Edkins, Jenny. 2003. *Trauma and the Memory of Politics.* Cambridge: Cambridge University Press.

Eisenstadt, S. N., ed. 1968. *Max Weber: On Charisma and Institution-Building.* Chicago: University of Chicago Press.

El Koshary Today. 2011. "Egypt's National Security Agency Helps Former Torturers Find 'Inner-Child'." July 4. http://elkoshary.com/features/egypts-national-security-agency-helps-former-torturers-find-inner-child.

Ellis, Stephen. 2009. *Movers and Shakers Social Movements in Africa.* Leiden: Brill.

Engle Merry, Sally. 2006. "Transnational Human Rights and Local Activism: Mapping the Middle." *American Anthropologist* 108(1): 38–51.

Entman, Robert. 1993. "Framing: Toward Clarification of a Fractured Paradigm." *Journal of Communication* 43(4): 51–58.

Epstein, Helen. 2011. "Talking Their Way Out of a Population Crisis." *New York Times*, October 22. http://www.nytimes.com/2011/10/23/opinion/sunday/talking-their-way-out-of-a-population-crisis.html?pagewanted=all.

Escarey, Ashley. 2006. *"Caught between State and Society: The Commercial News Media in China."* Ph.D. thesis. Columbia University.

Esman, Milton. 1994. *Ethnic Politics.* Ithaca, NY: Cornell University Press.

Exposing CEDAW, 110th Cong. 2008 (testimony of Janice Shaw Crouse).

"The Facebook Freedom Fighter." 2011. *Newsweek Magazine.* June 13. http://www.thedailybeast.com/newsweek/2011/02/13/the-facebook-freedom-fighter.html.

Farmer, Paul. 2005. *Pathologies of Power.* Berkeley: University of California Press.

Fassihi, Farnaz. 2009a. "Fighting a Regime He Helped Create." *Wall Street Journal.* December 3. http://online.wsj.com/article/SB125980542530173987.html?mod=article-outset-box.

Fassihi, Farnaz. 2009b. "Iranian Crackdown Goes Global." *Wall Street Journal.* December 3. http://online.wsj.com/article/SB125978649644673331.html.

"Fast for Justice Press Conference Draws Attention to Global Cycle of Genocide." 2011. *United Human Rights Council.* April 18. http://www.unitedhuman-rights.org/2007/01/%E2%80%98fast-for-justice%E2%80%99-press-con-ference-draws-attention-to-global-cycle-of-genocide.

Fathi, Nazila. 2009. "Chanting Iranian Militiamen Try to Cow Opposition Figure." *New York Times*, November 27.

Faul, Michelle. 2010. "A Second Rwanda Genocide Is Revealed in Congo." *Breaking News, Weather, Business, Health, Entertainment, Sports, Politics, Travel, Science, Technology, Local, US & World News—Msnbc.com*. http://www.msnbc.msn.com/id/39603000/ns/world_news-africa/.

"Female Genital Mutilation" n.d. *Medécins Sans Frontières*. http://www.msf.org.au/resources/special-features/womens-health/obstetrics/other-obstetrics-issues.html

FCLCA (Friends Committee on Legislation in California). 2012. "History of Abolitionism." http://www.fclca.org/legislative-issues/death-penalty.html.

"FDLR Arming for War with Congolese Children." 2010. *Rwanda News Agency*. December 20. http://www.rnanews.com/regional/4580-fdlr-arming-for-war-with-congolese-children-

Kittay, Eva Feder, and Ellen K. Feder. 2002. eds. *The subject of care: feminist perspectives on dependency*. Lanham, Md: Rowman & Littlefield Publishers.

Fei Shin, et al. 2009. "Online Network Size, Efficacy and Opinion Expression." *International Journal of Public Opinion Research 21*(4): 00-00.

Felice, William. 2003. *The Global New Deal: Economic and Social Rights in World Politics*. Landham, MD: Rowman and Littlefield.

Felman, Shoshana. 2001. "Theaters of Justice: Arendt in Jersualem, the Eichmann Trial, and the Redefinition of Legal Meaning in the Wake of the Holocaust." *Theoretical Inquiries in Law. 1* (2): 1–43.

Finnemore, Martha, and Sikkink, Kathryn. 1998. "International Norm Dynamics and Political Change." *International Organization* 52(4): 887–917.

Fisher, Ali. 2010. "Bullets with Butterfly Wings: Tweets, Protest Networks, and the Iranian Election." In *Media, Power, and Politics in the Digital Age: The 2009 Presidential Election Uprising in Iran*, ed. Yahya Kamalipour. Lanham, MD: Rowman & Littlefield Publishers.

Fletcher, Angus. 1964. *Allegory, the Theory of a Symbolic Mode*. Ithaca, NY: Cornell University Press.

Flyvbjerg, Bent. 1998. "Habermas and Foucault: Thinkers for Civil Society?" *British Journal of Sociology* 49: 2.

Forsythe, David. 2005. *Human Rights in World Politics*. New York: Cambridge University Press.

Forsythe, David. 2007. "The United States: Protecting Human Dignity in an Era of Insecurity." In *National Insecurity and Human Rights: Democracies in Debate Counterterrorism*, ed. Alison Brysk and Gershon Shafir. Berkeley: University of California Press.

Fox, Nick J. 1998. "Foucault, Foucauldians and Sociology." *British Journal of Sociology*. 49(3): 415–433.

Franklin, James C. 2008. "Shame on You: The Impact of Human Rights Criticism on Political Repression in Latin America." *International Studies Quarterly* 5(1): 187–212.

Frisco, Michelle L., and Kristi Williams. 2003. "Perceived Housework Equity, Marital Happiness, and Divorce in Dual-Earner Households." *Journal of Family Issues.* (24): 51–73.

GAATW (Global Alliance Against Traffic in Women), Anti-Slavery International, La Strada International, Buhay Foundation, Philippines, LSCW, Cambodia and Sodireitos, Brazil. 2009. "Statement on a Monitoring Mechanism for the United Nations Convention Against Transnational Organized Crime and Each of the Protocols Thereto with Specific Attention to the Protocol to Prevent, Suppress and Punish Trafficking in Persons (the Human Trafficking Protocol)." October 13. www.gaatw.org/statements/Statement_on_a_Monitoring_Mechanism-COPS08.pdf.

Galchinsky, Michael. 2008. *Jews and Human Rights: Dancing at Three Weddings.* Lanham, MD: Rowman and Littlefield.

Gamson, William. 1995. "Constructing Social Protest." In *Social Movements and Culture*, ed. Hank Johnston and Bert Klandermans. Minneapolis: University of Minnesota Press.

Ganguly, Swagato. 2011. "It's the Middle Class, Stupid." *Times of India.* August 19. http://articles.timesofindia.indiatimes.com/2011-08-19/edit-page/29901076_1_middle-class-anna-hazare-protests.

Garay, Luis Jorge. 2003. "Colombia's Political Economy." *ReVista: Harvard Review of Latin America*, Spring. http://www.drclas.harvard.edu/publications/revistaonline/spring-2003/colombias-political-economy

Garber, Megan. 2012. "How Kony 2012's Big Event Fizzled Out." *The Atlantic.* April 24. http://www.theatlantic.com/technology/archive/2012/04/how-kony-2012s-big-event-fizzled-out/256261/

Garsten, Bryan. 2006. *Saving Persuasion.* Cambridge, MA: Harvard University Press.

Gbowee, Leymah. 2011a. *Mighty Be Our Powers.* Philadelphia: Beast Books.

Gbowee, Leymah. 2011b. "Mighty Be Our Powers." University of California Santa Barbara Arts & Lectures. October 2.

Geertz, Clifford. 1983. *Local Knowledge: Further Essays in Interpretive Anthropology.* New York: Basic Books.

Gheytanchi, Elham. 2010. "Symbols, Signs, and Slogans of the Demonstrations in Iran." In *Media, Power, and Politics in the Digital Age: The 2009 Presidential Election Uprising in Iran*, ed. Yahya Kamalipour. Lanham, MD: Rowman & Littlefield Publishers.

Ghonim, Wael. 2012. *Revolution 2.0.* Boston: Houghton Mifflin Harcourt.

Ghosh, Palash R. 2012. "Hamas' Condemnation of Palestinian Visit to Auschwitz Underscores Holocaust Denial in Arab World. *International Business Times.* August 2. http://www.ibtimes.com/hamas-condemnation-palestinian-visit-auschwitz-underscores-holocaust-denial-arab-world-737331

Giddens, Anthony. 1979. *Central Problems in Social Theory.* Berkeley: University of California Press.

Gitlin, Todd. 2003. *The Whole World is Watching: Media in the Making and Unmaking of the New Left.* Berkeley: University of California Press.

Giugni, Marco, and Frederic Passy. 2000. *Political Altruism?: Solidarity Movements in International Perspective.* Lanham, MD: Rowman & Littlefield.

Gladstone, Brooke. 2011. "Egypt Finds Its Own 'Jon Stewart.'" *National Public Radio.* April 15.

Goodale, Mark, ed. 2012. *Human Rights at the Crossroads.* New York: Oxford University Press.

Goodhart, Michael, ed. 2009. *Human Rights: Politics and Practice.* New York: Oxford University Press.

Goodhart, Michael. 2012. "Human Rights and the Politics of Contestation." In *Human Rights at the Crossroads.* ed. Mark Goodale. New York: Oxford University Press.

Goodman, David J., and Jennifer Preston. 2012. "How the Kony Video Went Viral." *The New York Times*, March 9. http://www.anunconventionalwar.com/uploads/How_Kony_Video_Went_Viral.pdf.

Goodman, Peter S. 2011. "China Invests Heavily in Sudan's Oil Industry." *Washington Post—Politics, National, World & D.C. Area News and Headlines—Washingtonpost.com.* January 23. http://www.washingtonpost.com/wp-dyn/articles/A21143-2004Dec22.html.

Goodwin, J., J. Jasper, and F. Polletta, eds. 2001. *Passionate Politics: Emotions and Social Movements.* Chicago: Chicago University Press.

Gottschall, Jonathan. 2012. *The Storytelling Animal: How Stories Make Us Human.* New York: Houghton Mifflin Harcourt.

Gourevitch, Philip. 1999. *We Wish to Inform You That Tomorrow We will be Killed with our Families.* London: Picador Press.

Griffin, Dustin. 1994. *Satire: A Critical Reintroduction.* Lexington: University Press of Kentucky.

Gunn, Giles. 2001. *Beyond Solidarity: Pragmatism and Difference in a Globalized World.* Chicago: University of Chicago Press

Haas, Peter. 1989. "Do Regimes Matter? Epistemic Communities and Mediterranean Pollution Control." *International Organization* 43(3): 377–403.

Habermas, Jürgen. 1984. *The Theory of Communicative Action.* Translated by T. McCarthy. Boston: Beacon Press.

Habermas, Jürgen. 1990. *Moral Consciousness and Communicative Action.* Translated by Christian Lenhardt and Shierry Weber Nicholsen. Cambridge, UK: Polity Press.

Habermas, Jürgen. 1996. *Between Facts and Norms: Contributions to a Discourse Theory of Law and Democracy.* Cambridge, MA: MIT Press.

Haidt, Jonathan. 2012. *The Righteous Mind: Why Good People are Divided by Politics and Religion.* New York: Pantheon Books.

Hammer, Joshua. 2011. "A Free Woman: Can Aung San Suu Kyi Unite a Badly Weakened Opposition?" *The New Yorker*, January 24. http://www.newyorker.com/reporting/2011/01/24/110124fa_fact_hammer.

Hanks, William F. 1987. "Discourse Genres in a Theory of Practice." *American Ethnologist.* 14 (4): 668-692.

Hare, A. Paul, and Herbert H. Blumberg. 1988. *Dramaturgical analysis of social interaction.* New York: Praeger.

Harris, Ben. 2007. "ADL Recognizes Armenian Genocide." *JTA: The Global News Service of the Jewish People*, August 21. http://jta.org/news/article/2007/08/21/103755/adlgenocide.

Harris, David. 1999. "From 'Warlord' to 'Democratic' President: How Charles Taylor Won the 1997 Liberian Elections." *Journal of Modern African Studies* 37(3). 431–455.

Harris, Ruth. 2010. *Dreyfus: politics, emotion, and the scandal of the century.* New York: Metropolitan Books.

Hasday, Judy. 2007. *Aung San Suu Kyi: Activist for Democracy in Myanmar.* New York: Chelsea House.

Havel, Vaclav, and John Keane. 1985. *The Power of the Powerless: Citizens Against the State in Central-Eastern Europe.* London: Hutchinson.

Held, Virginia. 2006. *The Ethics of Care: Personal, Political, and Global.* New York: Oxford University Press.

Higgens, Michael. 2011. "Police Beating of 'Girl in the Blue Bra' Becomes New Rallying Call for Egyptians." *National Post*, December 20. http://news.nationalpost.com/2011/12/20/beating-of-blue-bra-woman-reignites-egyptian-protests/.

Hoffman, Robert Louis. 1980. *More than a Trial: The Struggle over Captain Dreyfus.* New York: Free Press.

Hollinger, David A. 2006. *Cosmopolitanism and Solidarity: Studies in Ethnoracial, Religious, and Professional Affiliation in the United States.* Madison: University of Wisconsin Press.

Hopgood, Stephen. 2006. *Keepers of the flame: understanding Amnesty International.* Ithaca, N.Y.: Cornell University Press.

Horowitz, Donald. 1985. *Ethnic Groups in Conflict.* Berkeley: University of California Press.

Hosken, Fran. 1982. *The Hosken Report: Genital and Sexual Mutilation of Females.* Lexington, MA: Women's International Network News.

Howard, Phillip N., Aiden Duffy, Deen Freelon, Muzammil Hussain, Will Mari and Marwa Mazaid. 2011. "Opening Closed Regimes: What was the Role of Social media During the Arab Spring?". Working Paper. Project on Information Technology and Political Islam, University of Washington Available online: http://pitpi.org/wp-content/uploads/2013/02/2011_Howard-Duffy-Freelon-Hussain-Mari-Mazaid_pITPI.pdf

Human Rights Commission Report. 2009. http://tb.ohchr.org/default.aspx?ConvType=12&docType=36. (ch. 5)

Human Rights Watch 2006a. *Mexico: The Second Assault. Obstructing Access to Legal Abortion after Rape in Mexico.* New York: Human Rights Watch.

Human Rights Watch. 2006b. "Swept under the Rug: Abuses against Domestic Workers Worldwide." July 28. http://www.hrw.org/en/reports/2006/07/27/swept-under-rug.

Human Rights Watch. 2008. *My Rights, and My Right to Know: Lack of Access to Therapeutic Abortion in Peru.* New York: Human Rights Watch.

Human Rights Watch. 2012. "US/Texas: Halt Execution of Man with Intellectual Disabilities." August 7. http://www.hrw.org/news/2012/08/07/ustexas-halt-execution-man-intellectual-disabilities.

Hunt, Lynn. 2007. *Inventing human rights: a history.* New York: W.W. Norton & Co.

Huyssen, Andreas. 1980. "The Politics of Identification: "Holocaust" and West German Drama". *New German Critique.* (19): 117–136.

"ICC Charges Bashir with Genocide—Africa—Al Jazeera English." 2010. *AJE—Al Jazeera English.* July 12. http://english.aljazeera.net/news/africa/2010/07/2010712141336556321.html.

Innocenti Research Centre/UNICEF. 2010. *The Dynamics of Social Change: Towards the Elimination of Female Genital Mutilation/Cutting in Five African Countries.* UNICEF.

Inter-American Court of Human Rights. 2001. Report 52/01. Case 12.243. *Juan Raul Garza v. United States.* April 4. http://cidh.org/annualrep/2000eng/ChapterIII/Merits/USA12.243.htm.

International Commission on Intervention and State Sovereignty. 2001. *The Responsibility to Protect.* United Nations. http://www.cfr.org/international-peace-and-security/international-commission-intervention-state-sovereignty-responsibility-protect-report/p24228

International Council on Human Rights Policy. 2009. *Corruption and Human Rights: Making the Connection.* Versoix, Switzerland: International Council on Human Rights Policy.

International Criminal Court (ICC). 2010. *Callixte Mbarushimana Arrested in France for Crimes against Humanity and War Crimes Allegedly Committed in the Kivus (Democratic Republic of the Congo). International Criminal Court.* 10 Nov. 2010. http://www.icc-cpi.int/en_menus/icc/situations%20and%20cases/situations/situation%20icc%200104/related%20cases/icc01040110/press%20releases/Pages/pr581.aspx

International Crisis Group (ICP). 2007. *Colombia's New Armed Groups: Crisis Group Latin America report 20.* Brussels: International Crisis Group.

International Human Rights Law Institute. 2005. *In Modern Bondage: Sex Trafficking in the Americas (2nd revised ed.).* DePaul University College of Law. http://www.law.depaul.edu/centers_institutes/ihrli/publications/.

International Rescue Committee. 2007. "Mortality in the Democratic Republic of Congo: an Ongoing Crisis". http://www.rescue.org/sites/default/files/resource-file/2006-7_congoMortalitySurvey.pdf

Ioffe, Julia. 2011. "The Condomnation of Vladimir Putin," *Foreign Policy,* December 16.

"JACL Director Honored by Islamic Cultural Center." 2008. *Islamic Cultural Center of Fresno.* http://www.icfresno.org/multimedia/04e.htm

Jacobs, Andrew. 2009. "China's Answer to a Crime Includes Amateur Sleuths." *New York Times,* February 25.

Jacobs, Charles. 2003. "There are 27 Million Slaves; Where are the Abolitionists?" In *Slavery in the 21st Century,* Worldviews for the 21st Century: An Occasional Monograph Series, Volume 1, Number 2. Global Connections Foundation and

University of South Florida's Global Perspectives Office and Political Science Department.

Japanese American Citizens League. 2001. "JACL Urges Caution in Aftermath of Terrorist Attack." JACL news release, September 12.

Japanese American Citizens League. 2007. "It's Time to Restore Law and Justice." September 18. http://www.jacl.org/public_policy/pdf/09-18-07RestoreLawAndJustice.pdf.

Jenkins, Rob, and Anne Marie Goetz. 1999. "Accounts and Accountability: Theoretical Implications of the Right-to-Information Movement in India." *Third World Quarterly* 20(3): 603–622.

Jepperson, R., A. Wendt, and P. J. Katzenstein. 1996. "Norms, Identity, and Culture in National Security." In *The Culture of National Security*, ed. P. J. Katzenstein. New York: Columbia University Press.

Jordt, Ingrid. 2007. *Burma's Mass Lay Meditation Movement: Buddhism and the Cultural Construction of Power*. Athens: Ohio University Press.

Just, Marion, Ann Crigler, and Todd Belt. 2007. "Don't Give Up Hope: Emotions, Candidate Appraisals and Votes." In *The Affect Effect: Dynamics of Emotion in Political Thinking and Behavior*, ed. W. Russell Neuman, George E. Marcus, Ann N. Crigler, and Michael Mackuen. Chicago: University of Chicago Press.

Kalla, Avinash. 2011. "Here's the Real Foreign Hand." *Times of India*. August 21.

Kamalipour, Yahya R., ed. 2010. *Media, Power, and Politics in the Digital Age: The 2009 Presidential Election Uprising in Iran*. Lanham, MD: Rowman & Littlefield Publishers.

Kane, J. 1998. *Sold for Sex*. Aldershot, UK: Ashgate.

Karon, Tony. 2006. "Why Holocaust Denial Hurts the Palestinian Cause." Time. December 14. http://www.time.com/time/world/article/0,8599,1570116,00.html

Katzenstein, P. J. 1996. *Cultural Norms and National Security: Police and Military in Postwar Japan*. Ithaca, NY: Cornell University Press.

Keck, Margaret, and Sikkink, Kathryn. 1998. *Activists Beyond Borders*. Ithaca, NY: Cornell University Press.

Kempadoo, Kamala, and Jo Doezema. eds. 1998. *Global Sex Workers: Rights, Resistance, and Redefinition*. New York: Routledge.

Kennedy, David. 2004. *The Dark Sides of Virtue: Reassessing International Humanitarianism*. Princeton, NJ: Princeton University Press.

Kenyatta, Jomo. 1938. *Facing Mount Kenya: The Tribal Life of the Kikuyu*. London: L. Secker and Warburg.

Khan, Omer Farooq. 2011. "And Now a Fast in Pakistan." *Times of India*. August 21. http://articles.timesofindia.indiatimes.com/2011-08-21/special-report/29911719_1_military-spending-military-budget-end-poverty.

Khong, Yuen Foong. 1992. *Analogies at War: Korea, Munich, Dien Bien Phu, and the Vietnam Decisions of 1965*. Princeton, NJ: Princeton University Press.

Kidder, Tracy. 2003. *Mountains Beyond Mountains*. New York: Random House.

Kinley, David. 2009. *Civilising Globalisation*. New York: Cambridge University Press.

Kleeblatt, Norman. 1987. *The Dreyfus Affair: Art, Truth, and Justice.* University of California Press.

Klotz, A. 1995. "Norms Reconstituting Interests: Global Racial Equality and U.S. Sanctions against South Africa." *International Organization* 49(3): 451–478.

Knauer, James T. 1980. "Motive and Goal in Hannah Arendt's Concept of Political Action." *American Political Science Review* 74(3): 721–733.

Knickmeyer, Ellen. 2004. "Darfur Slaughter Rooted in Arab-African Slavery." *The Seattle Times | Seattle Times Newspaper.* July 2. http://seattletimes.nwsource.com/html/nationworld/2001970382_slavery02.html.

Kohen, Ari. 2012. "An Overlapping Consensus on Human Rights and Human Dignity." In *Human Rights at the Crossroads*, ed. Mark Goodale. New York: Oxford University Press.

Kondolojy, Amanda. 2012. "Late Night TV Ratings for the Week of April 16–April 20, 2012." http://tvbythenumbers.zap2it.com/2012/04/26/late-night-tv-ratings-for-the-week-of-april-16-april-20-2012/130901/.

Koopmans, R. 2004. "Protest in Time and Space: The Evolution of Waves of Contention." In D. Snow, S. A. Soule, & H. Kriesi (Eds.), *The Blackwell Companion to Social Movements.* Malden, MA: Blackwell Publishing.

Kovalev, Alexey. 2011. "Russians Express Their Frustration with Explosion in Political Satire." *The Guardian,* December 22. http://www.guardian.co.uk/world/2011/dec/22/russia-frustration-leadership-political-satire.

Krammer, Arnold. 1969. "Germans Against Hitler: The Thaelmann Brigade." *Journal of Contemporary History* 4(2): 65–81.

Kreager, Philip. 1991. "Aung San Suu Kyi and the Peaceful Struggle for Human Rights in Burma." In *Freedom from Fear and Other Writings*, by Aung San Suu Kyi. New York: Penguin.

Krenn, Michael L. 1999. *The African-American Voice in U.S. Foreign Policy since World War II.* New York: Routledge.

Kristof, Nicholas. 2004. "Bargaining for Freedom." *New York Times*, January 21.

Kristof, Nicholas. 2005. "Illiterate Surgeon." *New York Times*, June 12.

Kristof, Nicholas. 2007. "Darfur and Congo." *New York Times.* June 20. http://kristof.blogs.nytimes.com/2007/06/20/darfur-and-congo/.

Kristof, Nicholas. 2008. "Misogyny vs. Sexism." *New York Times*, April 7.

Kristof, Nicholas. 2009a. "Hillary Clinton on Women in Foreign Policy." *New York Times*, January 13.

Kristof, Nicholas. 2009c. "The Senate Discovers Women." *New York Times*, February 5.

Kristof, Nicholas, and Wu Dunn, S. 2009a. "The Women's Crusade." *The New York Times Magazine.* August 23.

Kristof, Nicholas, and Wu Dunn, S. 2009b. *Half the Sky: Turning Oppression into Opportunity for Women Worldwide.* New York: Alfred Knopf.

Kumar, Raj. 2011. *Corruption and Human Rights in India.* London: Oxford University Press.

Kuo, James. 2010. "Jester in the King's Court: The Role of Political Satire in 21st Century American Politics." Senior Honors' Thesis. University of California, Irvine.

Kuper, Andrew. 2005. *Global Responsibilities: Who Must Deliver on Human Rights?* New York: Routledge.

Kuper, Simon. 2005. "Why Did Denmark Jews Survive while Dutch Jews Died in the Holocaust?" *London Financial Times Weekend Magazine*, January 22.

Kurczy, Stephen. 2010. "US, Brazil lead Google's Top 10 Censorship List; China off the Chart." *Christian Science Monitor*, April 21.

Kyle, David, and Ray Koslowski, eds. 2001. *Global Human Smuggling: Comparative Perspectives*. Baltimore: Johns Hopkins University Press.

Lakoff, George. 1990. *Women, Fire, and Dangerous Things: What Categories Reveal about the Mind*. Chicago: University of Chicago Press.

Landesman, Peter. 2004. "The Girls Next Door." *New York Times Magazine*, January 25

Langer, Maximo. 2007. "Revolution in Latin American Criminal Procedure: Diffusion of Legal Ideas from the Periphery." *The American Journal of Comparative Law*, (55): 617–676.

La Strada International. 2008. *Violation of Women's Rights: A Cause and Consequence of Trafficking in Women*. http://lastradainternational.org/lsidocs/431%20LSI-%20 violation%20of%20womens%20rights.pdf

Lau, J. T. F., X. L. Yang, Q. S. Wang, Y. M. Cheng, H. Y. Tsui, and J. H. Kim. 2006. "Gender Power and Marital Relationship as Predictors of Sexual Dysfunction and Sexual Satisfaction among Young Married Couples in Rural China—A Population Based Study." *Urology* 67(3): 579–585.

Laumann, Edward O., Alfredo Nicolosi, Dale B. Glasser, Anthony Paik, C. Gingell, E. Moreira, and T. Wang. 2004. "Sexual problems among women and men aged 40–80: prevalence and correlates identified in the Global Study of Sexual Attitudes and Behaviors." *International Journal of Impotence Research* 17 (1): 39–57.

Legler, Thomas, Sharon F. Lean, and Dexter Boniface, eds. 2007. *Promoting Democracy in the Americas*. Baltimore: Johns Hopkins University Press.

Legro, Jeffrey. 2005. *Rethinking the World: Great Power Strategies and International Order*. Ithaca, NY: Cornell University Press.

Lemere, Maggie, and Zoe West. 2011. *Nowhere to be home: narratives from survivors of Burma's military regime*. San Francisco: McSweeneys Books.

Lerner, Michael, and Cornel West. 1995. *Jews and Blacks: Let the Healing Begin*. New York: G. P. Putnam's Sons.

Levesque, Roger. 1999. *Sexual Abuse of Children: A Human Rights Perspective*. Bloomington: Indiana University Press.

Levy, Clifford. 2010. "Russia Uses Microsoft to Suppress Dissent." *New York Times*, September 11. http://www.nytimes.com/2010/09/12/world/europe/12raids. html?pagewanted=all.

"Leymah Gbowee: A Powerful Voice for Peace." 2010. Interview by Kwami Nyamidie. *Yes Magazine*, June 10.

Liang, Guo. 2007. "China Internet Project Survey Report 2007." Center for Social Development, Chinese Academy of Sciences/The Markle Foundation. November 2007.

Li, Chenyang. 2003. "Globalizing Cultural Values: International Human Rights Discourse as Moral Persuasion." In *Constructing Human Rights in the Age of*

Globalization, ed. Mahmood Monshipouri, Neil Englehart, Andrew J. Nathan, and Kavita Philip. Armonk, NY: M. E. Sharpe.

Lien, Pei-te, and M. Margaret Conway. 2000. "Comparing Support for Affirmative Action." In *Black and Multiracial Politics in America*, ed. Yvette M. Alex-Assensoh and Lawrence Hanks. New York: New York University Press.

Lipset, Seymour Martin, and Earl Raab. 1995. *Jews and the New American Scene.* Cambridge, MA: Harvard University Press.

Lipton, Eric, and Steven R. Weisman. 2008. "Lobby for Colombia Trade Pact Casts a Wide Net in Washington." *New York Times*, April 8.

Loyn, David. 2008. "Impossible Task for UN in DR Congo." *BBC News—Home.* 18 November 12. http://news.bbc.co.uk/2/hi/africa/7725344.stm.

Lukes, Steven, ed. 1986. *Power.* New York: New York University Press.

Lynch, Marc. 2006. *Voices of the New Arab Public: Iraq, Al-Jazeera, and Middle East Politics Today.* New York: Columbia University Press.

Mackey, Robert. 2012. "Ai Weiwei Covers 'Gangnam Style' Video." *New York Times: The Lede—Blogging the News,* October 24. http://thelede.blogs.nytimes.com/2012/10/24/ai-weiwei-covers-gangnam-style-video/

Majtenyi, C. 2009. "Catholic Church in Kenya Promotes Alternative to Female Circumcision." http://www.voanews.com/english/2009-07-11-voa22.cfm.

Mamdani, M. 2009. *Saviors and Survivors: Darfur, Politics, and the War on Terror.* New York: Pantheon Books.

Mar, Raymond A., and Keith Oatley. 2008. "The Function of Fictions is the Abstraction and Simulation of Social Experience." *Perspectives on Psychological Science* 3(3): 172–192.

Martin, Susan Taylor. 2006. "In Ireland, a Roadmap from Terror to Truce." *St. Petersburg Times* (Florida), March 19.

Mauss, Marcel. 2000. *The Gift: The Form and Reason for Exchange in Archaic Societies.* Translated by W. D. Halls. New York: W. W. Norton.

May, Ernest R. 1973. *"Lessons" of the Past: The Use and Misuse of History in American Foreign Policy.* New York: Oxford University Press.

McElwee, Joshua J. 2011. "Over 150 Theologians Call for Abolition of Death Penalty." *National Catholic Reporter.* September 26. http://ncronline.org/news/peace-justice/over-150-theologians-call-abolition-death-penalty.

McGrath, Charles. 2012. "How Many Stephen Colberts Are There?" *New York Times Magazine*, January 4.

McLuhan, Marshall. 1960. *Explorations in Communication.* Boston: Beacon Press.

"Mentally Retarded and on Death Row." 2012. *New York Times.* August 3. Opinion. http://www.nytimes.com/2012/08/04/opinion/mentally-retarded-and-on-death-row.html?_r=2.

Meyer, John W., John Boli, George M. Thomas, and Francisco O. Ramirez. 1997. "World Society and the Nation-State." *American Journal of Sociology* 103/1 (July): 144–181.

Miller, Arthur. 1977. *Death of a Salesman.* New York: Penguin Classics.

Miller, Rory. 2005. *Ireland and the Palestine Question, 1948–2004.* Dublin: Irish Academic Press.

Misztal, Barbara A. 2007. *Intellectuals and the Public Good: Creativity and Civil Courage.* New York: Cambridge University Press.

Mitchell, David. 2004. *Cloud Atlas.* New York: Random House Trade Paperbacks.

Mittleman, Alan, Jonathan D. Sarna, and Robert Licht, eds. 2002. *Jewish Polity and American Civil Society: Communal Agencies and Religious Movements in the American Public Sphere.* Lanham, MD: Rowman & Littlefield.

"Momentum Builds in North Jersey for Genocide." 2009. *Armenian National Committee of America | Home.* October 30. http://www.armenianweekly.com/2009/11/04/momentum-builds-in-north-jersey-for-genocide-workshop/.

Monroe, Kristen Renwick. 1996. *The Heart of Altruism: Perceptions of a Common Humanity.* Princeton, NJ: Princeton University Press.

Monroe, Kristen R. 2004 *The Hand of Compassion: Portraits of Moral Choice during the Holocaust.* Princeton, NJ: Princeton University Press.

Moon, Ban K. 2010. "Intensification of Efforts to Eliminate All Forms of Violence against Women: Report of the Secretary-General." August 2. http://www.unhcr.org/refworld/category,REFERENCE,UNGA,,,4cf4e25a2,0.html

Mori, Floyd. 2008. Personal Interview. Irvine, CA. June 30.

Morozov, Evgeny. 2010. "Think Again: The Internet." *Foreign Policy* May/June. http://www.foreignpolicy.com/articles/2010/04/26/think_again_the_internet

Muhammad, Jehron. 2010. "Scarce Water the Root Cause of Darfur Conflict?" *FinalCall.com News—Uncompromised National and World News and Perspectives.* March 9. http://www.finalcall.com/artman/publish/World_News_3/article_6808.shtml.

Mukherji, Anahita. 2011. "Indians Abroad Come Aboard Hazare's Anti-Corruption Crusade." August 19. http://articles.timesofindia.indiatimes.com/2011-08-19/mumbai/29904996_1_anti-corruption-anna-hazare-twitter-and-facebook.

Mydans, Seth. 2008. "Malay Blogger Fights a System He Perfected." *New York Times,* November 6. http://www.nytimes.com/2008/11/06/world/asia/06blogger.html?pagewanted=print

Naber, Nadine. 2002. "So Our History Doesn't Become Your Future: The Local and Global Politics of Coalition Building Post September 11th." *Journal of Asian American Studies* 5(3): 217–242.

Nafisi, Azar. 2003. *Reading Lolita in Tehran.* New York: Random House.

Nair, P. M., and Sen, S. 2005. *Trafficking in Women and Children in India.* National Human Rights Commission. New Delhi: Orient Longman.

National Poverty Center, University of Michigan. 2010. "2010 Poverty Facts." http://www.npc.umich.edu/poverty/.

Nelson, Paul, and Ellen Dorsey. 2008. *New Rights Advocacy: Changing Strategies of Development and Human Rights NGOs.* Washington, DC: Georgetown University Press.

Nesbitt, Francis Njubi. 2004. *Race for Sanctions: African Americans against Apartheid, 1946-1994.* Bloomington: Indiana University Press.

Norris, Pippa. 2002. "Democratic Phoenix: Reinventing Political Activism." Cambridge University Press.

Novick, Peter. 2000. *The Holocaust in American Life.* New York: Mariner Books.

Nussbaum, Martha. 1995. *Poetic Justice: The Literary Imagination and Public Life.* Boston: Beacon Press.

Nussbaum, Martha. 1997. "Capabilities and Human Rights." *Fordham Law Review* 66. 273–300

Nussbaum, Martha. 2002. "The Future of Feminist Liberalism." In *The Subject of Care: Feminist Perspectives on Dependency*, eds. Eva Feder Kittay and Ellen K Feder. Lanham, MD: Rowman & Littlefield Publishers.

Nussbaum, Martha, and Amartya Sen, eds. 2003. *The Quality of Life.* New York: Oxford University Press.

OHCHR, UNAIDS, UNDP, UNECA, UNESCO, UNFPA, UNHCR, UNICEF, UNIFEM, and WHO. 2008. "Eliminating Female Genital Mutilation: An Interagency Statement." http://www.un.org/womenwatch/daw/csw/csw52/statements_missions/Interagency_Statement_on_Eliminating_FGM.pdf.

Olesen, Thomas. 2005. *International Zapatismo: The Construction of Solidarity in an Age of Globalization.* London: Zed Press.

O'Neill, Barry. 1999. *Honor, Symbols, and War.* Ann Arbor: University of Michigan Press.

"On the Darfur Accountability and Divestment Act." 2007. *Armenian Assembly of America.* http://www.aaainc.org/index.php?id=274&type=98.

Orbinski, James. 2009. *An Imperfect Offering: Humanitarian Action for the Twenty-First Century.* New York: Walker.

Orden, Erika and Nicholas Bariyo. 2012. "Viral Video Puts Spotlight on Uganda Rebel." *Wall Street Journal*, March 9. http://online.wsj.com/article/SB10001424052970204781804577269781172772516.html

Orwell, George. 1950. *1984.* Signet Classic.

Oyston, Grant. 2012. "Show Me the Money." *Visible Children.* March 11. http://visible-children.tumblr.com/post/19134664367/show-me-the-money.

Parker-Pope, T. 2011. "The Generous Marriage." *New York Times Magazine*, December 8.

Paul, Annie. 2012. "Your Brain on Fiction." *New York Times*, March 17.

Penta, Leo J. 1996. "Hannah Arendt: On Power." *Journal of Speculative Philosophy,* New Series, 10(3): 210–229.

Perry, Benjamin J. 2004. "The Relationship between Equity and Marital Quality among Hispanics, African Americans and Caucasians." Ph.D. thesis, Ohio State University. http://etd.ohiolink.edu/view.cgi?acc_num=osu1078783478.

Perry, Michael. 2000. *The Idea of Human Rights.* New York: Oxford University Press.

Pew Research Center. 2010. "Few Say Religion Shapes Immigration, Environment Views: Results from the 2010 Annual Religion and Public Life Survey." *The Pew Forum on Religion and Public Life.* http://www.pewforum.org/Politics-and-Elections/Few-Say-Religion-Shapes-Immigration-Environment-Views.aspx#4.

Pinker, Steven. 2008. *The Stuff of Thought: Language as a Window into Human Nature.* Lonon: Penguin.

Pinker, Steven. 2011. *The Better Angels of Our Nature: Why Violence has Declined.* New York: Viking.

Pisani, Elizabeth. 2008. *The Wisdom of Whores: Bureaucrats, Brothels, and the Business of AIDS.* New York: W. W. Norton & Co.

Pleming, Sue. 2009. "U.S. State Department Speaks to Twitter over Iran." *Reuters.* June 16. http://www.reuters.com/article/2009/06/16/us-iran-election-twitter-usa-idUSWBT01137420090616.

Popper, Karl. 1971. *The Open Society and Its Enemies.* Princeton, NJ: Princeton University Press.

Power, Samantha. 2002. *A Problem from Hell: America and the Age of Genocide.* New York: Basic Books.

Pradham, Ashok. 2011. "Anna Wave Sweeps Students in Orissa." *Times of India.* August 22. http://articles.timesofindia.indiatimes.com/2011-08-22/bhubaneswar/29914647_1_anna-hazare-corruption-free-country-team-anna.

Pray the Devil Back to Hell. 2008. Documentary. Directed by Gini Reticker. New York: Fork Films.

Press, Eyal. 2012. *Beautiful Souls: Saying No, Breaking Ranks, and Heeding the Voice of Conscience in Dark Times.* New York: Farrar, Straus and Giroux.

Preston, Paul. 2012. *The Spanish Holocaust.* London: Harper Collins UK.

Prose, Francine. 2009. *Anne Frank: The Book, The Life, the Afterlife.* New York: Harper.

Putnam, Robert. 2002. *Democracies in Flux: The Evolution of Social Capital in Contemporary Society.* New York: Oxford University Press.

Quirk, Joel. 2012. "Uncomfortable Silences: Contemporary Slavery and the 'Lessons' of History." In *Human Trafficking and Human Rights: Rethinking Contemporary Slavery,* ed. Alison Brysk and Austin Choi-Fitzpatrick. Philadelphia: University of Pennsylvania Press.

Rae, Paul. 2009. *Theatre and Human Rights.* New York: Palgrave Macmillan.

Rahman, Annika, and Nahid Toubia, eds. 2000. *Female Genital Mutilation: A Guide to Laws and Policies Worldwide.* New York: St. Martin's Press.

Read, Piers Paul. 2012. *The Dreyfus Affair.* London: Bloomsbury.

Reeves, Eric. 2005. "Genocide in Darfur—How the Horror Began." *Sudan Tribune: Plural News and Views on Sudan.* September 3. http://www.sudantribune.com/Genocide-in-Darfur-How-the-Horror,11445.

Reporters Without Borders. 2005. *Cucuta: Colombia, Reporters at the Crossroads of Dangers.* April. Paris: Reporters Without Borders.

"Representatives Berman and Pence Introduce Genocide Accountability Act." 2007. *Armenian Assembly of America.* May 31. http://www.aaainc.org/index.php?id=343&type=98.

Rhoads, Christopher, and Loretta Chao. 2009. "Iran's Web Spying Aided by Western Technology." *Wall Street Journal,* June 22. http://online.wsj.com/article/SB124562668777335653.html

Ribando, Clare M. 2007. *Congressional Research Service Report for Congress: Trafficking in Persons.* http://www.au.af.mil/au/awc/awcgate/crs/rl30545.pdf

Rice, Xan. 2010. " 'Stench of Death' in Congo Confirms Resurgence of Lord's Resistance Army." *The Guardian.* March 27. http://www.guardian.co.uk/world/2010/mar/28/lra-congo-uganda-un.

Rich, Adrienne. 1993. *The Dream of a Common Language: Poems 1974-1977.* New York: W. W. Norton.

Risse, Thomas. 2000. "Let's Argue! Communicative Action in World Politics." *International Organization* 54(1): 1–39.

Risse, Thomas, Steven Ropp, and Kathryn Sikkink, eds. 1999. *The Power of Human Rights.* Cambridge: Cambridge University Press.

Risse-Kappen, Thomas. 1994. "Ideas Do Not Float Freely: Transnational Coalitions, Democratic Structures, and the End of the Cold War." *International Organization* 48: 185–214.

Robinson, Randall. 1999. *Defending the Spirit: A Black Life in America.* New York: Dutton.

Rodley, Nigel. 1993. "Can Armed Opposition Groups Violate Human Rights?," pp. 297–318 in Kathleen Mahoney and Paul Mahoney (eds.) *Human Rights in the Twenty-first Century: A Global Challenge.* Dordrecht: Kluwer-Martinus Nijhoff Publishers, 1993.

Romero, Simon. 2008a. "Colombia Inflates Rebel Toll with Slain Civilians." *New York Times,* October 30.

Romero, Simon. 2008b. "Facing Crises, Colombia Chief Hails Democratic and Economic Gains." *New York Times,* April 23.

Rorty, Richard. 1989. *Contingency, Irony, and Solidarity.* Cambridge: Cambridge University Press.

Rorty, Richard. 1993. "Human Rights, Rationality, and Sentimentality." In *On Human Rights: The Oxford Amnesty Lectures 1993.* New York: Basic Books.

Rosen, Jeffrey. 2008. "Google's Gatekeepers." *New York Times Magazine,* November 30.

Rosenbaum, Alan S. 2001. *Is the Holocaust Unique? Perspectives on Comparative Genocide.* 2d ed. Boulder, CO: Westview Press.

Rosenstone, Robert A. 1967. "The Men of the Abraham Lincoln Battalion." *Journal of American History* 54(2): 327–338.

Rubin, Elizabeth. 2010. "Studio Kabul: Advancing Female Empowerment in Afghanistan." *New York Times Magazine,* October 21.

Rudman, L. A., and J. E. Pehlan. 2007. "The Interpersonal Power of Feminism: Is Feminism Good for Relationship?" *Sex Roles: A Journal of Research* 57(11–12): 787–799.

Rummel, J. R. 1994. *Death by Government.* New Brunswick, NJ: Transaction Publishers.

Rumsfeld v. Padilla. 542 U.S. 426. (2004). http://www.law.cornell.edu/supct/html/03-1027.ZS.html

Ryzik, Melena. 2012. "Carefully Calibrated for Protest." *New York Times.*

SAFE California. 2012. http://www.safecalifornia.org/.

Sanders, Gabriel. 2008. "Protecting the Graveless." *Jewish Daily Forward,* February 28. http://forward.com/articles/12790/protecting-the-graveless-/

Santa Cruz, Arturo. 2005. *International Election Monitoring, Sovereignty, and the Western Hemisphere Idea: The Emergence of an International Norm.* New York: Routledge.

Santos, Boaventura. 2002. *Toward a New Legal Common Sense: Law, Globalization, and Emancipation.* London: Butterworth's LexisNexis.

Santos, Boaventura, and Cesar Rodriguez-Garavito, eds. 2005. *Law and Globalization from Below: Towards a Cosmopolitan Legality.* New York: Cambridge University Press.

Saxena, Deshdeep. 2011. "22 Babies Named After Anna Hazare in MP District." *Times of India.* August 23. http://articles.timesofindia.indiatimes.com/2011-08-23/india/29918532_1_anna-hazare-corruption-protest-hospital-staff.

Schaffer, Kay, and Sidonie Smith. 2004. *Human Rights and Narrated Lives: The Ethics of Recognition.* New York: Palgrave Macmillan.

Schulz, William. 2001. *In Our Own Best Interest.* Boston: Beacon Press.

Seib, Phillip. 2007. "New Media and Prospects for Democratization." In *New Media and the New Middle East,* ed. Phillip Seib. New York: Palgrave Macmillan.

Sen, Amartya. 1990. "More than 100 Million Women are Missing." *New York Review of Books*, December 20.

Sen, Amartya. 1998. "Autobiography (Nobel Prize)." http://nobelprize.org/nobel_prizes/economics/laureates/1998/sen-autobio.html.

Sen, Amartya. 1999a. "Democracy as a Universal Value." *Journal of Democracy.* 10 (3): 3–17.

Sen, Amartya. 1999b. *Development as Freedom.* New York: Anchor Books.

Sen, Amartya. 2001. "Many Faces of Gender Inequality." *The Frontline* 18(22). http://www.hinduonnet.com/fline/fl1822/18220040.htm.

Sen, Amartya. 2003. "Missing Women Revisited." *BMJ* 327: 1297. http://www.bmj.com/content/327/7427/1297.full.

Sengupta, Mitu. 2012. "Anna Hazare and the Idea of Gandhi." *Journal of Asian Studies* 71(3): 593–601.

Sengupta, Somini. 2003. "Child Traffickers Prey on Bangladesh." *New York Times*, January 24.

Shafir, Gershon, and Alison Brysk. 2006. "The Globalization of Rights: From Citizenship to Human Rights," *Citizenship Studies*, Special Issue on Human Rights and Citizenship Rights, 10(3).

Shils, Edward. 1965. "Charisma, Order, and Status." *American Sociological Review* 40(2): 199–213.

Shue, Henry. 1980. *Basic Rights: Subsistence, Affluence, and U.S. Foreign Policy.* Princeton, NJ: Princeton University Press.

Shuster, Simon. 2012. "Russia's Pussy Riot Trial: A Kangaroo Court Goes on a Witch Hunt." *Time.* August 2. http://world.time.com/2012/08/02/russias-pussy-riot-trial-a-kangaroo-court-goes-on-a-witch-hunt/.

Sisken, Alison and Liana Sun Wyler. 2010. "Trafficking in Persons: U.S. Policy and Issues for Congress" *Congressional Research Service.* http://www.fas.org/sgp/crs/misc/RL34317.pdf

Skaine, Rosemarie. 2005. *Female Genital Mutilation: Legal, Cultural and Medical Issues.* Jefferson, NC: McFarland & Company, Inc.

Slackman, Michael. 2011. "When a Punch Line is No Longer a Lifeline for Egyptians." *New York Times*, April 5.

Slaughter, Joseph. 2009. "Humanitarian Reading" *Humanitarianism and suffering: the mobilization of empathy,* eds. Richard Wilson and Richard Brown. Cambridge: Cambridge University Press.

Slovic, Paul. 2007. "Numbed by Numbers." *Foreign Policy,* March 13.

Smith, Adam. 2007. *The Theory of Moral Sentiments.* New York: Cambridge University Press. Originally published 1759.

Smith, Bonnie, ed. 2000. *Global Feminisms since 1945.* New York: Routledge.

Snow, David A., and Robert D. Benford. 1988. "Ideology, Frame Resonance, and Participant Mobilization." *International Social Movement Research* 1: 197–217.

Snow, David, Sarah A. Soule, and Hanspeter Kriesi, eds. 2004. *The Blackwell Companion to Social Movements.* Malden, MA: Blackwell Publishing.

Sodhi, Prerna. 2011. "Maidan Doesn't Sleep, Volunteers Up at Dawn." *Times of India.* August 24. http://articles.timesofindia.indiatimes.com/2011-08-24/delhi/29921918_1_volunteers-full-support-ramlila-maidan.

Solomon, Deborah. 2008. "Keeping the Faith." *New York Times Magazine,* October 5. http://www.nytimes.com/2008/10/05/magazine/05wwln-q4-t.html?gwh=EBFA C732E23EC268BD119DF4AEA05FB3

Solzhenitsyn, Aleksandr. 1968. *The First Circle.* Translated by Max Hayward, Manya Harari, and Michael Glenny. London: Collins.

Sonenshein, Raphael J. 2001. "When Ideologies Agree and Interests Collide, What's a Leader to Do? The Prospects for Latino-Jewish Coalition in Los Angeles." In *Governing American Cities: Interethnic Coalitions, Competition, and Conflict,* ed. Michael Jones-Correa. New York: Russell Sage Foundation.

Sontag, Susan. 2003. *Regarding the Pain of Others.* New York: Farrar, Straus and Giroux.

Spiegel, Steven L. 2001. "Israel and Beyond: American Jews and U.S. Foreign Policy." In *Jews in American Politics,* ed. L. Sandy Maisel and Ira N. Forman. Lanham, MD: Rowman and Littlefield.

Staub, Eric. 1989. *The Roots of Evil: The Origins of Genocide and Other Group Violence.* New York: Cambridge University Press.

Steele, Jonathon. 2001. "Food for Thought: The Guardian Profile: Amartya Sen." *The Guardian,* March 30. http://www.guardian.co.uk/books/2001/mar/31/society. politics

Steger, Manfred. 2008. *The Rise of the Global Imaginary: Political Ideologies from the French Revolution to the Global War on Terror.* New York: Oxford University Press.

Stelter, Brian and Brad Stone. 2009. "Web Pries Lid of Iranian Censorship". *New York Times* June 23. http://www.nytimes.com/2009/06/23/world/middleeast/23censor. html

Stone, Brad and Noam Cohen. 2009. "Social Networks Spread Defiance Online." *New York Times.* June 15. http://www.nytimes.com/2009/06/16/world/middleeast/16media.html

Stephan, Maria J., and Erica Chenoweth. 2008 "Why Civil Resistance Works: The Strategic Logic of Nonviolent Conflict." *International Security* 33(1): 7–44.

Stephen Roth Institute. 2004. "Anti-Semitism and Racism Report for Ireland 2004." Tel Aviv University.

Stohlberg, Sheryl Gay. 2011. "Shy U.S. Intellectual Created Playbook Used in a Revolution." *New York Times*, February 16.

Stone, Brad, and Noam Cohen. 2009. "Social Network Spread Iranian Defiance Online." *New York Times*, June 16.

Sullivan, Denis. 2010. "The Death Penalty Loses Its Mind: An Interview with James Acker." *Contemporary Justice Review* 13(4): 477–486.

Sullivan, Donna. 1995. "The Public/Private Distinction in International Human Rights Law." In *Women's Rights Human Rights: International Feminist Perspectives,* ed. J. Peters and A. Wolper. New York: Routledge.

Sunstein, Cass. 2008. *Infotopia: How Many Minds Produce Knowledge.* New York: Oxford University Press.

Tarrow, Sidney. 2008. *Power in Movement: Social Movements and Contentious Politics.* Cambridge: Cambridge University Press.

Tate, Winifred. 2007. *Counting the Dead: The Culture and Politics of Human Rights Activism in Colombia.* Berkeley: University of California Press.

Tessler, Mark. 2003. "Arab and Muslim Political Attitudes: Stereotypes and Evidence from Survey Research." *International Studies Perspectives* 4: 175–181.

Tethong, Tenzin. Personal interview and public talk, UC Santa Barbara, January 28, 2013.

Thakur, Ramesh, Andrew F. Cooper, and John English, eds. 2006. *International Commissions and the Power of Ideas.* New York: United Nations Press.

Thistlethwaite, Susan. 2012. "Lisa Brown, silenced on the Michigan House floor, helps read 'Vagina Monologues' on statehouse steps". *Washington Post.* June 19. http://www.washingtonpost.com/blogs/guest-voices/post/lisa-brown-silenced-on-the-michigan-house-floor-helps-read-vagina-monolgues-on-statehouse-steps/2012/06/19/gJQAwcGEoV_blog.html

Thomas, Hugh. 2001. *The Spanish Civil War.* New York: Modern Library.

Thomas, Laurence Mordekhai. 1999. "Suffering as a Moral Beacon: Blacks and Jews." In *The Americanization of the Holocaust,* ed. Hilene Flanzbaum. Baltimore: Johns Hopkins University Press.

Tilly, Charles. 2008. *Contentious Performances.* New York: Cambridge University Press.

Trade Union Friends of Palestine. 2008. "Irish Union Passes Motions in Support of Palestine." ICTU statement. June 5. http://electronicintifada.net/v2/article9586.shtml.

Transparency International. 2010. "Corruption Index Results." http://www.transparency.org/policy_research/surveys_indices/cpi/2010/results.

UNICEF (United Nations Children's Fund) 2011. *Profiting from Abuse: An Investigation into the Sexual Exploitation of Our Children.* New York: UNICEF.

United Nations. 1968. United Nations Conference on Human Rights, Proclamation of Tehran, 22 April to 13 May, 1968. A/CONF. 32/41. Reproduced in *American Journal of International Law* 63/3 (1969): 674–677.

United Nations. 1990. "General Recommendation No. 14, Female Circumcision." Ninth session. http://www.un.org/womenwatch/daw/cedaw/recommendations/recomm.htm.

United Nations. 1996. *"Beijing Declaration and Platform for Action."* http://www.un.org/womenwatch/daw/beijing/platform/.

United Nations Development Fund for Women. 2010. *Making the MDGs Work Better for Women: Implementing Gender Responsive National Development Plans and Programmes.* New York.

United Nations General Assembly. 1993. "Resolution 48/104: Declaration on the Elimination of Violence against Women." December 20. http://www.ohchr.org/english/law/eliminationvaw.htm.

United Nations Office on Drugs and Crime. 2006. *Trafficking in Persons: Global Patterns.* United Nations. http://www.unodc.org/pdf/traffickinginpersons_report_2006ver2.pdf

United Nations Population Fund. 2010. *Partnering with Men to End Gender Based Violence: Practices That Work from Eastern Europe and Central Asia.* New York.

"UN Report: CNDP, Congolese Soldiers Involved in Illegal Mining Operations | Congo Planet." 2011. *Congo Planet—News, Music, Videos, Pictures from the Congo.* 23 January 23. http://congoplanet.com/news/1779/un-report-cndp-congolese-soldiers-involved-in-illegal-mining-operations-exploitation-eastern-congo.jsp.

"U.N. Tones Down Congo 'Genocide' Report." 2010. *CBS News.* September 30. http://www.cbsnews.com/stories/2010/09/30/world/main6915478.shtml.

US Department of Health and Human Services. http://www.hhs.gov/.

US Department of Health and Human Services. 2012. "Infant Mortality and African Americans." http://minorityhealth.hhs.gov/templates/content.aspx?ID=3021.

US Department of State. 2001. "Second Reply of the Government of the United States to August 21, 2000 Response by Petitioner." http://www.state.gov/documents/organization/6594.doc.

US Department of State. 2009. *Trafficking in Persons Report.* http://www.state.gov/g/tip/rls/tiprpt/2009/.

US Department of State. 2010. "U.S. Government Anti-Trafficking in Persons Project Funding Fact Sheet." http://www.state.gov/j/tip/rls/fs/2010/144670.htm.

"US Expands Human Trafficking Black List to 23." 2011. *NBC news.* http://www.nbc-news.com/id/43554910/ns/world_news-mideast_n_africa/#.UT7H_9HwKag.

Verma, Ravi K., Julie Pulerwitz, Vaishali Mahendra, Sujata Khandekar, Gary Barker, P. Fulpagare, and S. K. Singh. 2006. "Challenging and Changing Gender Attitudes among Young Men in Mumbai, India." *Reproductive Health Matters* 14(28): 135–143.

"Vienna Declaration and Programme of Action." 1993. Adopted by the World Conference on Human Rights in Vienna on June 25, 1993. http://www.ohchr.org/english/law/vienna.htm.

Volpp, Leti. 2002. "The Citizen and the Terrorist." *UCLA Law Review* 1574. University of California Regents. June 15.

Wagner, Gerhard, and Heinz Zipprian. 1989. "Habermas on Power and Rationality." *Sociological Theory* 7(1): 102–109.

Walker, Alice. 1992. *Possessing the Secret of Joy.* New York: Harcourt Brace Jovanovich.

Walker, Alice, and Pratibha Parmar. 1993. *Warrior Marks.* New York: Distributed by Women Make Movies.

Walley, Christine J. 1997. "Searching for 'Voices': Feminism, Anthropology, and the Global Debate over Female Genital Operations." *Cultural Anthropology* 12(3): 405–438.

Weber, Max. 1964. *Theory of Social and Economic Organization.* New York: Free Press.

Weber, Max. 1994. "The Nation." In *Nationalism*, ed. John Hutchinson and Anthony D. Smith. Oxford: Oxford University Press.

Wehrenfennig, Daniel. 2008. "Conflict Management and Communicative Action: Second Track Diplomacy from a Habermasian Perspective." *Communication Theory* 18(3): 356–375.

Wehrenfennig, Daniel. 2009. *The missing link: citizen dialogue in Northern Ireland and Israel/Palestine.* Irvine, Calif: University of California, Irvine. http://proquest.umi.com/pqdweb?did=1919564851&sid=6&Fmt=2&clientId=48051&RQT=309&VName=PQD.

Wendt, Alexander. 1999. *A Social Theory of International Politics.* Cambridge: Cambridge University Press.

West, Robin. 2002. "The Right to Care." In *The Subject of Care: Feminist Perspectives on Dependency*, eds. Eva Feder Kittay and Ellen K Feder. Lanham, MD: Rowman & Littlefield Publishers.

White, Hayden. 1987. *The Content of the Form: Narrative Discourse and Historical Representation.* Baltimore: Johns Hopkins University Press.

White, Stephen K. 1986. "Foucault's Challenge to Critical Theory." *American Political Science Review* 80(2): 419–432.

"Widely Seen Video of Young Woman's Death Resonates with Protesters in Iran." 2009. *New York Times*, June 23.

Wiesel, Elie. 1982. *Night.* New York: Bantam Books.

Wilkerson, Michael. 2012. "Joseph Kony is not in Uganda (and Other Complicated Things)." *Foreign Policy.* March 7. http://blog.foreignpolicy.com/posts/2012/03/07/guest_post_joseph_kony_is_not_in_uganda_and_other_complicated_things.

Williams, Alex. 2008. "Trying to Put a Name to the Face of Evil." *New York Times.* http://www.nytimes.com/2008/05/04/fashion/04myanmar.html.

Williams, Timothy. 2010. "Wanted—Jihadists to Marry Widows." *New York Times,* July 9.

Wilson, Richard, and Richard D. Brown. 2009. *Humanitarianism and suffering: the mobilization of empathy.* Cambridge: Cambridge University Press.

Wines, Michael. 2009a. "In Latest Upheaval, China Applies New Strategies to Control Flow of Information." *New York Times*, July 7. http://www.nytimes.com/2009/07/08/world/asia/08beijing.html

Wines, Michael. 2009b. "Mythical Beast (A Dirty Pun) Tweaks China's Web Censors." *New York Times*, March 12. http://www.nytimes.com/2009/03/12/world/asia/12beast.html?gwh=70AD38D3896110AFE01735AB7AEEBF13

Winright, T. 2011. "A Catholic Call to Abolish the Death Penalty." September 27. http://catholicmoraltheology.com/a-catholic-call-to-abolish-the-death-penalty/.

Winston, Morton Emanuel. 1999. *Indivisibility and Interdependence of Human Rights.* Lincoln: University of Nebraska-Lincoln.

World Health Organization, United Nations Children's Fund, and United Nations Population Fund. 1997. Female Genital Mutilation. A Joint WHO/UNICEF/UNFPA Statement. Geneva, World Health Organization.

World Health Organization. 1999. *Female Genital Mutilation: Programmes to Date: What Works and What Doesn't. A Review.* http://www.who.int/reproductive-health/publications/fgm/en/index.html.

World Health Organization. 2000. *Female Genital Mutilation: A Handbook for Frontline Workers.* http://www.who.int/reproductivehealth/publications/fgm/en/index.html.

World Health Organization. 2001a. *Female Genital Mutilation: Integrating the Prevention and the Management of the Health Complications into the Curricula of Nursing and Midwifery. A Student's Guide.* http://www.who.int/reproductivehealth/publications/fgm/en/index.html.

World Health Organization. 2001b. *Female Genital Mutilation: The Prevention and the Management of the Health Complications. Policy Guidelines for Nurses and Midwives.* http://www.who.int/reproductivehealth/publications/fgm/en/index.html.

World Health Organization. 2006. "Female Genital Mutilation and Obstetric Outcome: WHO Collaborative Prospective Study in Six African Countries." *The Lancet* 367: 1835–1841.

World Health Organization. 2008a. Eliminating Female Genital Mutilation: An Interagency Statement—OHCHR, UNAIDS, UNDP, UNECA, UNESCO, UNFPA, UNHCR, UNICEF, UNIFEM, WHO. http://www.who.int/reproductivehealth/publications/fgm/9789241596442/en/.

World Health Organization. 2008b. *Sexual Reproductive Health: Research and Action in Support of the Millennium Development Goals: Biennial Report 2006-2007.* Geneva: World Health Organization.

World Medical Association. 1993. Policy: The World Medical Association Statement on Female Genital Mutilation, adopted by the 45th World Medical Assembly, Budapest, Hungary, October. http://www.wma.net/e/policy/c10.htm.

World Medical Association. 1997. Female Circumcision (2). http://www.wma.net/en/40news/20archives/1997/1997_11/.

World Medical Association. 2003. "New WMA President Condemns Ill Treatment of Children." http://www.wma.net/en/40news/20archives/2003/2003_17/

Yaffa, Joshua. 2012. "The Kremlin's Not Laughing Now." New York Times, February 25.

Yang, Guobin. 2009. *The Power of the Internet in China: Citizen Activism Online.* New York: Columbia University Press.

Yang, Guobin. 2011. "Technology and Its Contents: Issues in the Study of the Chinese Internet" *The Journal of Asian Studies* 70(4): 1043-1050

Yardley, Jim. 2011a. "Anticorruption Bill Stalls as Indian Lawmakers Prepare to Adjourn." *New York Times*, December 29.

Yardley, Jim. 2011b. "Protests Awaken a Goliath in India." *New York Times*, October 29.

Yerushalmi, Isaac. 2010. "Transformation." *Expressions/Impressions.* Spring. Irvine: University of California, Irvine.

Young, Iris Marion. 2000. *Inclusion and Democracy.* Oxford: Oxford University Press.

Young, James. 1993. *The Texture of Memory: Holocaust Memorials and Meaning*. New Haven, CT: Yale University Press.

Zak, Dan. 2010. "Stephen Colbert, in GOP Pundit Character, Testifies on Immigration in D.C." *Washington Post*. September 25. http://www.washingtonpost.com/wp-dyn/content/article/2010/09/24/AR2010092402734.html.

Zielinski, Siegfried, and Gloria Custance. 1981. "History as Entertainment and Provocation: The TV Series 'Holocaust' in West Germany". *New German Critique: An Interdisciplinary Journal of German Studies*. 19: 81–96.

Zimmer, Ben. 2011. "How the War of Words Was Won in Cairo." *New York Times*, February 12.

Zivi, Karen. 2012. *Making Rights Claims: A Practice of Democratic Citizenship*. New York: Oxford University Press.

INDEX